From Facts to Values
Certainty, Order, Balance and Their Universal Implications

Mehran Banaei
Nadeem Haque

OPTAGON PUBLICATIONS LTD.

From Facts to Values: Certainty, Order, Balance and Their Universal Implications

First Edition
Printed In Canada

All rights reserved under the International Copyright Convention. No part of this publication may be reproduced, stored in a retrieval system or transmitted in any form or by any means, electronic, mechanical, photocopying, recording or otherwise, without the prior permission of the publisher, except in the case of brief quotations embodied in reviews, articles and books.

Copyright © 1995 by Mehran Banaei and Nadeem Haque

Optagon Publications Ltd.
P.O. Box 572
Postal Station "P"
Toronto, Ontario, Canada
M5S 2T1

Canadian Cataloguing in Publication Data
Banaei, Mehran, 1960–
From facts to values
Includes bibliographical references and index.
ISBN 0-9699605-0-6
1. Knowledge, Theory of. I. Haque, Nadeem, 1960–
II. Title.
BD161.B35 1995   121   C95-931539-X

This book is dedicated to all those who have dared to speak the truth throughout the ages — those who were ostracized, resented, discriminated against, excommunicated, oppressed, persecuted or murdered.

Contents

Chapter 1
The Current State of Affairs 2

Introduction – Seeking a Viable Solution – Relativism: Licence to Pure Nonsense – Relativism and Language: Does Language Shape Reality? – Problem of Mysticism and its Inherent Demise.

Chapter 2
The Certainty of Human Knowledge 28

Towards the Establishment of the Universal Reality Principle – Methodology – Knowledge – Dogma – Background: Induction or Deduction in the Realm of Science? – The Inductive Method: Is it Reliable? – Rational vs. Pathological Sceptical Challenge – Deductivism, a possible alternative? – Falsification and its Limitations – Resolution by Consistency – Scientific Dogmatism – Big Bang and Biological Evolution: Theory or Fact? – The Status of Biological Evolution – Implications of the Big Bang – The Big Bang 'Controversy'? – The Teleological Argument Revisited and Re-established – Is the Universe Goal-Directed? – Teleology in Question: Purpose versus Randomness – Statistical Fallacy – Certainty and Quantum Mechanics – Is the Concept of 'God' a Placebo? – Knowledge: Its Integrated Nature – Scientific Investigation and Ethics.

Chapter 3
The Equigenic Principle:
The Foundation of Absolute Values — 118

> The Usage of Facts – Justice and Rights – The Problematic Nature of Conventional Rights and Systems of 'Justice' Built on a Relativistic Foundation – 'Natural Rights' as Understood by Previous and Contemporary Philosophers – Natural Rights: "Nonsense upon Stilts"? – 'Natural Law' and Mystical Movements – The Circular Dilemma of Positivism – The Foundation of All Rights – The Equigenic Principle – Nationhood and Racism – Justice in the Distribution of Resources – Justice, Gender and Nature – Animal Rights Under Equigenic Principle – Competition or Cooperation? – The All-Embrasive Feature of Equigenic Rights – The Parameters of Freedom in Nature – Boundaries of Civil Rights Under Equigenic Principle – "Is-Ought" dilemma? – Is Democracy a Possible Alternative? – Conclusion.

Chapter 4
The 'New Humanism': Is it Really New? — 236

> Consistency and the Concept of 'Revelation' – Background Information – Convergence Between the Quran and the Equigenic Principle – Islam: The Misrepresented 'New Humanism' – Convergence Between the Quran and the Equigenic Principle – Epilogue.

Bibliography — 268

Index — 283

Acknowledgements

The authors wish to express their deep appreciation to all colleagues and individuals who read the manuscript in various stages of completion, and were kind enough to provide us with their valuable comments and suggestions. We benefited greatly from their feedback.

There are also many other individuals who have made immense contributions to this book without necessarily knowing it. We are in debt to all of them. We would, finally, also like to thank the individuals who assisted us in formatting this book.

Chapter One

The Current State of Affairs

What would one, indeed, attain if one gains the whole world, but loses oneself. It would be just like multiplying infinity by zero.

-Sage

Introduction

The greatest danger associated with pervasive irrational human behaviour is when it is approved by social norms and is acted upon collectively. This mode of conduct is extremely perilous because it renders society blind to the threats of destructive norms. Today, more than ever, humankind is engulfed in an invidious situation, characterized by prolonged systemic and collective self-delusion. We now live in an era that thrives on trivia, propaganda and falsehoods. What passes for serious thought is the ever-illusive pursuit of instant pleasure, steeped in a plethora of fantasies and ephemeral illusions. Deception has become a way of life for modern man. It is present everywhere: in business, law, human relationships, personal self-analysis, international politics, etc.

Contemporary man has developed a pathological preference not to choose that which is wise, but to choose that which 'feels good'. Humanity today is in exclusive devotion to the satisfaction of bodily needs and uncontrolled desires, without any due consideration for the dire consequences. The pleasures of flesh and unruly passions are sought obsessively. This uninhibited adherence to immediate gratification has led to a total disregard for values, reason, rationality or, in short, for the reality principle. Any reference to rationality is seen as a psychological threat to the pursuits of desire. Speaking against anything which is well cherished by the 'worshippers of pleasure' is openly resented. Most people have completely abandoned their own minds, intellects and are heedlessly following their whims, cultures, traditions, leaders or favourite media role-models. The irony is that they do so without taking the time to find out that what they are following may be detrimental. Tragically, all of this is done under the pretext of faith, loyalty, fashion or in the name of progression and modernism. No doubt, the price that one pays to escape reality is high and regrettable. Yet sadly, there are many of us who do not mind destroying our lives totally, so long as there is 'glory' today and destruction tomorrow.

From Facts to Values

This short-sighted preference is indeed the main reason behind most miseries which befall humanity.

Consider the current dilemmas that the world is facing. Our social problems are escalating at an unprecedented skyrocketing pace, being inseparable from the way we set our values and the way we choose to conduct our lives. There certainly must be something fundamentally wrong with our outlooks, attitudes and lifestyles when generations of innocent men, women and children die in one half of the world, while in the other half many are illusively engrossed in having a 'good time'. Thousands upon thousands of people are butchered on every single continent, while all eyes remain hypnotically transfixed to television screens, following vacuous Hollywood shows and senseless commercialized 'game sports'. Homeless beggars die on the streets, while the affluent shop for new coats for their cherished pets in Pets' Department Stores. Generations of children grow up illiterate, while irresponsible governments spend billions of dollars on armaments.

Racial strife has torn apart the fabric of most societies, leaving behind a drenched trail, soaked in the blood of innocents. The rate of narcotic addiction, alcoholism, poverty, crime and divorce persists to climb. The breakdown of the family has never before occurred on such an enormous scale. The generation gap is getting wider and deeper. Elderly parents and grandparents are forsaken in the black hole of nursing homes to perish. Battered wives suffer horrendously, abused children commit suicide, yet business goes on as usual for the careless and heartless society. The younger generations of society have been kidnapped from their own brains; they are floating in a reality manufactured by MTV and the likes. Sexual anarchy is so pervasive that it is persistently ubiquitous in: 'advertisement', 'music', 'art', 'entertainment', social behaviour, male/female workplace interactions and in the so-called relationships. Despite the fact that our personal experiences repeatedly remind us that great things in life are usually expensive and hard to find, nowadays, having a

The Current State of Affairs

'relationship' has become as cheap as Bubble Gum. Breaking up its fragile bond is just as easy as establishing it.

Yes, we are indeed living in an age when most people have forgotten the most fundamental and deepest truths of our existence. We are so busy getting our kicks and thrills that we have become blind to greater realities of life. This is an age in which individualism, materialistic ambition and egotistical desires have usurped reason and rational inquiry. The genuine tendency to care and help has become a relic of the past to most people in our today's competitive world. The whole social structure continues to decay under the weight of human apathy and dereliction. Up above is the captivating blue sky but down here, people have built a living hell. Indeed, at the turn of the century, we are faced with pandemic alienation, isolation, hopelessness, depression and desperation that floods human societies. And yet it is disguised by TV, flamboyant movie stars, polished politicians and the frivolities of Saturday Nights in 'high-class' bars. The irony is that we call this trash 'modern civilization'. Yet, everyday things are getting worse, and everyday there are more people creating more problems than there are people looking for alternatives and solutions. Mostly, everybody is busy following everybody else, though none of them really knows where in the blazes they are heading to. In this moribund atmosphere, everybody tries to be 'politically correct'; hardly anyone ever wants to be factually correct, in spite of prevailing and overwhelming clear-cut facts. Yet, it is puzzling as to how on earth we could assume that living in such a manner would not have any drawbacks.

Humanity is in a state of loss due to centuries of neglect and inadequate approaches to fundamental social issues with the result that now, mankind in general is poised at the precipice of ever-deeper confusion on basic matters, with the emergence of nihilism, relativism, new age mysticism and various other forms of fabricative 'isms'. One may wonder, how it could be that we have allowed the conditions for such an aberrational melange of ignorance to sprout like

From Facts to Values

mushrooms and become so pervasive, as an acceptable normative set of beliefs and lifestyles? It is surprising to see that most people think that deviations and high risk behaviour are free from hazards! Although, history proves quite the opposite, what is the use of proof when the mind, eyes and ears are blocked, polluted or cling to the pleasure principle? As Caleb Colton once beautifully summarized it: "The soundest argument will produce no more conviction in an empty head than the most superficial declamation; a feather and the guinea [coin] fall with equal velocity in a vacuum." When the mind resembles a vacuum, the pleasure principle becomes the moment of inertia of the polluted mind, leading to ever-increasing disorder. The pleasure principle in this case, becomes the directional force leading to mental pollution, which is indeed the 'mother of all' pollutions. It cannot be separated from any other pollution, for somewhere along the network of cause and effect interrelationships, mental pollution will inevitably lead to many other forms of pollution.

It seems that no-one really wants to confront the issues at the fundamental level. Policy-makers are primarily concerned with the generated income rather than the degenerative outcome of their policies. Rather than approaching each problem at its foundational level, our so-called intellectuals and experts, attempt to narrowly deal only with symptoms related to their respective fields, whilst languishing in their opulent ivory towers. As a result, far from resolving anything, things are getting worse and worse in this interconnective and multidimensional web of issues. One need not delve into the socio-economic statistics to know this — anyone who is not living in an isolated cave would be all too familiar. Yet, the problem outside the cave of unconcern is not that of the west or the east; rather, it is a global human problem in a world that has become tightly interconnected through revolutions in transportation, information-technology and state-of-the-art telecommunication systems.

The Current State of Affairs

The above-mentioned problems are only some of the tiny symptoms of the twentieth century breakdown, characterized by a degraded lifestyle, adopted by the elite and promoted by them through its instruments of mass communication. In fact, part of the problem is the very profusion of information being marketed, sold or used as a means of indoctrination by whoever has control of the airwaves and various other means of communication to the masses. Television, in particular, has become the remote control of the brain. Never before in history, has humankind been subjected to such an intense bombardment of propaganda seeking to win their wallets, their allegiance and their souls.

Generally, if we are not mindful, what we happen to see or hear depends a lot on what we want to see or hear. Furthermore, the information which is gathered by our faculties of hearing and vision needs to be connected in the proper way to understand reality. If facts are misrepresented and reality is distorted, then it makes it much easier to mislead the masses. With the advancement of modern electronic technology the masses are easily brainwashed for various purposes through *misrepresentation by false association*. The subtle messages being conveyed appeal only to vulnerable emotions. This is exclusively the sight, sound, and vibes' zone; there is no cerebral content at all. The idea is to short-circuit the intellect and operate exclusively on the pleasure principle, by bringing to bear liberal doses of alluring images that promote various popularized lifestyles. These messages are intrinsically degrading, since they devalue the intellect and the human potential.

The common strategy is first to create the need, and then boost the product. The propagandists are as diverse as they could be — from marketers of chewing gum, to the manufactures of political ideology and religion. For example, since smoking is not a human need and it is utterly impossible to promote smoking by appealing to reason and logic, smoking is, therefore, promoted by false association with a sporty lifestyle, sex, prestige, glamour, social status and

From Facts to Values

sophistication. Likewise, the beer commercials sell their harmful product by painting a deceptive association with the idea of 'having a good time'. Through this cunning scheme the 'worshippers of pleasure' come to believe in that which is intrinsically so false to be so true. The idea is that once the target is hooked onto the hedonistic lifestyle, not only will the product sell, but the target will start to chase down the product, just as if a prey were chasing its predator — a fatally convoluted inversion.

Certainly, such insidious advertising tricks will never work on a thoughtful individual who is functioning on the level of truth and pure honesty. For such an individual, things will always be judged on the basis of their consequences, not on the projected image. Only the naive would fall for such subterfuges, those who, when they receive information, never bother to enquire about its origin and validity. For such people who are operating on the level of the pleasure principle, the idea of consequences might be the criterion only up to the point where it serves their interests. Indeed, when the human mind has sunk to the centre of the gravitational force of desire, it is certainly crippled to operate on the basis of the reality principle. Therefore, it becomes very difficult to spread globally interconnected rational ideas when such a self-serving principle becomes the dominating factor for the individual and society. Under this scenario, *'misrepresentation by false association'* becomes an ideal tool with which the elites fabricate information to bolster or reinforce false concepts to preserve errant and inconsistent 'belief structures', in order to make fast bundles. Indeed, the world is being plundered just for the sake of more dollars. Where is the sense of integrity? It has certainly diminished to the vanishing point.

The bottom line is, if our problems are associated with our thought patterns, mixed-up priorities and resulting lifestyles, be they environmental, economic or social, or more precisely, be they AIDS, alcoholism, nationalism or depletion of ozone layer, then a cure is not possible without a

The Current State of Affairs

fundamental change in our outlook, both on the individual and collective levels. Truly, any other approach is a waste of time and efforts. Indeed, the denigration of thought is the fundamental disease. AIDS, alcoholism, etc. are only a few of the many symptoms which have emanated from the overarching cancer of systemic falsehood and misinformation, where we have not kept abreast of the truth. Thus, if humanity truly wants to change the way it is dying, it simply ought to change the way it is living, and that too, is possible only before it becomes too late. This is because, if we do not make the right choices today, we may end up with absolutely no choice tomorrow. Of course, the intention here is not to say that there is nothing good out there, but to point out that due to the way things are heading, humanity as a whole is in deep trouble. There is an urgent need to wake up and take the appropriate and necessary actions. After all, the future generations who are going to inherent this mess from us are our very own dear children.

Seeking a Viable Solution
Unfortunately, what we have been offered as solutions, i.e. feminism, socialism, pluralism and positivism (conventionalism) are themselves highly problematic; all doomed to collapse into vacuum. They are all like water which just looks like water; not only does it not quench thirst, but it makes the mouth even dryer with every sip. Each of the above-mentioned 'isms' is solely and biasly concerned about the affairs of its own segment. Each one offers a band-aid solution which overlooks the sources of folly and the conditions under which the predicament occurs. Therefore, it is bound to be problematic, ineffective and a false comfort. What is lacking here, is an intervolved system of thought which corresponds with the whole of reality and is thereby able to reconstruct humanity in consonance with that whole. In fact, this notion of something corresponding with the totality of reality has become entirely foreign to latter day generations. Yet, it is one thing to identify and describe the

problem and quite another to find the optimal solution for it — a solution which is free from any side-effects, a solution which is truly a remedy, not another disease.

On the other hand, there are many disenchanted individuals today, particularly those in the social and environmental movements who have come to know, face to face, the reality of that which most men have ridiculed. These group of people believe that the only way by which humanity and the natural world can be saved is by introducing a 'new religion'. Such individuals and groups do recognize the seriousness of our contemporary problems; yet some of them are hopeless about the future and some are vague about the solution. They have, however, two things in common in their assessments. Firstly, they strongly denounce man's anthropocentric attitude with his egotistical desires as the deciding factor for his mode of conduct. Secondly, they recognize man's need for attachment to some sort of novel sagacious ecumenical moral principle, since they feel that our old religions have failed us. For example, geneticist David Suzuki, a leading analyst of social and environmental issues sees a need for a new 'spiritual faith' similar to that of native Indians. Novelist and environmentalist, Walker Percy blames the present state of affairs to be a blow due to the estrangement of self in our naked secular society. Recently it was diagnosed by two environmentalists, King and Schneider, that there are two phenomena which are going in opposite directions:

> There is indeed a weakening of the moral sense of individuals, who feel cheated not only because the ethical structure that used to serve as their reference and to which they willingly submitted has collapsed, but also because the great threats of the contemporary world have frightened them into a chilly self-withdrawal. Simultaneously, there is a progressive collective awareness of the great problems of the world, old and

new, which is encouraging expectations and research. The spiritual and ethical dimension is no longer an object of scorn or indifference; it is perceived as a necessity that should lead to a new humanism.[1]

Similarly, physicist Heinz R. Pagels, commenting on our so-called civilization feels that:

> The challenge to our civilization which has come from our knowledge of the cosmic energies that fuel the star, the movement of light and electrons through matter, the intricate molecular order which is the biological basis of life, must be met by the creation of a moral and political order which will accommodate these forces or we shall be destroyed. It will try our deepest resources of reason and compassion.[2]

If the solution lies within the bounds of identifying and implementing a 'new humanism' or a 'new religion' as an alternative to the old ones, then, in so doing let us turn our competition to competition for a better human condition. Environmentalists are pleading to save the ecosystem. They are convincingly arguing that a potential drug against an unknown forthcoming plague might be lost for ever, due to an unwitting destruction of the rainforests. Similarly, the destruction of something of life sustaining value is not limited to the ecological sphere, but also applies to the realm of thought from which the socio-political environment springs. It is, therefore, crucial that an atmosphere of intellectual growth,

---

[1]. King, Alexander and Schneider, Bertrand. (1991), *The First Global Revolution: A Report by the Council of the Club of Rome*, p. 244.

[2]. Pagels, Heinz R. (1984), *The Cosmic Code: Quantum Physics as the Language of Nature,* p. 309.

From Facts to Values

tolerance and accurate portrayal of substantial holistic systems of value be discovered, lest they become lost in the ignorance of trivialization. We may lose sight of an optimal unified system that is capable of not only protecting our natural environment, but also capable of protecting and guiding rational human achievement towards the creation of a healthy society. We must remember that the best and most protective guard against corrupting influences is offered by the faculty of discernment which can only derive from the proper recognition, understanding and application of reality.

The authors of this book venture to direct the readers towards the suggested 'new humanism'. We shall try to offer an approach which will go beyond identification. The proposed approach of the book may be appealing to those individuals who are concerned and conscious of the great dilemmas we are facing on the earth today and are striving to discover how these problems can be addressed at their root level, by thinking things through for themselves, free from any external constraints. Such individuals are ones who would strive to reflect clearly, in age of utter confusion, for they would value being rational above anything else. They have already realized that all of the multiple problems on earth have resulted from selfish, incorrect or unfinished human thinking.

The first chapter of this book sees that the nature of our multifarious problems is deeply entrenched in the predominant acceptability of the belief that truth is relative. It attempts to debunk relativism and establish that reality, far from being relative, is in fact absolute. Consequently, in the second chapter we attempt to establish the methodology which identifies how we can arrive at the realization of the Absolute with certainty. In it, we shall deal with issues of a more 'scientific' nature and then, in the process, show that this methodology is not limited to the realm of 'natural science', but rather, is universal, permeating both the natural and social domains. The third chapter, using the proposed methodology and its implications, tackles the pressing socio-

The Current State of Affairs

economic, socio-political and socio-ecological issues. It seeks to establish a viable foundation for a value system by the use of first principles: using our mind and the signs in the universe, endowments readily accessible to any human beings, anywhere on this planet, at any time. We will evolve an argument which derives values from facts. Here, it was necessary to coin new terminology — the Equigenic Principle — to dissociate our ideas from the centuries' old misapprehension of 'natural law'. This chapter is a follow-up from certainty and absolutism. It is a follow-up since it extends the methodology of thought and its most salient and fundamental conclusions towards an analysis of the basis of rights. It shall be argued that if the foundation is realized, it should help transform society towards a consistent system of justice for all, be the recipients white or black; men or women; human or non-human. Indeed, if we truly want a panacea we would have to go to the foundation of things, to see what has caused the cracks in the structure we are a part of and how we can make amends. Anything less than an attempt at addressing the issues from the foundational level will be false comfort and superficial at best. Let us therefore avoid superficiality and get to the heart of the foundational issues that concern every thinking human being. Having dealt with foundational issues the final chapter is a brief introduction to the 'new humanism' commensurable with the Equigenic Principle and its associated concepts.

Although, we shall attempt to irrefutably and logically resolve these very issues; the ideas that have been proposed do, nonetheless, remain open to rational and constructive criticism. In particular, given the sensitive nature of the topics under discussion in this book, we would welcome any constructive feedback, discussion and a challenge on any of the arguments which are posited, in the spirit of gaining further understanding and steps towards the global reconstruction of human thought and society.

From Facts to Values

Relativism: Licence to Pure Nonsense

The lack of objectivity, sound judgement, mixed-up priorities and the widespread belief that truth is relative have all created a fertile ground for the emergence of ineffectual belief systems that are devoid of substance. The perniciously toxic underlying ingredient behind all these belief systems is no doubt the enticing face of easygoing Relativism. It should be emphasized at the very outset, that the kind of relativism that is under discussion in this section has nothing to do with taste, preference, art, beauty or the intensity of an emotional experience, etc. By all means, all of these notions may very well be relative, depending on the eye of the beholder. What is under discussion here is far deeper: it is the foundation of knowledge, justice, values and truth. It will be argued that none of these can be relative, circumstantial or arbitrary.

The dogmatic absurdity of Relativism has been exposed by many[3], yet this myopic outlook is predominantly embraced among both natural and social scientists, and is continuously propagated in educational settings[4]. Let us examine its baseless position.

What exactly is Relativism? Relativism is the popular view that truth is subjective and varies from individual to individual, group to group, culture to culture and time to time — it has no objective standard. All that is claimed to be the truth is merely a matter of personal opinion or customs. Therefore, it rejects any notion of absolute reality. That is to say, according to implications of relativism 2 X 2 is equal to 4, simply because

---

[3]. Harris, James F. (1992), *Against Relativism*.

Masters, Roger D. (1993), *Beyond Relativism: Science and Human Values*.

Siegal, Harvey (1987), *Relativism Refuted: A Critique of Contemporary Epistemological Relativism*.

[4]. Bloom, Allan. (1987), *The Closing of the American Mind*.

The Current State of Affairs

we are used to it. However, apart from the absurd implications of this illogical doctrine, the argument itself is incoherent and self-referential. In a nutshell, relativism suffers from what is sometimes referred to as the *glasshouse syndrome*[5], where arguments used against others, would equally apply to one's own position and arguments in defence of one's own position are also equally applicable to one's opponent's position. Let us probe this further.

There are only two possibilities: Either relativism is false or is true. If it is false, then it is naturally invalid and that is the end of it. But, if it is true, it is then actually false by its very own implications! How so? Suppose that we characterize the above argument as the proposition 'A' — that 'everything is indeed relative'. Now, it appears that if 'A' is true, that indeed everything is relative, then this should also apply to 'A' itself. In this case, 'A' must also turn out to be relative. However, if this is the case, then 'A' cannot serve as a premise to establish any valid assertion, due to its relative nature. That is to say, 'A' is nothing but a helpless product of the relativist's very own thought or culture. But if it is not so, that is, that 'A' is false (that is, 'A' is not relative), then not everything could be relative because 'A' is at least one thing which is not relative! In this case, it seems that 'A' is taken to be absolute: universal for every individual, group and time. Consequently, 'A' seems to have sadly refuted itself. Consider the following example where, philosopher Joseph Margolis, gives an elaborated account of relativism in his most recent book *The Truth about Relativism*.[6] Margolis spends 224 pages to defend and justify

---

[5]. This is the notion which basically reminds one of one's own state of severe vulnerability. For example, those whose house is made of glass had better remember not to cast any stone.

[6]. Margolis, Joseph. (1991), *The Truth about Relativism*.

relativism. Here is indeed a rare case where one can truly judge a book by its title. *Is the proposed truth about relativism relative or absolute?* As explained above, in either case his proposition turns out to be false, and his 224 page book, which can be debunked with one sentence, is indeed an embarrassing waste of paper and ink.

Moreover, if a relativist asserts that every individual or nation has a different reality, then it would be absurd to find a relativist disputing anything with anyone. For example, a relativist, such as Margolis, cannot argue against an absolutist that reality is not absolute, which is basically what he argues for, since absolutism is the relative reality of an absolutist. This would mean that, if the reader would also like to indulge in the murky waters of relativism, he or she cannot possibly tell me that I am wrong in holding my view, since my position that there is such a thing as absolute 'Truth' with the capital 'T' is my relative reality with a small 'r'. Unless we admit that there is an absolute objective standard by which we can judge, from a relativistic point of view, I cannot even be challenged, let alone be refuted! However, if we do agree upon the existence of an objective standard for judgement, then the case is closed; there would be no need for further discussions impinging upon relativism.

The catastrophic implication of relativism is that, firstly, there are no inherent principles of value. Secondly, it creates the ground for every nonsensical and indefensible view to be justifiable or at least believable. Without any standard of judgement, one man's opinion becomes just as good as another's. What he thinks to be true, is as likely to be true as what you think. Therefore, he is okay, you are okay, I am okay, everybody is okay, 'let us all hug each other'. Allan Bloom, professor of social thought states:

> I have never met a person who says, "I believe what I believe; these are just my values." There are always arguments. Nazis had them; Communists have them. Thieves and pimps have them ...

> However, these words are not reasons, nor were they intended to be reasons. All to the contrary, they were meant to show that our deep human need to know what we are doing [needs excuses] ... By some miracle these very terms became our justification: nihilism as moralism. It is not the immorality of relativism that I find appalling. What is astounding and degrading is the dogmatism with which we accept such relativism, and our easygoing lack of concern about what that means for our lives.[7]

Thirdly, relativism implies that facts are doubtable, and thereby, by the destruction of the possibility of certainty, it produces a polluted atmosphere in which it is felt that there is nothing that one can ever rely upon. "You cannot be certain about anything," is often said by relativists. If so, then, one should simply ask them, how did they become certain about that assertion?

By not responding to reason, relativism is nothing but pure dogmatism. It is, in fact, a dogmatic version of absolutism, rejecting rational absolutism which is supported by reason. Relativism is a psychological way of discrediting indisputable evidence. As such, relativism is a disease. It is like a cancerous growth stifling intellectual development. Indeed, relativism is the true opium of the mind. Relativism clings like a leech to desires; such a doctrine is not a product of intellectual inquiry, for it is an artifice which suppresses, distorts and hides the evidence. Despite its rampant profusion in society, there is not even one single shred of evidence to support it. For instance, a relativist cannot claim support for his position by arguments patterned on things which have to do with contextual situations such as, 'one man's medicine is

---

[7]. Bloom, Allan. (1987), *The Closing of the American Mind*, pp. 238-239.

From Facts to Values

another's poison'. Nor can the idea of some strange practice in a far off country be construed as being the truth for that particular society, but false for us, just because we never would engage in that exotic practice. This is because the reason why people engage in differing practices or have different values is connected to the way they 'perceive reality' and their extent of knowledge. For example, someone in the middle of a jungle may sacrifice a human to the god of thunder because he feels that his god would be pleased. That society may grow to accept this over time — it would become their entrenched 'value' as being something which is good to perform. However, this idea is based on a false notion and therefore cannot be true, because rain or thunder is not dependent on sacrifices to stone gods.

Moreover, if every individual and every society has its own particular version of reality, then who are we to condemn or criticize, for example, the corporate polluters, the disastrous deforestation of the Amazon rainforest, the racist neo-Nazis — after all, is their behaviour not their reality, and our discontentment lacking an absolute foundation?

Another strategy adopted to defend relativism is that which argues that there are many versions of relativism: the so-called 'naive-relativism', the 'epistemological relativism', the 'logical relativism' and the 'ontological relativism'. Quine, Goodman, Kuhn are the major culprits in the propagation of the sophisticated versions. An epistemological and logical relativist would claim that everything which has been said here is only a straw man attack on the epistemological, logical and ontological relativism, which he may agree with only to some extent. However, the epistemological relativist would retort that, unlike the naive relativist, his position is irrefutable. He holds the view that there is no objective knowledge of reality that is independent of the knower.

The arguments presented in defence of the sophisticated relativism are nothing but 'word games'. Take W.V. Quine's famous logical relativistic postulation that "No statement is immune to revision". If that is so, then in a similar vein, the statement that "no statement is immune to revision" is also subject to definite revision. After all, nothing is constant as it is suggested. Of course, if we take this "revision" to mean a simple amendment of statement and ideas, no one would argue with Quine. Yet, Quine is using the word "revision" as a Trojan horse, which hides the true import of its fundamental relativistic ramifications. In other words, the word "revision" is being used to mean something more than *upgrading*. Quine's postulation falls under the category of 'Fallacy of Counter-Suggestion' or 'Fallacy of Ambiguity'. In the former case, one says something, but in essence means something totally different. In the latter case, the essence of an argument is presented by a word which has more than one meaning, in this case *revision*. As such, his statement would not hold water with the relativistic connotation of the word revision. In fact, Quine's position in defence of sophisticated relativism is very much closer to the version advocated by 'naive-relativist'. He states that:

> The totality of our so-called knowledge or beliefs, from the most casual matters of geography and history to the profoundest laws of atomic physics or even of pure mathematics and logic, is a man-made fabric which impinges on experience only along the edges.[8]

Once again, we are witness to an argument that, if it is taken to be true, would immediately refute itself by its own implications. It seems that the so-called sophisticated logical relativism does not appear to be so sophisticated when analyzed even surficially. The schemes of Margolis, Quine, Goodman, Kuhn, etc., in essence, boil down to self-contradiction, because their postulations cannot escape the basic rules of logic. Whether one says that languages are

---

[8]. Quine, W.V. (1953), *From a Logical Point of View*, p. 42.

relative in colouring various fundamental notions of existence (Quine), or that we are all fixed by frames of reference (Goodman), or that all we have are ever-changing paradigms which are incommensurable, meaning that they cannot be compared to each other (Kuhn), their schemes cannot escape self-contradiction. That is because upon careful analysis they become subject to their own criticism. What these relativists are all essentially saying is that we perceive everything through frames of reference, regardless of the details of these frames, and that the human being is bound by them. As it has been repeatedly pointed out, though, this is just a typical case of suffering from the *glasshouse syndrome*, where one can equally counter-pose the valid question, as to what are the frames of reference for their assertions, which are dubiously taken to be absolute? It is not difficult to observe that the so-called sophisticated relativism indeed devolves into its primitive essence: naive relativism. Thus, needless to say, in essence, there is no difference at all between the naive and epistemological versions of relativism, as the confabulations of sophisticated relativism are just clothed in publications exhibiting verbose and convoluted statements and paragraphs, used as covering mechanisms. So much for the dissertations of sophisticated logical relativism!

Considering what relativism presupposes, no objective and honest person in his right mind would justify what relativism entails and stands for. For example, no academic relativist would go around behaving like a relativist in daily life, especially when his/her interest is at stake. When it comes to their own dear interests, all relativists suddenly become absolutists. All of this means that justice, values and human knowledge cannot be relative, but rather are absolute, and universal reality cannot vary from culture to culture. None of these attempts establish the validity of Relativism.

Relativism and Language: Does Language Shape Reality?
The latest arguments in support of relativism come from some philosophers and linguists who state that language shapes our

The Current State of Affairs

perception of reality. This group argues for the dependence of human thoughts on language, in such a way that language somehow determines or constitutes what one perceives, thereby shaping reality. This would imply that our notions of what belongs to the domain of reality is rendered for us in the language that we use.

The use of the 'language-creates-reality argument' is only one of the many which have emerged and will no doubt yet emerge from the odious bag of relativism. They all have the common indefensible position that tries to explain why something is relative. This argument appears to be so absurd that it is indeed not even worthy of analysis. Just like so many other self-referential fallacies, it takes only one line to demolish its utterly baseless position. If language shapes reality, then how can language itself be used to express and describe this postulation. That is to say, how can the human mind objectively use ordinary language to describe the limitation of human subjective thought due to the subjectivity and limitations of ordinary language? Those who use the 'language argument' are trying to say that everything is relative; however, they are using 'language' to say this. The use of this argument implies that cause and effect are an illusion dependent on language, and that language therefore causes this illusion. But, once again this is a contradiction, because then what is being said is that language causes the illusion (cause and effect). But, if cause and effect are an illusion, then how can language cause 'cause and effect'?

Consider the following example, if one's description of gravity is different than that of Newton's, i.e. that it is the opposite of how Newton perceived gravity, would this then mean that this individual would start floating in space at the onset of such a belief? Language is a description of cause and effect relations but it does not alter cause and effect. Death is death — no matter what language you use to describe it. Also, for instance, the Inuit have many words for snow — each one of which describes the subtle variations in the softness and shape of snow. They are more sensitive to it — they have a greater perception. However, snowfall itself is a fact and their language never shaped that! Language, therefore, does not shape the forces of reality; it may only create different understandings — however there is only one reality out there. Language has nothing to do with foundation of human understanding, for words translate human thought and language is the mapping of thought.

It is often claimed that if there are, for example, two different societies that have different languages, then their world pictures will be different and their realities likewise. However, if the context for particular situations is the same in each of these societies, there may be no difference in their understanding of reality because cause and effect relations are universally the same in nature and any sane description of them with accuracy would be the same no matter which society one emanates from. The context is universal.

Finally, for the sake of argument, suppose that it is granted that in some cases language shapes one's perception and understanding of reality. If from these specific cases we conclude that language, in general, shapes reality, then are we not making a profound mistake that the anti-inductivists try to warn us about — the error of making an illegitimate move from a particular instance to the universal truth? We shall come to this type of assertion in more detail in the second chapter.

In general it is becoming more and more apparent that whenever human beings try to escape an absolute and consistent system by resorting to relativity as described above, they are actually undoing their own arguments due to self-referentiality where, when the basic statement(s) of the relativistic scheme are analyzed, at the meta-level, the system contradicts itself. It is almost as if one were trying to escape the gravitational field of the earth with inadequate propulsion, being forced back to its surface each time.

Despite the lack of foundation, why is it that relativism enjoys such popularity? For various reasons: Firstly, it is because of its false association with the notions of democracy

The Current State of Affairs

and liberal tolerance. Secondly, because it fosters and protects the pleasure principle by shielding untutored desires. It is a covering mechanism which allows individuals and societies to indulge in pursuits based on whims rather than reason. The German poet Goethe said: "Let us not dream that reason can ever be popular. Passions, emotions may be made popular, but reason remains ever the property of the few."

Problem of Mysticism and its Inherent Demise

Another popular, yet monumentally faulty belief in society which appears in various guises is mysticism. Mysticism is in fact an offspring of relativism. Just like its parent, it is so appealing to desires, as opposed to the mind. The most common argument quite often used by those who attempt to defend mysticism is an appeal to personal experience — experiences which are sometimes supernatural and sometimes ordinary. However, one's personal experience is subjective, and unless it is objectified, it cannot possibly serve as the foundation for a universal belief system.

The kernel of mysticism is that, firstly, one cannot know the ultimate truth through the usage of reason. Truth ought to be inexplicable by its nature. Thus, those who subscribe to the notion of mysticism are urged to nurture a way of life based on blind faith. They accept things without reason and evidence, in order to obtain some type of Assurance. However, what is totally unacceptable here is that one cannot claim something to be true and then acknowledge its inconsistencies and its attendant difficulties, which tend to disintegrate its quasi-interconnections. That which is illogical to human intellect and cannot be understood explicitly with the support of reason and evidence cannot be vital. Ironically, even those who ardently propose non-rational answers to the question "why?" always attempt to rationalize irrationality by giving what they consider to be 'reasons' for believing, thus once again contradicting themselves at the very outset of their discourse (See Proposition 1, in the next chapter).

From Facts to Values

It must be pointed out that to defend a mystical proposition, any explanations which are offered, are merely explanations, not proofs. To prove means to give reasons why such is such. Thus, an explanation can never replace a proof. In addition, these explanations do not possess the quality of uniqueness, which is essential for Truth and Certainty. For example, someone may not be able to give a rational reason for his belief, but may then simply say: "I believe in it because my book say so", "I believe it, because it was manifested in my dream", or "I believe in it because that is what my forefathers believed." But, this is what all other different brands of mystical systems claim — so are they all true? Besides, in the first two responses, no amount of staunch belief can produce facts. In the third case, it seems that belief becomes hereditary and genetically passable onto the next generations. Not to mention, that even if one's forefathers somehow 'believed' it, so what? Why should anyone be loyal to wrong ideas, even if one's forefathers earnestly cherished those ideas?

Secondly, the followers of mystical schools seek recourse to some authority figure, or some intermediary between man and their notion of reality. However, the need for an authority figure and their notions of proof are distorted and are devoid of any logical connections with the fundamental questions of life. For example, the purported ability of a 'master' being able to levitate in mid-air, does not prove any non-rational idea such as "three gods created the cosmos" and that one must therefore follow the biddings of such a levitating master. Furthermore, why does one need a master, when one can always maintain an open mind? All to the contrary, the need for a so-called leading master arises only when one goes cognitively blind.

Another point of commonality in many brands of mysticism is that they do not possess the property of timelessness or universality. If you do not belong to a particular region, or a particular tribe, or if you do not believe in a particular person who may be regarded as divine or semi-divine, who exists now, or perhaps did so in the past, you cannot be saved. The question which arises here is: What about the multitude of people before the time of the advent of such a particular saviour. Are they all doomed? If no, then their system is not necessary. If yes, then their system is not fair because it treats people differentially, just because they happened to be born in the wrong time or place by 'accident of birth'.

One of the great fallacies in mysticism is the notion that truth can be arrived at instantaneously, when one achieves a disconnection with cause and effect relations — where one would merge into or see the Truth or some type of Divine Essence. The claimants of this assumption say that they do not rely on the analytical mind for this purported achievement, but transcend the mind and all reason by intuition? However, the great flaw in this argument is that the mind is an integrated unit which operates in space and time and is dependent wholly on space and time, cause and effect, and that therefore, in this universe one cannot separate intuition from the other processes such as analytical thought, if we want to determine reality. Most mystics always talk about oneness of being and purpose, yet, they blatantly contradict the notion of the integration of the mind when it comes to the issue of thinking, and the integrated and convergent nature of evidence.

Since mysticism is irrational and yet is spreading rapidly in most human societies, it is causing a breakdown of the natural pattern in the social fabric by allowing irrationality to become the accepted norm of thinking. This consequently, manifests itself in concomitant problematic social behaviour.

The negation of relativism and its offspring mysticism, indicates the existence of an epistemological absolutism and certainty. However, there are some serious misapprehensions surrounding the concept of absolutism which need to be clarified. Most people, in general, are fearful of anything which is presented as absolute. This is because the notion of absolutism is often falsely associated with intolerance, extremism, authoritarianism, radicalism and so on. It is due to such harsh and grim images that people psychologically drift away from absolutism and are, conversely, attracted to easygoing relativism. However, the proper notion of absolutism is free from all of the above erroneous associations. Absolutism has nothing to do with coercion; it is only an epistemological contrast to relativism. It means that truth and values are not relative but absolute and unchangeable. They can also be objectively determined. Unlike relativism, they are not subject to the vicissitudes of time, culture and human perception. They are absolute by their inherent nature not by any external coercion. However, if that is so, what is the Absolute Truth? How can we be absolutely certain of anything? This fundamental issue is the subject of the next chapter.

Chapter Two

The Certainty of Human Knowledge

The highest wisdom has but one science — the science of explaining the whole creation and man's place in it.

Leo Tolstoy

Towards Establishment of the Universal Reality Principle

The question of Certainty comes naturally to any thinking individual. In particular, it is the most crucial concern for those who wish to be confident and secure about what they believe in. That is, those who are concerned about the Reality Principle. Yet, the crux of the matter is: If the Reality Principle is the ultimate deciding guideline, then how can reality be determined? How can one differentiate sense from nonsense, facts from myths, appearances from reality — if one ever can at all! Indeed, for that matter, is there really such a thing as Reality? And if there is, is it discoverable by human intellect? On the other hand, if it is not discoverable by human intellect, then how can we ever be certain that there is indeed no such thing as reality. If everything is just a matter of opinion and interpretation, then it makes one wonder which of those diverse opinions is true. However, if there is such a thing as Reality, then how can reality ever be determined? Whatever the answer is, it would have to be based on absolute certainty. This leads us to ask: How can we become certain of either case? And if certainty is obtainable, then how do we go about becoming certain? What are the criteria? Specifically, what exactly is the methodology required to bring us to the Certainty of the Reality?

There are those who seriously advocate that the whole of existence is just a grand illusion. However, such proponents seem to circumvent the blatantly obvious fact that there is indeed such a thing as Reality. Not only do we derive this conclusion from our lifetime experiences which would, for one thing, tell us that we are not living a dream, but also from the fact that reality must exist, because if we assume that "there is no such thing as reality", then the concept that "there is no such thing as reality" must, in fact, be the absolute, immutable, and concrete universal reality, which contradicts the very assertion in the first place.

Contrary to the popular belief that Certainty is unreachable, in this chapter, it is being argued that it is indeed reachable by the usage of reason and evidence, integrally accompanied by the methodology of consistency, which alone is the measure for determining truth and falsity. With this approach, the relationship between knowledge and the process of reaching the certainty of the Truth shall be discussed — for in order to recognize what the Truth is, one has to have a true concept of the Truth, for which the validity of the true concept itself has to be established. A proposal for the methodology of science in this process is also being offered in order to resolve the shortcomings of present scientific methodological schemes, such as 'falsifiability' and 'paradigm shifts'. Most importantly, it will be shown that scientific inquiry is only an extension of common-sense in the urge to verify beliefs and assumptions. Such an inquiry, is not the exclusive property of something which happens in labs by those who wear white coats. Furthermore, it will be shown that no separation and difference exists between science and 'metaphysics' from a methodological perspective, in our attempts to discover the ultimate existence and nature of things. Any such separation is only a result of erroneous reasoning and incomplete thoughts. A proof for the existence of a Singular Creator is also provided in this context. Among the issues discussed, by way of example, are the major ideas in physics and biology, such as the Big-Bang, biological evolution and teleology. In the light of the various methodologies dealing with thought and the evidence, an attempt has been made to examine these matters decisively, so as to determine whether they belong to the category of fiction, theory or fact.

Methodology
In order to determine the certainty of human knowledge, one ought to start from correct premises. From the most obvious notions, we must then advance further, step by step, making .sure that at each step, the argument is absolutely indisputable. In this process one must never blindly rely on the authority of supposed 'experts', without examining their

The Certainty of Human Knowledge

purported evidence, in particular, when such supposed experts are basing their theories on relativism and conventionalism. To discover anything of value, one ought not to regurgitate the works of other 'scholars' in an attempt to fathom the answers, since mistakes and inconsistencies can be passed on from writer to writer, generation to generation, particularly when no one has confirmed the veracity of their findings. The veracity of one's scholarly paper does not at all depend on the quantity of one's references handed in as a collage of multifarious quotations bound together, nor does it depend on the 'authority' of the 'scholars' being referred to; rather, it solely depends on the quality of the contents and process. The quality is directly dependent on the soundness of the methodology applied. The methodology must be based on the keen observation of what is happening around us and in the universe, by the usage of one's mind. Hence, in order to seek the absolute foundation of knowledge, we are left with only one viable option, which is, to set aside all our biases and preconceptions and start from scratch, using what is available to our faculties. The internal faculty — the mind — must always objectively interact with the external reality — the universe. Our methodology must be in absolute congruity with the universe of cause and effect, and furthermore, it ought to be consistent within itself — throughout. To set aside one's biases and preconceptions means to start with a totally objective approach. However, is total objectivity possible in life? The reason why some people are imprisoned by their biases, is because they have particular mindsets which function on the pleasure principle as opposed to the reality principle. However, there are other individuals who are willing to step outside of themselves and view the entire situation, including themselves, in order to make sound judgements, even if they may be against their preferences. Finally, if one wishes to dismiss the possibility of total objectivity, then one ought to approach the debate in a non-subjective manner; however, what is the non-subjective manner other than the objective approach. That is to say, if one proclaims that there is no objectivity, then this means that the statement is either subjective or objective, and as it has already been established it is a self-refuting approach. We shall deal in more detail with this kind of a futile approach in the next chapter (under Proposition 1).

In order to accomplish the vital task of ascertaining the foundations of absolutism, we must apply knowledge, as opposed to dogma. However, at the very outset we must clearly define what constitutes knowledge and dogma, in order to avoid the emergence of any rebuttles involving any red herring, straw-man and ad hominem fallacies.

Knowledge
Certainty is connected to the state of knowledge. But, what exactly is knowledge? Knowledge is the awareness of reality and the concomitant proper action that follows therefrom. Actions which correspond with reality are the outwardly visible measures of knowledge. To correspond with reality means that all of our concepts must be both *internally self-consistent, and externally consistent* with the universe or the world outside. Knowledge must also be consistent with the natural processes, in that, it must be a non-contradictory description of the rule of cause and effect. Therefore, only the proper organization of information is knowledge, just as only the proper assemblage of pieces of wood is a table. This is what separates knowledge from mere valid or invalid un-integrated pieces of information, piled up, as it were, in a heap. Indeed, knowledge is not the accumulation of information, as it is commonly assumed; rather, it is the proper organization of all the relevant information directed towards a specific goal — the meaning and purpose of all.

Knowledge can only be acquired by the proper usage of our mind and senses. What is meant by "the proper usage of the mind and senses" is the usage of the faculty of reason. Reason is the natural interconnection of information which corresponds with the concrete reality in this universe of cause and effect relations. This implies that anyone having an impressive university education with a PhD., BSc., LLd., MBA,

The Certainty of Human Knowledge

and any other permutation and combination of alphabets appended to his or her name, certainly cannot be deemed as being truly knowledgeable, if, for instance, that individual consistently engages in the destruction of oneself, the social and the natural environment. For example, a medical doctor who smokes and drinks is not at all acting as an intelligent or a knowledgeable individual. He is just like a donkey carrying medical books — so oblivious as to their content. After all, what is the use of knowing all that information if it does not manifest itself in one's behaviour.

On the other hand, an 'illiterate' farmer in an obscure village, who sees the interconnectivity of the causal order and consistently utilises his social and natural environment in the most harmonious way is indeed truly knowledgeable. This presupposes that the individual in question looks at the factual relations and evidence in the universe without covering the facts and accepts reality for what it is, irrespective of his possible personal 'losses' and erroneous preconceptions. It is only when the implications of what one sees to be the case is freely and unhesitantly expressed in behaviour, is one then said to be a knowledgeable person. The mere acknowledgement of knowing that such and such is the case is not sufficient criteria for knowledgeablity. The manifestation of the implications in one's daily public and private conduct is the only true indicator for possessing knowledge.

Towards gaining knowledge, the sought after evidence does not depend upon the proclamations of an 'authority', but rather, on the value of the proclamation in relation to how it fits with the totality of reality in terms of correspondence and global stability — stability in the sense of not causing any disruption, leading to harm.

Dogma

Keeping the above-mentioned definition of knowledge in mind, dogma is counter-knowledge or pseudo-knowledge, trying to pass off as knowledge. Dogma is an unsubstantiable

From Facts to Values

quasi-'belief' wrapped up with pseudo-intellectual trappings and jargon. It is devoid of evidence and proof. It is a spurious construct engulfed in selfish desires which arrogantly or blindly denies reality and insults human intelligence.

Dogma is not necessarily associated with superstitious beliefs and the inane approaches of the dark ages. It could also be ubiquitous in the modern era of science, technology and academic circles. In fact, these days the most noxious form of dogma is vividly present where it is least expected — in universities, among the academics, the so-called 'guardians of knowledge'. The present day universities are institutions that are intellectually bankrupt. They have turned into arenas for pseudo-intellectual wrestling among academics. Particularly in fields of humanities and social sciences, professors while reclining in the comforts of their opulent ivory towers, discuss the semantics of how many camels could conceivably dance on the head of a pin. Many of them have become more concerned about the status quo to remain as faculty members, than about genuine research and authenticity. It is here, where knowledge far from being sought, is in fact suppressed. Indeed, universities are not a place to enlighten pupils, but to endarken them. As such, universities foster an environment which is very hostile to growth of knowledge as defined above. Speaking the truth is often considered an offensive act. Students are penalized in subtle ways for challenging the prevailing dominant view of their department. "How dare you make sense, you're not suppose to reason, but to repeat," is reverberated in many a lecture. The whole system is set up to get students to regurgitate foolish ideas without any cognitive activity taking place within.

These modern day dogmatic educational institutions like other hypocritical institutions are threatened by the promotion of knowledge as defined here. Students who spend years in universities to be educated are in fact being de-educated, programmed towards certain goals and 'politically correct' ideologies. The idea is not to give them any education at all,

The Certainty of Human Knowledge

because once they are truly educated, of course, they all start to pose a serious threat to the whole de-intellectualized system. What they are given instead is enough tunnel-vision training to be productive within the existing system. All they learn in four years is how to make living, not how to live. As such, in universities today, it is indeed dogma which is being manufactured and deposited, not knowledge.

One of the facets of dogma is the lack of integration or interconnection in the thought structure of the individual. Such a perspective is so narrow that it precludes the inclusion of other pertinent information[9] which has a bearing on the question at hand, simply because, for instance, it may not be the specialization of that particular individual. In this respect, the hidden dogmatism which is often committed by pseudo-intellectuals of our time, is when they try to analyze and measure the cost and benefit of an action, in isolation, not in relation to other interconnected issues. Most of them even fail to detect the connection. Another facet of dogma is the incompleteness of ongoing thought processes. Often, an individual may start an intelligent analysis, but suddenly stop the thinking process when the discoveries conflict with that individual's desires and self-interests. Knowingly cutting short the path which leads to evidential conclusions is a sure sign of dogmatic inclinations.

A good historical example of dogma in action is when Bruno was burned at the stake by the dogmatic Church for saying that the earth was not at the centre of the universe, just because it visually appears so. Bruno stated:

> If therefore the Universe is infinite, why place the earth at its centre? The sun, the father of life, is the centre of our world; but the centre of the infinite universe is in all things...for the

---

[9]. In logic, this is referred to as 'special pleading', a presentation of only that portion of the information, which suits one's vested interests.

> centre of the universe is neither the sun nor in the sun, neither the earth, nor in the earth, nor in any place whatever... Therefore, there are as many centres as there are worlds...[10]

However, when we connect all the relevant facts, our findings testify against the erroneous notion of geocentrism. Therefore, it could well be said that Bruno was certainly not the one holding onto dogma. Bruno was using the very same methodology suggested in this chapter (at least in this respect) — the sole usage of the mind together with the observations of the celestial phenomena. However, the illogical and unintegrated approach of the Church was at the zenith of dogmatism. Bruno resisted the anti-Copernican view despite the violent pressures imposed by the institution and the masses who were under their ecclesiastical influence. As in the Middle Ages there are many modern day Brunos who oppose popular ideas backed up by various governmental, corporate and pedagogical institutions. Such individuals may pose a threat to the established norms — norms which may, in actuality, be totally fallacious, having no medium of support and evidence.

For a truly knowledgeable and intelligent person the network of cause and effect is undeniable: This universe functions according to various causal processes. For example, we know that food is necessary for life, that there is oxygen, that there is gravity which makes life possible on earth and that there is death. We know about these things from the collection and processing of information, by the usage of our mind and senses. It is only from these faculties that we can gain knowledge of the reality of these cause and effect relations and hence possess Certainty or move towards Certainty.

---

[10]. Fowler, W.S. (1962), *The Development of Scientific Method*, pp. 40-41.

The Certainty of Human Knowledge

One aspect of knowledge is the description and explanation of the physical processes in this universe, from a quantitative perspective known as the 'natural or physical sciences'. Scientists aim to discover reality by means of what most of them classify as two mutually exclusive methodologies: induction or deduction. Using induction or deduction, they hope to distinguish between science and pseudoscience, and between theory and fact. Yet, these classifications of methodology and their corollaries have been criticised over the ages by the anti-deductivists, or conversely, by the anti-inductivists, as having their respective limitations. Before we enter into a discussion of the proposed solution to the whole problem of induction and deduction and scientific methodology in general, let us examine the historical and contemporary views on the issue of scientific investigation itself. Attempts have been made to resolve the many shortcomings, but so far the various thinkers on these issues have not come up with a satisfactory universal resolution.

From Facts to Values

Background: Induction or Deduction in the Realm of Science?

Over the millennia, a large number of philosophers have attempted to answer the fundamental questions of how we come to know things. Unfortunately, instead of providing solutions to these basic issues, in most cases, their attempts have been counterproductive. This is because their approach has been extremely fragmented and disconnected. They were often so busy trying to refute one another, that the main issue was sometimes lost. In seventeenth century Europe, Rene Descartes exerted himself to establish a foundation for the certainty of human knowledge.[11] Yet, he failed to develop an adequate methodology. His proposed approach was too confined and narrow in scope. To defeat the sceptics of his time, he only managed to prove the existence of an individual's own internal self, neglecting to address the issue of global certainty adequately.

The Inductive Method, is it Reliable?

Let us first deal with induction. Induction refers to the method of basing *general* statements derived from accumulated observations of *specific* instances. More precisely, induction involves proceeding from sets of particular observations to general laws. For example, if scientists find that every metal which they expose to heat, expands, then inductively they could argue that *all* metals must expand when heated.

However, induction, though plausible, could end up being a fallible exercise requiring a great deal of caution. For example, often, many biological, anthropological, and psychological theories are said to be provisional. This means

---

[11]. Descartes, Rene. *A Discourse on the Method*, (1637) and *Meditations on First Philosophy*, (1641), in the *Philosophical Works of Descartes*, translated by E.S. Haldane & G.R.T. Ross, (1968).

The Certainty of Human Knowledge

that an explanation which accounts for all observations, is put forward with the acknowledgement that some other theory may account for the same observations. In other words, a different explanation might account for the same data. In the application of an inductive methodology, one has to be cautious of the fact that an explanation is not a proof and that it may certainly not be the only possible causal explanation. For example, the over-population of seals may account for decline of Atlantic fisheries, but is this the only possible explanation for the loss of cod fish? Often when scientists, politicians, or theologians are asked to prove their positions, they may go on and on *explaining* them, rather than *proving* them.

Since the seventeenth century many scientists and philosophers like Hume, Whewell, Mill and Eddington have radically argued that no number of observations, however large, could logically justify an unrestrictive general statement. They claim that if one constantly observes that B is always followed by A, it is simply the description of the events in the past, and that regular past events cannot predict future events. Therefore, according to them, although we may come to expect that B will always be followed by A, this may not necessarily be due to the logical sequence, but rather, may be the result of classical conditioning. Hume believed that tendency towards justifying a claim by appealing to past regular experiences is a fact of psychology, and therefore, the exercise is bound to be futile. For example, the fact that the sun has been rising every morning, for the past billions of years, is not enough to conclude that it will rise and shine tomorrow morning. These critics are quick to completely dismiss induction as a credible foundation for human knowledge.

Induction is no doubt a dependable method to falsify a theory, but it has some weaknesses in proving a theory. The crucial point is that, although we can rely on inductive investigation, we should also recognize its limitations and at times its lack of finality. We should acknowledge that both observations and experimentations could sometimes be inconclusive, since scientists cannot observe and absorb everything all at once — they can only do so gradually. Nevertheless, modifications in scientific findings should emanate from a constant pursuit of careful inductive generalizations, where superficial observations and experimentations are cautiously avoided. With the use of such a methodology, we only have to bear in mind that the credibility of the inductive approach depends on important factors such as considering the conditions under which an observation is conducted, by evaluating all the possible variables. Therefore, the sceptics' criticisms are valid only to the extent that unless the conditions are known, the observation is worthless or unreliable. This is as far as their criticism can be valid. They can only argue, for example, that a claim such as, "a certain liquid boils at $100°$ C" has no value, if we do not observe: the density of the liquid, its purity and its atmospheric pressure. However, once all of these factors have been taken into consideration, the conclusions are perfectly valid and so indeed is the methodology.

The opponents of induction, seemingly fail to acknowledge that many well established scientific facts were discovered through such calculated systematic observations. Many of these discoveries could later on be tested in the laboratories, in controlled natural settings, or could be defended mathematically and supported by rational thinking. It is indeed through the use of this system of scientific discovery, that human beings have uncovered a vast storehouse of knowledge about how the universe that surrounds us operates. This is, for example, the methodology that Galileo, Copernicus, and Kepler used to discover that the earth is neither flat nor at the centre of the universe. This is also the methodology that naturalists such as George Romans, Diane Fossey and Jane Goodall have used to study animal behaviour.

Moreover, no anti-inductivist, in the daily affairs of life, can be entirely a non-inductivist. Interestingly enough, *even the*

The Certainty of Human Knowledge

opponents of induction use inductive reasoning to discredit induction. Induction as it has already been mentioned proceeds from sets of specific observations to the universal. However, the anti-inductivists cite certain specific inconclusive inductive bits of reasoning to generalize that induction as a whole is unreliable. Their criticism, however, undermines their very own position. While it is true that certain regular sequential events are, for instance, habitual, this does not mean that all regular sequential events are habitual. Therefore, in order to dismiss induction, one is bound to use a non-inductive approach. Failing to do so, that is, by using the same methodology that one is trying to attack, one is actually arguing in its favour rather than against it, as intended.

By self-refutation we find many inductive inferences in Hume's empiricism — Hume being an ardent champion of anti-induction. For example, in his theory of animal intelligence he states that, "beasts are intelligent beings". Hume believes that an animal's intellectual inferiority to human beings is just a matter of degree. Hume, saw the source of animals' intelligence in their natural instinct, as well as in animals being able to learn many things from observation. In response to Descartes, who had earlier refuted animal intelligence, Hume states that:

> ...next to the ridicule of denying an evident truth, is that of taking much pain to defend it; and no truth appears to me more evident, than that beasts are endowed with thought and reason as well as men. The arguments in this case are so obvious, that they never escape the most stupid and ignorant.[12]

Needless to say, the formulation of this theory arises from past inductive inferences, deduced from inductive observations —

---

[12]. Hume, David. (1888), *A Treatise of Human Nature*, p. 176.

From Facts to Values

the very same methodology which he had already refuted. Indeed, Hume appears to have unwittingly fallen victim to his very own induction. Here is an individual who seems not to be convinced at all, logically speaking, that the sun will rise tomorrow, just because inductively we know that it has been rising every day since the beginning of the earth. Hume's approach to the sun-rising question and the question of animal intelligence is completely inconsistent. For we certainly have a clear and quantitative understanding of the orbits of celestial bodies such as the earth's motion. On the other hand, comparatively speaking, the nature of animal psychology is a more nebulous area and one would have to 'induce' many things before one makes such a pronouncement about animal behaviour. One could ask Hume: How do you know that an animal is intelligent? He would have to cite specific behavioural responses. But, we could then ask: How do you know that animal will respond again in the same manner, if the appropriate response or any other specific action is a measure of intelligence? If one surveys the argument closely, one would realize that the sun certainly appears to have set on Hume's inconsistent approach.

On the contrary, is there any evidence to give the slightest indication that the sun, for instance, will not rise tomorrow? Any kind of sceptical objection to the physical laws of nature must surely be based on the realm of reason and human experience — it should not pop-out of the blue and then cover the entire horizon. Moreover, when rational inductivists expect that the sun will rise tomorrow, they are implicitly expecting the condition that it will do so, if and only if the laws continue to operate as before. Therefore, to expect that the sun will rise tomorrow given the same conditions, indeed is a fact of logic, while the *denial* of this would be psychological, not logical.

Another and most recent indictment against induction comes from contemporary scientists and philosophers. There are those who state that to start an inductive investigation,

The Certainty of Human Knowledge

one needs first to formulate a hypothesis. In so doing, the formulated hypothesis may be culturally, socially or individually biased, or, may be influenced by the dominant ideological theories, models and ways of thinking in vogue at the time. According to this group, every scientist is a product of his social culture and is very much influenced by the predominant views of his scientific community. Therefore, in the process of investigation, data collection and analysis, one becomes inadvertently blind to other pertinent information. Such opponents of induction argue that an observer in the field only finds what he is looking for. He only sees things the way he expects them to be seen. The same charge applies to the manner and the set-up of experimentations conducted in a lab. Thus, as the result of such shortcomings, some crucial information might easily be overlooked.

However, without hesitation, it should be acknowledged that this is certainly the case in *some* instances, or may even very well be true in *most* instances, but can this be true in *all* instances? Can such limitation be characterized as an inherent property of induction? Certainly not, firstly, because the accusation is undoubtedly another inconclusive move from specific to general rule. Secondly, as it has already been indicated, the validity of induction solely depends on objectivity and consideration of all factors. Thirdly, once again the above charges seem to suffer from the glasshouse syndrome, since one can equally argue that the above statement is itself an inductive hypothesis. Therefore, one in processes of confirmation one has become inadvertently blind to the counter evidences which disproves it.

Rational vs. Pathological Sceptical Challenge

There are some who hold extreme positions against induction. A radical anti-inductive sceptic wishes to doubt everything which is proposed. His position is basically already set at the outset: "Do not bother defending your position, I will question anything you say!" Should we take such a sceptic seriously? Certainly not! For this approach is inconsistent with itself and the sceptic's objection does not contribute anything whatsoever to the discussion. Firstly, if one wishes to doubt everything, then one has to even doubt one's own doubt. Secondly, if one wants to doubt everything, then one will not even come to the beginning of the process where one starts to doubt. Even if somehow one starts to doubt everything one will get caught up in the infinite regress and not be able to stop doubting. Thirdly, the anti-inductive sceptic too, has to explain and defend his sceptical approach as having some validity and use. In this case one can equally and rightfully claim: "Do not bother defending your sceptical position, for I will question anything you say". So how does one begin in such an unfruitful system which would tend to leave one in a state of limbo? It seems that anti-inductivists are in the habit of constantly coming up with self-referential arguments.

To put the whole sceptical anti-inductivist approach in a nutshell, they claim that: since science keeps changing all the time and inductive reasoning cannot guarantee certainty "we can never be certain about anything." In this case one should respond by asking them, if they can be certain about that statement!

Deductivism, a possible alternative?

On the other hand, deductive reasoning is an approach to scientific inquiries in which it is impossible to come up with wrong conclusion(s) when one's premise(s) is valid. That is to say, it is impossible to deny the conclusion without contradicting what is explicitly given in the premise(s). The seventeenth century philosopher, Rene Descartes, whose aim was to achieve epistemological certainty, was one of the main proponents of the deductive approach. Descartes was impressed with mathematical certainty. Thus, he approached philosophy, metaphysics and natural science in a very similar manner to the basic methodology employed in mathematics. He believed, that knowledge derived through the inductive method such as by empirical means, can always deceive us. Thus, the inductive approach can never establish

The Certainty of Human Knowledge

epistemological certainty. Hence, according to Descartes, the deductive methodology is the only way by which man can emerge out of the confusion of contradictory opinions, towards clarity and security engendered by mathematical facts and evidence.

However, anti-deductivists argue that deduction, despite its universality brings no new knowledge. That is, they assert that, what is already implicit in the premise(s) is once again brought up, but just in a different form. They cite the example of deductive propositions such as: "all bachelors are unmarried" or "all bodies are extended", where the premises express the same propositions as the conclusions; hence, their negation is naturally contradictory. Moreover, the validity of deductive reasoning depends on the validity of information contained in the premise(s), which is often assumed to be true.

Although the anti-deductivists' criticisms may be valid in some cases, they are certainly not valid in general. What actually happens with deduction, despite its limitations, is that the existing information is re-interconnected, yielding new conclusion(s) from the finite sets of premises. Deduction is a helpful way of sorting out information which is already contained *implicitly* in the premise(s). For example, all formal mathematical reasoning used in science is deductive in nature. Such reasoning often fulfils its objectives. One cannot, therefore, easily dismiss deduction as a mere exercise in futility.

In general, in the pursuit of scientific investigation one could indeed use both induction and deduction, depending on the availability of information and what exactly it is that one is trying to ascertain. There ought not to be any artificial polarizations.

Falsification and its Limitations

Karl Popper, a philosopher of science, acknowledged the limitations of the inductive method. He suggested that although no number of empirical observations that "all swans are white", would logically allow us to derive the universal statement that "all swans are white", a single observation of a black swan, would logically allow us to derive the universal statement that "not all swans are white". This means that although scientific laws may not be conclusively verifiable, as Hume had pointed out, they can, however, be conclusively falsifiable. Here is Popper in his own words:

> If this decision is positive, that is, if the singular conclusions turn out to be acceptable, or *verified*, then the theory has, for the time being, passed its test: we have found no reason to discard it. But if the decision is negative, or in other words, if the conclusions have been *falsified*, then their falsification also falsifies the theory from which they were logically deduced.
>
> It should be noticed that a positive decision can only temporarily support the theory, for subsequent negative decisions may always overthrow it. So long as a theory withstands detailed and severe tests and is not superseded by another theory in the course of scientific progress, we may say that it has 'proved its mettle' or that it is *'corroborated'* by past experience.[13]

For Popper, falsification is the criterion which demarcates science and non-science. Hence, one is able to use the

---

[13]. Popper, Karl R. (1975), *The Logic of Scientific Discovery,* p. 33.

The Certainty of Human Knowledge

falsifiability criterion to dismiss Parapsychology, Psychoanalysis, Eugenics, and Marxism as being totally unscientific, invalid and false. However, the suggested standard may not be able to be satisfied even by those theories which are 'respectable'. According to Alan Chalmers, a contemporary philosopher of science, Popper's methodology is problematic, if the falsification rule is followed in its strictest sense:

> Suppose, for instance, we take falsificationism to involve the demand that falsified theories be rejected. Then, unless 'Falsified' is interpreted so weakly as to be ineffective, exemplary scientific theories fail to meet the demand. For instance, throughout its dramatically successful history, Newton's astronomy was confronted by observations incompatible with it, ranging from observations of the moon's orbit to those of the orbit of the planet Mercury.[14]

Also, for example, over two thousand years ago, the Greek philosopher Democritus, claimed that all physical things in nature are divisible into atoms (atomism), yet during his days he had no means of testing his theory or offering any predictions for falsification. Similarly, physicist David Bohm, in response to the question of whether new experiment could be conducted to test his novel new theory of Quantum Mechanics, retorts that:

> [Such testing of my theory] is a bit premature, because we are in a peculiar situation, as when Democritus proposed the atomic hypothesis several thousand years ago... There was no way at that time to propose an experiment. Even if anybody had

---

[14]. Chalmers, Alan. (1990), *Science and Its Fabrication*, p. 16.

> been ingenious enough to propose one, there was no equipment available that would have made it possible anyway. And yet the idea was still valuable ... It took 2,000 years to get enough content into atomic theory to propose an experiment. So what would you have said? That nobody should think about it until suddenly an idea would occur for an experiment. Experiments would never have been done if nobody had thought about it.[15]

According to Popper's scheme, Democritus' view could not have been, at the time, classified as a scientific theory or hypothesis. However now, we have discovered that things are comprised of atoms — even though atoms are not like billiard balls and are divisible. Therefore, Popper's approach seems to have fallen short of a comprehensive method by which to explain that which is and is not science. We shall return to these two examples to analyze them in greater detail.

This state of 'intellectual ping-pong' has led to a conflict about what is science and pseudoscience, and what is fact and theory. Indeed, the pertinent question is: When does a theory come to be realized as being a fact, if it ever does?

---

[15]. Davies, P.C. & Brown, R.R. (1989), *The Ghost in the Atom*, p. 126.

Resolution by Consistency

The issue at hand is, how do I know what I know is true. More precisely, what is the methodology which one can firmly apply to distinguish between nonsense, theory and fact. In this chapter, the universal solution will be proposed and elaborated upon. Furthermore, it will be argued that the following three propositions that will unfold in the course of discussion are the only sound methodology employable:

> **Proposition 1:** *Any proposition which is internally inconsistent is neither a fact nor a theory. It is pure nonsense.*

Internal consistency means that there should be no contradictions from within. There are two kinds of internal inconsistency. The first is the one in which the two ideas put together are mutually exclusive. The second is the case where the idea proposed is inherently self-consuming. In any proposition, one aspect of a claim should not refute the whole of the claim or another aspect of it, for otherwise the claim becomes a self-implosive construct.[16] For example, consider Nietzsche's well-known proclamation. As a cultural relativist, he believed that: "There is no such a thing as fact, but only interpretation." The proposition presented here by Nietzsche is a typical case of self-contradictory paradox. The question is: Is the above proposition itself a fact? Or, is it merely one's subjective interpretation? Needless to say, if it is a subjective interpretation, then it is biased and cannot lead to certainty. The above example can only be taken seriously if it is offered as fact. If so, it seems then, that it both affirms and denies its basic assertion. Such a proposition is simultaneously both self-protective and self-destructive, as it is condemned by its own

---

[16]. Johnson, R.H. and Blair, J.A. (1983), *Logical Self-Defence,* pp. 59-63.

verdict. Thus, Nietzsche's assertion, due to its inherent self-referential nature falls into the category of pure *nonsense*.

In another example, consider the Freud's speculation that man's behaviour and daily activities are constantly motivated by unconscious sexual desires and power. As Allan Bloom has pointed out, if this argument is true, then this should also apply to Freud's account of psychology and his very own 'scientific' activities. However, Freud did not consider these hidden motives to explain his own view of psychoanalysis. That is to say, formulating theories inspired by sex and power is not at all objective science. Allan Bloom states:

> But if he can be a true scientist, i.e., motivated by love of the truth, so can other men, and his description of their motives is thus morally flawed. Or if he is motivated by sex or power, he is not a scientist, and his science is only one means among many possible to attain those ends.[17]

Thus, similar to Nietzsche, Freud's supposition also easily falls into the category of pure *nonsense*. Both views suffer from the *glasshouse syndrome*.

Another blatant case of internal inconsistency can be found in the Christian doctrine of deity: a being who is at the same time both man and God, both the Creator and createe, both mortal and immortal, both finite and infinite. This doctrine is also internally inconsistent because the two concepts of humanity and divinity are mutually exclusive and cannot co-exist together. To be one means not to be the other, just like the imaginary concept of square-circle. A square-circle is a sheer contradiction — a case of logical impossibility. Therefore, in all three cases mentioned here, the issue does not even reach the level of whether one ought to employ induction, deduction or falsification to establish the

---

[17]. Bloom, Allan. (1987), *The Closing of the American Mind*, p. 204.

certainty of the claim. Such claims themselves are structurally absurd, regardless of who proclaims them.

Although **Proposition 1** may seem very obvious, it is quite often abandoned due to pressures imposed by the notions of relativism, political correctness and the paradigm shifts among the academic community. It is interesting to note that all these three notions which give support to the likes of fundamental contradictory elements within the philosophies of Nietzsche, Freud and Christianity fall into the category of *nonsense*.

Now, once we separate nonsense from theory and fact, how do we come to separate fact from theory? The issue of induction, deduction and verification is resolvable by the 'methodology of consistency'. As stated earlier, our notions and concepts must be internally and externally[18] consistent. If one proposes an explanation for the way something works in nature, then if that explanation is internally inconsistent, it is automatically false. This is what should easily distinguish science from pseudoscience. The difficulty arises when there is no *internal* inconsistency. According to Popperian methodology, for example, Democritus' idea could not have been classified as being scientific. As it has already been pointed out, it is clear to us today that the world is comprised of atoms and yet smaller subatomic particles.

In the light of these shortcomings, we should be asking: Is there a universal methodology which could encompass Democritus' notion, and any other idea explaining things in nature? We shall argue that the following proposition is the only sound methodology employable:

---

[18]. External consistency means that the explanation must not contradict any known facts. For example, if it is claimed that the moon is made of Swiss cheese, it contradicts geological reality and is externally inconsistent as opposed to being externally consistent.

From Facts to Values

Proposition 2: *An explanation of the way something in nature works remains a theory, only so long as there is no external inconsistency, given that its internal consistency is already established.*

We should take note, however, that the thrust of this proposition stipulates checking for the negative postulation, that is, *inconsistency* as opposed to consistency. Thus, using this methodology we can re-assess Democritus' theory of atomism and can see that it would have been perfectly valid as it was internally consistent and also remained externally consistent, because no-one could prove that there was any external inconsistency over the ages. And so would Newton's Universal Gravitational Theory, as it remained internally and externally consistent. However, we must assess Universal Gravity further, as it is a more complex issue. Firstly, it may be asked whether, historically, scientists had been regularly operating consciously or unconsciously using Popper's methodology? To answer this, let us assess Universal Gravitational Theory in the light of the way it was actually perceived. Upon analysis, it will be realized that scientists after Newton were, in fact, trying to *explain* the motions encompassed by the general theory of Universal Gravity more than they were trying to *falsify* it; they were, for example, trying to explain the motions of planets. Philosopher Hilary Putnam elaborates on this further stating that even where there was an attempt to falsify Newton's explanation for the cosmic motions, these falsifications did not apply to his general theory but rather to Auxiliary Hypotheses:[19]

---

[19]. Auxiliary Hypotheses or statements are any claims conjoined with a hypothesis that is under test, in order to derive observable predictions from the hypothesis. For example, if someone is ill and one hypothesizes that the sickness is due to pneumonia, then the auxiliary hypotheses or statement could be that the person's temperature will not be normal. This could be easily confirmed or refuted by use of

The Certainty of Human Knowledge

> All this is not to deny that scientists do sometimes derive predictions from theories and A.S. [Auxiliary Statements] in order to test the theories. If Newton had not been able to derive Kepler's laws, for example, he would not have even put forward U.G. [the Theory of Universal Gravity]. But even if the predictions Newton had obtained from U.G. had been wildly wrong, U.G. might still have been true: the A.S. might have been wrong. Thus, even if a theory is 'knocked out' by an experimental test, the theory may still be right, and the theory may come back in at a later stage when it is discovered the A.S. were not useful approximations to the true situation. As has previously been pointed out, falsification in science is no more conclusive than verification.[20]

On the other hand, other theories were postulated allowing for falsification at the outset. These certainly fit Popper's falsification methodology. Therefore, the Popperian methodology cannot be discounted, but must be relegated as a subset of a more general approach — the methodology of consistency — which is simply based on commonsense. This is why this proposal based on consistency, must be considered as the foundation for scientific inquiry, because it does not insist that one has to come up with predictions at the

---

a thermometer. However, note that if the auxiliary hypothesis is falsified it does not necessarily mean that the person definitely does not have pneumonia. Popper refers to Auxiliary Hypotheses as "Initial Conditions".

[20]. Putnam, Hilary. (1978), *The 'Corroboration' of Theories,* in *The Philosophy of Science,* edited by Richard Boyd, Philip Gasper and J.D. Trout, (1991), p. 127.

outset. If one uses the methodology advocated in this book, one will certainly be asking for proof and seeking a means of testing the hypothesis or theory. However, one would not dismiss an idea just because one cannot test it. If a means of testing were to be discovered, then one would indeed test the predictions of the hypothesis by experimentation. Falsifiability is, therefore, indeed one of the tools used to establish inconsistency, but cannot always be used as the *starting point* of an inquiry, since it is not wide enough in its scope. In this way, Popper's falsification methodology serves as a subset of a more embrasive approach. One can see that 'explanatory coherence' to use the term of Paul Thagard, has indeed been the main driving force behind the major "conceptual revolutions".[21]

The methodology of consistency as postulated above would close the doors on certain ideas at the very outset as it would regard them to be non-scientific or pseudoscientific. A good example of such pseudoscience is astrology. Astrology postulates that the movement of planets and stars light-years away affect human destiny. These ideas are plagued with external inconsistencies at the very outset. Conversely, however, the law of non-contradiction stressing and elevating 'consistency', as the overarching criterion, would favourably open up other areas to investigation which have been disregarded due to Popperian notions. Take for example acupuncture — is it science or a hoax? Is it a placebo or something real? It is conceivable that one could indeed have an explanation of acupuncture. One could ascribe energy flows through meridians as being the conveyors which are rechannelled by needles. However, although some of such theories may not be testable, perhaps due to lack of imagination, lack of apparatus etc., one cannot refute such explanations as being pseudoscientific hoaxes, because there is no observable *external inconsistency*. Yet, at the same time,

---

[21]. Thagard, Paul. (1992), *Conceptual Revolutions*.

one cannot as a critically thinking individual, regard the above-stated explanation for acupuncture, for example, as a proof and therefore, as a fact since there is no detection of energy pathways through 'meridians'. It would fall into the category of theory by the virtue of the proposal of consistency. Perhaps one could conduct experiments to determine energy flows and perhaps these energy flows might have more to do with the regular energy forms which we already know of, having a synergistic effect, or perhaps there is yet another explanation.

Many people, including scientists have blindly adhered to Hume's notion of not being able to verify any scientific laws, and further, have bought Popper's notion of being only able to falsify observations due to induction. Consequently, because of this they have come to think that we cannot become certain about things. However, these notions are totally erroneous. To take the famous generic example of the swans, although we may not be able to know by mere observation that all swans are white, we would not even need to observe all swans — we may be able to say one way or another for sure if we could tell from the genetic code whether all swans are indeed white or not. The point is that, if we reach a particular level of knowledge, in this case, for example, conclusive constraints set up by genetics, then it is indeed possible to know for sure. Yet Popper insists that:

> The old scientific ideal of *episteme* — of absolutely certain, demonstrable knowledge — has proved to be idol... every scientific statement must remain *tentative forever*. It may indeed be corroborated, but every corroboration is relative to other statements which, again, are tentative. Only in our subjective experiences of conviction, in our

subjective faith, can we be 'absolutely certain'.[22]

This self-refuting relativistic assertion can easily be shot dead by application of **Proposition 1**, as it is doomed by its own verdict. That is, if Popper's assertion is taken to be true, it seems that the above proclamation is bound to be a product of his 'subjective faith', 'subjective experience', 'tentative' and above all lacking the notion of 'absolute certainty'. Moreover, if what he claims is true, then, he should not propagate an idea, which he cannot be absolutely certain about with respect to its validity. One may be puzzled, as to how such nonsense can be taken so seriously and reach so far in academia and beyond. What is remarkable when it comes to such issues is the unfortunate blind reliance of people, both academic and non-academic, on so-called giants in philosophy and science as being the 'authorities' having the final word. The frequent natural urge to question and complete one's own thoughts seems to be entirely lacking. This unquestioning reliance often leads to dogmatism on various scientific issues. Yet, there is a misconception among the scientific community that, in science there is no room for dogmatism. However, this assumption is incorrect. There are at least two ways in which dogmatism may be present in scientific investigations. The most common one often arises from the inability to distinguish between fact and theory. This inability may lead many people to embark on building upon theories for centuries as if they were facts. Over history, certain so-called facts collapsed when more evidence to the contrary mounted and led to a new way of looking at things.

Due to such a state of affairs, a view has arisen, which holds that one cannot have a true explanation of the way nature works - all you have are paradigms, models of reality. Thomas Kuhn was one of those who propounded this notion

---

[22]. Popper, Karl R. (1975), *The Logic of Scientific Discovery*, p. 280.

The Certainty of Human Knowledge

of paradigm shifts.[23] However, if all we have are paradigms, or constantly fleeting models, then is not Kuhn's theory on theories also a paradigm and ephemeral as well, consequently being subject to rejection as have been all the others? Kuhn's idea too, therefore, implodes by self-refutation. Once again, this is another clear example of a theory being internally inconsistent. Thus, it falls into the category of *nonsense* regardless of who says it. Yet, despite its obvious self-implosive character, it has been blindly adopted by the scientific community for decades.

Reinforced by Kuhn's notion, and supported by Hume and Popper's fragmented philosophy, it is often asked: How can we be certain about the status of our knowledge, when knowledge itself keeps changing all the time? For example, it is often said that what was thought to be true yesterday is known to be false today. However, we should make the distinction that, it is not the case that the reality of this universe keeps changing, but it is our understanding of that reality which is improving. Therefore, what was known to be true, never was true in the first place, or was perhaps incomplete. For example, when it was discovered that the earth was not flat, but rather, a spheroid, the shape of the earth did not suddenly change at the moment of our realization to accommodate the new discovery. As to why it is that our understanding of reality changes from time to time, is because the methodology which was applied to discover reality was faulty or incomplete in the first place — the very same methodology that this book is criticising. We cannot expect to arrive at the absolute truth by using inconsistent methodologies or incomplete systems. There can never be a case when the root of the tree of thought is jumbled in confusion and disorder, and yet extends branches that are in complete clarity and order.

---

[23]. Kuhn, Thomas S. (1962), *The Structure of Scientific Revolutions.*

From Facts to Values

In addition, the increase in data accumulated will ultimately lead to new conclusions and discoveries, for learning is a gradual process. Psychologists James Gibson and Eleanor Gibson explain that human perception depends on the information that the world offers us.[24] If we happen to perceive an event, or a phenomenon incorrectly, such as geocentrism or the earth being flat, it is all because it naturally seems that way at first glance. However, after acquiring more accurate information, our conclusions will certainly prove to be otherwise. As we learn more, we gradually become 'skilled perceivers'. This would enable us to become more sensitive to the external reality in front of us. We then pick up more signs, detect new features and higher orders to which, as 'naive viewers' we were before blind to. Gibsons' analysis also accounts for the individual differences between two people in the perception of the same phenomenon, such as between an infant ('naive viewer') and an adult ('skilled perceiver'). The crux of the matter, however, is that learning, perception and our understanding changes not the fundamental facets of external reality which are indubitably constant.

---

[24]. Gibson, James J. (1966), *The Senses Considered as Perceptual Systems*.
Gibson, James J. (1979), *The Ecological Approach to Visual Perception*.
Gibson, Eleanor J. (1969), *Principles of Perceptual Learning and Development*.

The Certainty of Human Knowledge

Scientific Dogmatism

There are some theories which have persisted and still do continue to persist as 'facts'; this is what could be designated as being scientific dogmatism: the failure to distinguish fact from theory. That is to say, treating a proposed theory as though it is a proven to be a fact. For instance, the effect of taking Darwin's proposed theory of natural selection as the mechanism for evolution is a good example of such dogmatism. Ever since Darwin, this theory has been erroneously taken to be a fact by many. The assumption of natural selection has been taken to be completely valid and indeed has had a powerful dogmatic impact on most of the scientific research in psychology, sociology, anthropology and biology since the end of the nineteenth century. However, more than a century of research has failed to prove this theory.[25] Evolution shall be discussed at greater length, further on in this chapter.

The dogmatic outlook in science can also be detected in the use of faulty argumentation models, or in the abuse of valid argumentation models. Some scientists today have adopted fallacious models, incomplete models or may misuse a legitimate model for formulating their theories. One notable scheme is the approach of selectivity, disguised under scientific investigation. Most scientists use Stephen Toulmin's model for laying out arguments. Toulmin's model consists of:

---

[25]. Denton, Michael. (1986), *Evolution: A Theory in Crisis*.

Koestler, Arthur & Smythies, J.R. (1972), *Beyond Reductionism: New Perspectives in the Life Sciences: Proceedings of the Alpbach Symposium*.

Thaxton, Charles B. & Bradley, Walter L. & Olsen, Roger L. (1984), *The Mystery of Life's Origin: Reassessing Current Theories*.

From Facts to Values

Data, warrant, qualifier and claim.[26] Here, data refers to factual information which is used to support the claim, warrant is the support for the conclusion based on the data presented, qualifier is the consideration for exceptions and finally there is the claim, which is the theory or the concluding statement(s). Some other researchers use the notorious Aristotelian model of constructing arguments, which consists of premise(s), support(s) for the premise(s) and finally the conclusion(s). Now, although these models do seem plausible at first glance, they are indeed quite *vulnerable* to be *misused* and turned into a major fallacy known as 'special pleading'. Special pleading is nothing but the representation of only half of the truth, making an argument look sound with the purposeful selection of only that information or set of data which supports one's theory, at the expense of ignoring that which is unfavourable to one's position. As such, all the data, premises, warrants and supports put forward, although valid will not establish anything. In short, while much has been said, what has been left unsaid? In fact, the concealed information, if finally revealed, may force a completely different conclusion. In this respect, half of the truth becomes like half a parachute — it is completely useless. Therefore, it is not sufficient to attempt to validate a claim by putting forth that which supports it, and disregard that which puts it under question.

Such a devious approach of argumentation is quite often used in the formulation of theories in the area of experimental psychology, particularly in the nature/nurture debate. Many researchers have taken the attitude that so long as one has some support such as citing certain studies or statistics to back up one's theory, it is enough licence to formulate claims. However, before making any such claims, even in the case where the researchers are not dishonest or biased, they have

---

[26]. Toulmin, Stephen E. (1969), *The Use of Arguments*, Ch. 3.

The Certainty of Human Knowledge

yet to account for all the existing counter-arguments in their theories. For example, there are some 'scientific studies' which suggest that smoking is not addictive or harmful at all. Although, procedurally these studies might, by the prevailing standards, be acceptable and valid, surely the researchers of the tobacco industries cannot conclude that smoking is not addictive and harmful, when there are numerous studies which indicate otherwise, as for example, that smoking is the major cause of lung cancer and heart disease. The use of such a special pleading model runs rampant in every scientific discipline today. Everyday, one hears about competing groups of scientists confronting each other, persisting that their theories are more viable than those of their opponents, while they all use the very same faulty approach. The common ingredient in all of these 'controversies' is the form — what differs is the context. One day it may be over a nature/nurture issue, another day on the greenhouse effect, or, for instance, the harmfulness of cholesterol levels. Such ongoing debates by scientists, subliminally reinforce in the collective mind of the populace, the notion that there is no certainty and that there are no answers — that many issues are controversial and unresolvable, whereas they are indeed resolvable.

From Facts to Values

Big Bang and Biological Evolution: Theory or Fact?

Using the above-discussed proposition of *consistency* and *inconsistency*, our outlook on two major developments in science turn out to be different than what is being erroneously clung onto in general. These two major issues are: the *Big Bang*, and *Biological Evolution*. Many contemporary scientists and philosophers think that the "Big Bang" is a theory, whereas "Biological Evolution" is a fact. It will be argued in this section that it is just the converse: The Big Bang is a fact; Biological Evolution is a theory. Here, the Biblical account of creation, is not being defended at all. Rather, what is being determined is the status of Biological Evolution — is it fact or theory?

First, let us consider the 'Big Bang'. When one refers to the 'Big Bang' what exactly is one talking about? Is one referring to the development of the universe after the initial origin? Or is one talking about the actual point of origin of the universe? Or both? What has been concluded by the writers is the following: The Big Bang origination of the universe is most assuredly a fact, but the details of how exactly the galaxies etc. got structured thereafter remains theoretical.

Once there was no space and time. This is an established fact. Why? The proof that the universe had an origin lies in the fact that the universe has been, and still is, constantly expanding. This logically means that the galaxies etc. were together at one point. One does not need to see the actual state of the universe, x billion years ago to know this. This is assuredly extrapolable. For example, if one is six feet tall, then there must have been a point when one was two or three feet tall. This is a conclusive proof of development. In a similar way we can realize for a fact that the universe once occupied a smaller volume. We can come to know this for a fact.

Other evidence for the Big Bang is the constant background radiation permeating the whole of space. This background noise, detectable on radiowave antenna — is no doubt the primeval remnant of that 'explosive' beginning.

The Certainty of Human Knowledge

Then, there is also the evidence of the quantity of helium and hydrogen found in the Universe, which exactly matches that which was predicted by the Big Bang. Recently, the puzzle as to how galaxies got formed or how the gases got clumped together has been resolved by the discovery that the 3° K background radiation in the universe is not distributed uniformly, but with fluctuations; the gases have congregated around the various distributional intensities of the early radiation, producing galaxies in some regions and none in others.[27] However, one does not need thousands of proofs — all that is required is one proof. In the case of the Big Bang a proof — such as the expansion of spacetime — is conclusive and enough. Any other proofs, however, would certainly add to our knowledge, making us see things from different angles. This leads us to the third proposition:

> **Proposition 3:** *A theory is either rejected by at least one external inconsistency, or is proven to be true by one or a series of interconnected evidences, and thus is a fact.*

Such proof would be conclusive and direct. Conclusive proof means that all possible alternatives for explaining the phenomenon have been rigorously exhausted by the process of 'elimination by contradiction'. Direct proof means that there is a continuity in the chain of evidence — evidence which is seen. However, to see does not necessarily mean to see visually, although it could include this. The process of elimination by contradiction is the process which forms the basis of the proof. It could, however, be conceivably counterposed that: How does one know that all the possibilities have been exhausted? To address this question, we will have to analyze the process of the process of elimination. In the

---

[27]. Powell, Corey S. (1992), "More Proof for the Big Bang: The Golden Age of Cosmology", *Scientific American,* pp. 17-22.

process of elimination we are trying to determine what is the possible cause for a given effect. Let us assume that there is an effect H and that we are examining a finite set of possibilities as causes: A, B, C, and D. If we start comparing each of these potential causes and come across inconsistencies in their relation to H, then we can eliminate them one by one. We may conceivably eliminate all of them, in which case there must be something else which caused H — something that we do not know of. If A is the most plausible of the four options but does not explain the whole effect, then we know that there must be some other cause(s) associated with A which must have produced the effect H. In this case, we should be talking about probabilities, not certainties. But, let us assume that B, C, and D are eliminated by checking for consistency. Does this automatically mean that A is the answer? One should not automatically jump to the conclusion that A is the cause. 'A' would only be the cause if it would be integrally connected with H by finding direct proof for its association with H, wherein there is no inconsistency. To take a simple, but practical example, if you had a set of four keys, but did not know which of them (if any) was correct one, how would you find out? The procedure is exactly as discussed. In the next section, let us utilize the established propositions to ask some questions concerning biological evolution.

The Status of Biological Evolution

Neo-Darwinian evolution postulates a mechanism for change — the drastic developmental change in species by chance, random and stochastic processes acting on natural selection at various levels. This, most scientist admit is a theory. They readily admit that the mechanism for the proposed transformations are theories. Yet most scientists think of the macro-transformation of species irrespective of mechanism to be fact. In other words, most scientists think of biological evolution to be a fact rather than a theory. This section argues just the opposite. The main problems with the theory of

The Certainty of Human Knowledge

evolution have to do with the 'continuity in the chain of evidence', the lack of direct evidence and the circumstantiality of the evidence. For example, although in the fossil records when one finds a change in the form of say a 'horse' from A to B, there is a problem of intermediate forms. Darwin had thought that the gaps in the fossil records would be filled in due course through research. However, over a hundred years have elapsed and these gaps have still have not been filled. Does this mean that evolution has not occurred? Some palaeontologists such as Stephen Jay Gould have suggested that there were long periods of stasis (no change) followed by 'sudden' jumps. However, if there were jumps then one needs to find a mechanism and an underlying cause for the jumps — otherwise evolution is just a theory and not a fact. Punctuated equilibrium — the name for this explanation — is indeed regarded as a theory by scientists, including Stephen Jay Gould. However, although many of such researchers regard punctuated equilibrium and other postulations as a *mechanism* they also maintain that evolution itself is a fact, not a theory. For example, the evolutionist Niles Eldredge states that:

> That evolution occurs no biologist worthy of the name doubts. But many biologists these days do openly wonder how complete and accurate our grasp of the mechanics of the evolutionary process really is.[28]

However, there is a subtle logical fallacy here, with respect to evolution being regarded as a fact. To discover this, let us look logically at the point of contention regarding the ascription of fact or theory to evolution. Firstly, the word evolution in English expresses the idea of a process, in which there is a change of a thing over time. Schematically then:

---

[28]. Eldredge, Niles. (1985), *Time Frames,* p. 14.

From Facts to Values

*If $a=b$
and $b=c$ then $a=c$
If $a=c$
and $c=d$ then $a=d$*

*Similarly, if:
evolution (a)=process (b)
process(b)=mechanism(c) => evolution(a)=mechanism(c)
and if,
evolution (a)=mechanism (c)
mechanism (c)=theory (d) => evolution (a)=theory(d)*

This all boils down to the fact that evolution cannot be a fact if the mechanism is not known. That evolution is not a fact is even admitted by Ernst Mayr, the pre-eminent contemporary Darwinian, when he states that there is "no clear evidence for any change of a species into a different genus or for the gradual origin of any evolutionary novelty."[29]

Now, someone could pose the counter-argument that one cannot equate process with mechanism and that: Two-hundred years ago, humankind, knew the process by which it rains. For example, they may have stated that it fell from the grey clouds which were 'vapoury'. However, they did not know the mechanism. Therefore, process is not equivalent to, or equal to mechanism. However, this counter-argument that "process is not equivalent to, or equal to mechanism" is not valid. We are not concerned with exactly what the nature of 'mechanism' is in this context; whatever is its exact nature, it is still a process. Even if one knows exactly how water vapour turns into raindrops, or how clouds nucleate, it would still just be a process, whether you call it a process, mechanism,

---

[29]. Mayr, Ernst. (1988), *Toward a New Philosophy of Biology,* pp. 529-530.

The Certainty of Human Knowledge

'heckanism' or by any other label. Therefore, mechanism is a process and any such counter-argument is only semantic quibbling on shades of meaning at most.

One possible way for proving evolution as a fact would be to find the genetic mechanism which causes macroevolutionary changes or the jumps, if there were indeed jumps. Such evidence would be direct and conclusive and would be one way to establish evolution as fact.

It has been stated that a theory is discovered to be a fact when one finds proof as discussed above. But what about Newton's ideas on gravity. Could one not argue that Newton's equation of universal gravitation was corroborated by the confirmation of the planetary motions and that his theory must then have been a fact by the methodology proposed in this chapter? But, if it is indeed a fact, why did Einstein's notion supplant Newton's? Here we must differentiate between an explanation of *how* things happen, in the sense *what* is the operative essence of something (processes), on the one hand, and *whether* it happened. We must be clear to make a distinction between these two categories. For example, did the event of evolution occur? If we do discover its mechanism, or its utter impossibility, then we will most certainly know whether it did or not happen. Regarding *how* things happen, such as what the basis of gravity is, we can only get closer and closer to an understanding of gravity, but our understanding may always remain incomplete. In actuality, when we try to explain "how" or "what" is the essence of something, then our postulations are either wrong (e.g. Ptolemaic system) or incomplete (approximations). Being incomplete though does not mean that one cannot gain factual answers from the theory, e.g. *force= mass x acceleration*. It makes sense that the ultimate understanding of the universal laws is incomplete because human knowledge is limited. However, this does not mean that we cannot get factual answers or close approximations. We must all learn to sort out apples from oranges.

From Facts to Values

In summary, the basic way to arrive at certainty is by first establishing internal consistency. If there is internal inconsistency then the particular postulation is false and *nonsense* and must be rejected (Proposition 1).

If internal consistency has been established then it remains as theory only so long as there is no external inconsistency (Proposition 2). This requirement for something deemed to be a valid theory does not use falsification with respect to us being able to put forward testable hypotheses which are to be falsified, for, given the circumstances and data it may not be possible to actually test anything. However, Popper's methodology becomes a special case of Proposition 2, which can be used in cases where we are able to put forward testable hypotheses.

If the external inconsistency for the central tenets or claims of the theory are found then the theory is false and must be rejected. If interconnected evidence is found, by the process of elimination by contradiction, then a theory is validated into fact and must be accepted (Proposition 3). The process of elimination by contradiction does not mean that we have to check an infinite number of possibilities and eliminate them because our theory (key) may fit an observation (key-hole) exactly and by turning that key we may open the door to fact and certainty.

The Certainty of Human Knowledge

Implications of the Big Bang

In the above postulations showing the 'transition' of the status of theory into fact, it has been mentioned that something does not have to be seen visually to be proven. We are unable to see many things, but we know that they exist by extrapolation or from their effects. For example, we do not see gravity but know it exists because things fall to the ground. We do not see oxygen but we know that it exists because we breath it. We cannot have an adequate mental picture of the applied mathematical concept of plus and minus infinity, however, we surely know that such concepts are facts. There are many ways to see the effects of something and therefore know of its existence. This is the rational methodology which leads to facts and certainty. Similarly, one of the effects of this universe is the intelligent way in which the Universe has been designed. The cause of the universe, therefore, must be an intelligence. Again we do not have to see this intelligence visually to know that this intelligence exists. We see all of the myriad effects in a remarkable universe that could only have been the outcome of the some creative singular intelligence. We, therefore, can see the *effects* of an intelligence. The intricate tapestry of nature is interconnected precisely and optimally to allow for a balance in the myriad systems of life, in the air we breath, in the oceans, in the distribution of the animal and plant life, in the location of our earth from the sun, in the sun's orbit amid a cluster of stars, which themselves swirl in an uncounted hierarchy of clustered formations, in an ever-expanding universe whose gravitational and expansional forces are poised at a knife-edge, in the interplay of this ordered universe.[30]

---

[30]. Goodwin, Brain. (1994), *How the Leopard Changed its Spots: The Evolution of Complexity.*

Huntley, H.E. (1970), *The Divine Proportion: A Study of Mathematical Beauty.*

Morrison, A Cressy. (1944), *Man Does not Stand Alone.*

From Facts to Values

Cressy Morrison, astronomer and former president of the New York Academy of Science, gives seven reasons to postulate why, as a scientist, he believes that there is an intelligent Creator, three of which are: Firstly, "By unwavering mathematical law we can prove that our universe was designed and executed by a great engineering Intelligence." Secondly: "The resourcefulness of life to accomplish its purpose is a manifestation of all-pervading Intelligence". Thirdly, "By the economy of nature, we are forced to realize that only infinite wisdom could have foreseen and prepared with such astute husbandry."[31]

Physicist Paul Davies remarks on the universe's origin:

> It is hard to resist the impression of something — some influence capable of transcending spacetime and the confinements of relativistic causality — possessing an overview of the entire cosmos at the instant of its creation, and manipulating all the causally disconnected parts to go bang with almost exactly the same vigour at the same time, and yet not so exactly coordinated as to preclude the small scale, slight irregularities that eventually formed the galaxies, and us.[32]

Pagels, Heinz R. (1986), *Perfect Symmetry*.
Schneck, Marcus. (1991), *Patterns in Nature: A World of Colour, Shape and Light*.
Thompson, D'arcy. (1990), *On Growth and Form*.

[31]. Morrison, Cressy. (1988), "Does God Exist?" in the *Philosophy and Contemporary Issues*, by John R. Burr and Milton Goldinger, pp. 98-101.

[32]. Davies, Paul. (1982), *The Accidental Universe,* p. 95.

The Certainty of Human Knowledge

Could the origin of all this wonderfully harmonious interpenetration of order be due to mere Chance — or Intelligence? The cumulative probabilities for the development of life-forms and everything else in the Universe, known and yet unknown, is mathematically zero if it were to be the product of Chance. In fact, the proof for the existence of a Singular Intelligence, that is, a creator who is a unique single entity is no different in methodology than trying to prove the existence or non-existence of, for example, leaking invisible carbon monoxide. In proving the existence of an invisible gas we can know of its existence by the effects it causes, and likewise for the existence of such a Creator we can realize such an entity's existence by the effect of intelligence engrained in the structures and processes in the Universe. Therefore, by the usage of the same process we can eliminate the artificial separation between physics and so-called metaphysics even though such a Creator is not subject to the confinements of space-time. In order to see this, let us examine the relationship between space-time and the purported existence of a singular Creator.

It has already been established that this universe of space and time had a conspicuous origin, and that the Big-Bang is a fact. We also know that from nothing comes nothing. This universe is something, so what was there when the universe was not in existence? Was there an infinity of universes before this one, or at least one eternal universe prior to this one? Or was there just One Singular Creator of this universe that we know of? Note, that in all cases, we have to contend with the notion of eternity, which surprisingly, is usually thought of as being problematic only when it comes to the question of a Creator, but not when it comes to an infinity of universes, (or one preceding infinite universe). However, if one is impartial, one will measure everything by the same yardstick for both scenarios. Eternity in itself, is not problematic when ascribed to this Intelligence. Space and time encapsulate beginnings and ends. But a Being not dependent on time-space does not have to suffer death, or be born and can be eternal. Opting for an infinity of the universes, however, does not in the least, explain the intelligence engrained in the cosmic system. Postulating a unique Originator, on the other hand, does explain its intelligently designed structures and functions. This Creator-Originator is the One who created the perspicaciously integrated, planned and guided interrelations in the processes of nature, which include the oftentimes arrogant but relatively infinitesimal created intelligences which have the capacity for volition called human beings. This intelligence may well have built biological evolution into the scheme of nature, as a goal directed enviro-biological mechanism.

In fact, resorting to the infinity of universes scenario, is akin to escapism; it is strikingly reminiscent of the theory for the origin of life which advances the idea that entities from distant planet — from another stellar system — seeded the earth with incipient lifeforms. Over time, these have developed into homo-sapiens. But, the question remains: What about that other distant planet, how did life originate there in the first instance? From yet another planet, and so on, ad infinitum... ? Infinite universes suffer the same regression.

The Big Bang 'Controversy'?

It has been shown in this chapter that the 'Big-Bang' is a fact. Yet there is the general impression among people that it is not legitimate for it to be considered as a fact, because the subject is 'controversial'. In this section what is being suggested is that it is not even controversial in the usual sense of 'controversy'. We must reflect on what 'controversy' really is. Controversial issues are more prevalent in moral dilemmas where there are some personal desires and vested interests influencing one's choice. For example: the usage of an innocent baboon's heart for saving the life of a helpless little girl is controversial. Any choice taken in this matter is emotional and would not be without controversies.

In the case of the Big Bang, there is no real controversy. Instead, what you have is a psychological reaction. The fact that the universe has had an origin is deeply disturbing for many individuals because it has an implication extending far

The Certainty of Human Knowledge

beyond the borders of 'science'. Indeed, this fact thrusts right into the consciousness of every human being because it implies a Creator and an Originator, something which many may want to deny, for one reason or another. If it is true that there is a Creator responsible for this universe, then his existence has a definite unpopular implication on people's desires, behaviour and codes of conduct. That is because, the existence of the Creator, would be at the basis of every single issue. On the other hand, if there is no Creator, for many people then conveniently there is no accountability. Another reason for this denial is that, when it is evidenced that there is a Creator, most people think of the type of Creator that is found in mystical and irrational belief systems such as the one in Christianity. For many reasons there has been a great counter-reaction against Christianity and other similar 'belief systems'— especially in the twentieth century. In some cases, in an attempt to reject particular mystical or anthropomorphic conceptions of God, people have rejected the existence of any type of Creator.

When the notion of "Big Bang" was first being developed and then when evidence was found for it, some scientists decided to concoct a rival theory — the steady-state theory — which would do away with an origin. However, this theory was debunked because it violated the principle of the conservation of matter and energy. Similar defective theories are, at present, being put forward; these are redundant and are being proposed solely for psychological reasons. For example, there is a theory that the universe is not expanding and that it is eternal, having evolved from pre-existent plasma. This was recently argued by Eric Lerner, in *The Big Bang Never Happened.* Lerner states that the Big Bang is erroneous because it does not explain adequately the formation of the galaxies after the Big Bang event; however the plasma theory does account for galactical formations.[33] But, as it was suggested earlier, the Big Bang is a fact and the question of the formation of the galaxies is theoretical — these are matters only of detail and therefore do not undermine the Big Bang origin event. However, Lerner's book, itself was written prior to the new discovery in 1992 which explains the fluctuations in the background radiation, explaining in principle the galactical formations. Indeed, because of this very fact and its ongoing re-corroboration, Lerner's book has been proven to be totally fallacious in its central tenets against the Big Bang. In an understandably re-published edition in 1992 (Vintage Books), in the new preface, he still dogmatically clings to the wrong notion, claiming that the information gained by the COBE satellite on the discovered fluctuations does not exactly show what was predicted by physicists. The difference between the measurement of COBE and theoretical expectations is only a matter of trivial detail, however, and does not in the least undermine the Big Bang. In cases like this, one has to fine tune or correct either the details with respect to calculations, or perhaps improve the technical resolutions of the measuring instruments. Astrophysicist Michael Rowan-Robinson, who was a leading participant in the mapping of the distribution of galaxies by the Infrared Astronomical Satellite (IRAS) comments on the meaning of the information COBE (Cosmic Background Explorer Satellite):

> The deeper meaning of the ripples, though, is that they show that we seem to understand the universe well enough to trace structure back to only 300,000 years after the Big Bang. Radio and microwave astronomers around the world have been trying for decades to

---

[33]. Lerner, Eric J. (1991), *The Big Bang Never Happened: A Startling Refutation of the Dominant Theory of the Origin of the Universe,* pp. 274-275.

The Certainty of Human Knowledge

find these ripples, to show that we really do know how galaxies and clusters arose from an initially smooth, hot universe dominated by radiation. Even if the COBE ripples do not exactly correspond to the density fluctuations from which galaxies will arise, because they are on much too large a scale, the detection of the smaller-scale fluctuations should not be long delayed now. Seventy years ago we knew nothing of the expanding universe. Fifty years ago we had no concept of the Hot Big Bang and it is less than thirty years ago that we saw the first evidence for such a picture. Now we can say with confidence that we broadly understand the evolution of the universe from a time 300,000 years after the Big Bang until today, thirteen billion years or so later (with lots of details to be filled in). Our understanding of the origin of the light elements shows that we safely extrapolate this picture back to a time one second after the Big Bang.[34]

It is remarkable that even many leading scientists have disconnected thinking when it comes to the question of origins. Take, for example, Stephen Hawking. He has suggested that there is no origin of the universe in time. In order to prove this, what he does is to construct an analogy. However, he then fallaciously thinks of the analogy as being reality. In fact, Hawking is presenting the model of reality for reality and has ignored the importance of a very crucial aspect of reality. We shall discuss this below. But first, let us see what he concludes regarding the question of origins:

---

[34]. Rowan-Robinson, Michael. (1993), *Ripples in the Cosmos,* pp. 194-195.

> The idea that space and time may form a closed surface without boundary also has profound implications for the role of God in the affairs of the universe. With the success of scientific theories in describing events, most people have come to believe that God allows the universe to evolve according to a set of laws and does not intervene in the universe to break these laws. However, the laws do not tell us what the universe should have looked like when it started — it would still be up to God to wind up the clockwork and choose how to start it off. So long as the universe had a beginning, we could suppose it had a creator. But if the universe is really completely self-contained, having no boundary or edge, it would have neither beginning nor end: it would simply be. What place, then, for a creator?[35]

Hawking proposes that at the beginning of the universe, time did not exist and was just homogeneous with space — just another space-like dimension. He has used the analogy of the balloon's surface (2 dimensions), as representing space (3 dimensions). He then says that real time can be considered as 'imaginary time'. Hence, there is no boundary in time, just as there is no boundary on the surface of a sphere, if for instance, an ant was walking on it. If there is no boundary in time (i.e. no origin) then the universe is eternal. Is it perhaps with a sleight of mind, that this eminent physicist appears to be trying to escape from the idea of the origin? The question is: why should one be forced to accept the notion of time as described in his analogy? In fact, Roger Penrose, the co-theorist with Hawking on singularities, holds quite the

---

[35]. Hawking, Stephen. (1988), *A Brief History of Time*, pp. 140-141.

The Certainty of Human Knowledge

opposite view. Indeed, what he says boils down to the fact that the origin of the universe — the origin of time and space — is so unique that for it to happen by chance is indeed a severe stretch of the imagination, to say the least:

> This [calculation] now tells us how precise the Creator's aim [to produce our universe from a phase space of possible universes] must have been: namely to an accuracy of one part in $10^{10^{123}}$.
>
> This is an extraordinary figure. One could not possibly even write the number down in full, in the ordinary denary notion: it would be '1' followed by 10^{123} successive '0's! Even if we were to write a '0' on each separate proton and on each separate neutron in the entire universe — and we could throw in all the other particles as well for good measure — we should fall far short of writing down the figure needed. The precision needed to set the universe on its course is seen to be in no way inferior to all that extraordinary precision that we have already become accustomed to in the superb dynamical equations (Newton's, Maxwell's, Einstein's) which govern the behaviour of things from moment to moment.[36]

Astonishingly, that which cannot be ignored in this discussion is often ignored by sceptical participants. That is, things like order, precision, complexity, growth, goal-directedness, purpose, harmony, balance, functionality, complementarity, optimality, beauty and perfection are not at all characteristics of chance and randomness. All to the contrary, they are

---

[36]. Penrose, Roger. (1989), *The Emperor's New Mind*, p. 344.

characteristics of supremely-crafted design. This assertion is surely open and beckons challenge and falsification by the sceptic. Consider the scenario of a vicious tornado, ravaging a car scrapyard, which, subsequent to its turbulent passage, after the dust has settled, happens to produce an elegant brand new 1995 White Lamborghini with AM/FM stereo and cruise control. What would be the probability of such an accidental outcome? Or, suppose that an earthquake occurs: What would be the probability for all the various necessary solutions in a medical lab to fall down and become an admixture of exactly the right proportion to produce a new medicine that could cure a deadly disease such as cancer? Or, what would be the probability for all the letters in this book unscrambling themselves to re-form these meaningful and structured sentences to produce this book by sheer coincidence? No sane person can argue that such events and cases are probable by chance? Now, compare these scenarios with the probability of one in $10^{10^{123}}$ of an accidental universe with numerous precise conditions which were necessary, in order for life on earth to have developed to the way it is now. Yet, there are many 'hotshot' scientists and philosophers who push their own cerebral matter and the public into thinking that the creation of the universe and life on earth were accidental processes from the very beginning to the present!

Interestingly, it must be noted, when referring to probabilities, that for practical purposes, mathematicians argue that events with a probability of less than one in 10^{50} are considered as impossible, since their likelihood of occurrence within a reasonable timeframe is negligible.[37] The probability calculated by Penrose for the chance occurrence of the cosmos is, needles to say, unimaginably smaller than that and hence impossible!

---

[37]. Hitching, Francis. (1982), *The Neck of the Giraffe: Darwin, Evolution, and the New Biology*, p. 53.

The Certainty of Human Knowledge

Penrose's view of the origin of the universe is realistic, not only for considering an extremely infinitesimal probability, but also because he takes into consideration that aspect which Hawking takes so lightly, namely, entropy. Entropy is associated with time and if we really want to understand the universe we cannot dissociate entropy from the rest of physics. We must seek ways to incorporate it, because this is the reality of the integrated universe.

Another attempt to make people, especially laymen, think that the Big Bang is highly controversial is the notion that a vacuum is not perfectly empty and that 'quantum or vacuum fluctuations' in it, produce something from almost nothing; therefore, if this is the case, then the singularity, that is, the origin of the Big Bang, was also produced from a vacuum, or a vacuum like state:

> Vacuum Fluctuation theories of the origin of the universe, in combination with inflationary views of the expansion of the universe, depict the Big Bang as the end-product of the quantum fluctuation of a primordial vacuum. A vacuum is seen here as being saturated with quantum fields and as being subject to fundamental fluctuations (a prediction of quantum physics). When strong enough, the fluctuating energy fields appear briefly as "virtual" particles and then disappear.[38]

However, the obvious point which is not brought up is that: How can one speak of the Big Bang arising out of a quantum field when there was no space at the origin? On the other hand, if there was some type of dimension, then that dimension was something akin to another type of a universe in which there would be this purported fluctuation. But, one could yet again legitimately ask: Why should there be a

---

[38]. Margenau, Henry and Varghese, Roy A. (1992), *Cosmos, Bios, Theos*, p. 8.

fluctuation in the first place — what could have been responsible for it? And where did that arise from — if it did? Here we get into the infinite regress problem once more. Physicist Heinz Pagels, one of the supporters of the Vacuum Fluctuation theory discusses his reservations:

> The nothingness 'before' the creation of the universe is the most complete void that we can imagine — no space, time or matter existed. It is a world without place, without duration or eternity, without number — it is what the mathematicians call 'empty set'. Yet this unthinkable void converts itself into the plenum of existence [and we would hasten to add the order, diversity and beauty of life on Earth] — a necessary consequence of physical laws. Where are these laws written into that void? What 'tells' the void that it is pregnant with a possible universe? It would seem that even the void is subject to law, a logic that exists prior to space and time.[39]

Anthony Flew, the champion of the atheists and a well-known scientific philosopher, admits candidly in the book *Cosmos, Bios, Theos*, that the Big Bang origin has created a profound problem for the atheistic dogma of an eternal universe:

> Remarkably, Professor Flew goes on to "confess" that the atheist "has to be embarrassed by the contemporary cosmological consensus. For it seems that the cosmologists are providing a scientific proof of what St. Thomas [Aquinas] contended could not be proved philosophically; namely, that the universe had a beginning. So long as the universe can be comfortably thought of as being not only

---

[39]. Ibid., p. 9.

> without end but also without beginning, it remains easy to urge that its brute existence, and whatever are found to be its most fundamental features, should be accepted as the explanatory ultimates. Although I believe that it remains still correct, it certainly is neither easy nor comfortable to maintain this position in the face of the Big Bang story.[40]

When questions of the origin, structure and processes of the universe are broached, most scientists, students and academics are suffering from either touches of relativism or full blown relativitis. The educational systems in the Western countries and indeed, for that matter in the Eastern countries, which are blindly emulating them are permeated with notions of relativism, where there is no consistent methodology for sorting out apples from oranges, science from pseudo-science, fact from theory, and truth from falsity.

Although, it has been proven that the Big Bang is a fact, there are still many who would reject it. This is due to the fact that most people, in our present day 'educational systems', have been trained not to accept it as fact because of relativistic outlooks. What needs to be emphasized is that the only way one can disprove the Big-Bang, is to prove that the universe is not expanding and that it is just an illusion or that one cannot extrapolate back to the origin, specifically for the Big Bang scenario. However, anyone who asserts this must bring forward concrete proof for the assertion.

---

[40]. Ibid., p. 15.

Is the Universe Goal-Directed?
The Teleological Argument Revisited and Re-established

The fact of the big-bang origin and the directionality of the universe attests to the fact that it appears to be pursuing an intention. All of the components in this universe, as well as those on the earth, as discussed earlier, have been clearly designed to fit and function together harmoniously. It is indeed impossible to dispense with the idea of purposiveness. However, due to a counterreaction of many thinkers against anthropomorphic and mystical notions of a deity, in addition to various psycho-sociological reasons, the obviousness of a goal directed purpose — 'teleology', in the jargon of philosophers — is either denied completely, or diffused by the misuse of language. For example, Ernst Mayr, the well-known contemporary evolutionary biologist, among others, attempts to disintegrate teleology by the usage of the words 'teleomatic' and 'teleonomy'[41]. However, the concept that embodies all these qualities of design, is still a supreme intelligence, incomparable to anything in this universe. To circumvent this intelligence, one would have to attribute it to something in this universe such as "Mother Nature". Scientists such as Mayr are simply playing futile word-games in an attempt to evade the interrelated purposiveness of both animate and inanimate things in this universe. Mayr reduces teleological into teleomatic and teleonomic, ascribing the latter to being a 'program'. In his scheme, the program is a

---

[41]. Mayr, Ernst. (1988), *Toward a New Philosophy of Biology*. As defined by Mayr in Chapter (3), teleonomic has to do with the "processes (behaviour) whose goal-directedness is controlled by a program". On the other hand, teleomatic: "processes which reach an end state caused by natural laws (e.g., gravity, first law of thermodynamics) but not by a program", p. 60.

The Certainty of Human Knowledge

function of 'natural selection' when it deals with organisms, which is governed by Chance, not Intelligence. However, if as he says, inanimate objects are programmed, then the concept of 'program' explicitly implies the concepts of origin, planning, purpose, goal directedness, integration and above all a *programmer*. One can, therefore, still rightfully ask: who is the programmer? Even if the word program is not used and some other word, such as 'algorithm', is used to describe the underlying mindlessness of development in the universe by natural selection, one cannot escape the fact that an algorithm has to be written by someone and does not arise by chance, and also the fact that the logical structuring of programs is through algorithms.[42] The factor of intelligence in the matrix of reality is wholly inescapable. Everything then, converges to question of a singular Intelligence which is what has historically and sociologically been put aside in our relativistic age of confusion — the Intelligence that set the program or the boundary conditions. Two contemporary American cosmologists, Barrow and Tipler elaborate on this issue:

> The limitation of explanation in terms of mechanical causality can perhaps best be understood by comparing a living being to a computer. As Michael Polanyi has pointed out the internal workings of a computer can of course be completely understood in terms of physical laws. What cannot be so explained is the computer's program. To explain the program requires reference to the *purpose* of the program, that is, to teleology.
>
> Even the evolution of a deterministic Universe cannot be completely understood in terms of the differential equations which

---

[42]. Dennett, Daniel C. (1995), "Darwins's Dangerous Ideas", *The Sciences,* pp. 36-37.

> govern the evolution. The boundary conditions of the differential equations must also be specified. These boundary conditions are not determined by the laws of physics which are the differential equations. The universal boundary conditions are as fundamental as the physical laws themselves; they must be included in any explanation on a par with the physical laws.[43]

Many have used the notion of biological evolution to escape the question of purpose and design. To tackle the question of evolution itself would require another book. However, in connection with the Darwinian belief that the only overall control process is natural selection, numerous problems exist, the greatest of which remains the question of intelligence. Richard Milton, science journalist elaborates in his critique of the Darwinian evolutionary theory:

> I believe that [even] if biological processes were so simple [that is, as simple as the most elaborate human designed computer spell-checking program], they too would become functionally corrupt unless there were some underlying or overall design process to which the simple mechanisms answered in a global way, and which were capable of taking action to correct mistakes. This is the mechanism that we see in action in the case of the 'eyeless fly', *Drosophila* [when artificially mutated flies return to normality after a few generations]; in Dreisch's experiment with the sea urchin and Balinsky's with the eye's of amphibians; and the 'field' that govern's the metamorphosis of

---

[43]. Barrow, John D. & Tipler, Frank J. (1988), *The Anthropic Cosmological Principle*, p. 75.

the butterfly or the re-constitution of the cells of sponges and vertebrates.

[The theory of] Natural selection works on populations, not individuals. It is capable only of making sure that creatures with massively fatal genetic defects die in infancy, or that populations that are genetically dispersed will eventually produce sterile offspring. It is a poor feedback mechanism in the sense of exercising an overall regulating effect... Because natural selection offers only death or glory it cannot provide the microscopic adjustments that the individual needs. Yet we are asked to believe that a mechanism of such crudity can creatively supervise a program of gene mutation.

This is plainly wishful thinking. The key question remains: what is the location of the supervisory agency that oversees somatic development? How does it work? What is its connection with the cell structure of the body? Whether they are Darwinists or vitalists, biologists have begun to talk in terms of 'morphogenetic fields'.[44]

Such questions that the freelancer, Milton asks, are not only never asked but are avoided much as a zebra runs away from a hungry lion.

However, let us complete Milton's assessment. We should ask: If there is a morphogenetic field as a governor, what governs and has devised that? Even if we assume that there is a special or supra-program controlling the subprogram of genetic shuffling, the question of a *Programmer* i.e. an Intelligence — a Supreme Mind behind the creation of space

---

[44]. Milton, Richard. (1992), *The Facts of Life: Shattering the Myth of Darwinism*, p. 201.

and time — not only still remains, but becomes even more viable because of the greater and greater sophistication that is revealed each time we peel the layer of designed controlling processes. Eventually, one may be certain that behind the 'programming' of the universe there must be a Singular Intelligence and that the entire universe has arisen from the creative act of this Intelligence. We may surmise from this certainty of an Intelligence, that every astrophysiological and biological development was encapsulated right from the very beginning with intentionality. The lack of following through one's thoughts, and concluding 'morphogenetic fields' or whatever as the ultimate source of creation, is a prime example of unfinished and erroneous thinking. Only by completing the thought process to its logical conclusion we would realize the existence of a Singular Intelligence behind the totality of existence.

What about the objections to the 'argument from design' or the teleological argument? The basic problem with the view which attacks the design argument has been the use of secondary non-fundamental arguments as a distractive mechanism which has had the tendency to detract from the question of the existence or non-existence of a Intelligence, which is the real issue at hand. For example, the leading British philosopher, A.J. Ayer said that: "[It is] to be noted that the analogy with the makers of human artefacts is still further weakened if we suppose the material world to have been created out of nothing at all."[45] Now, what Ayer is arguing here is that the design argument, which uses the analogy of human design to extrapolate a Divine creator and designer is deficient because, when human beings design things, they already have something to work with, and this type of rearrangement of matter to produce things is unlike the organization which results when God creates *ex nihilo* (out of nothing, thence by

---

[45]. Ayer A.J. (1982), *The Central Questions of Philosophy*, p. 219.

evolution etc.). However, this assertion does not refute the existence of a non-spatio-temporal Intelligent Being. It is only an argument against the *how* of the arrangement of order by an intelligence, not *if* or whether an Intelligence has created that order. If one were to pick-up any book arguing against the design argument over the past 150 years or so, the pattern of argumentation would be the same, where the denial of the existence of God is based on what one may term as being the fallacy of irrelevance, conflating the categories of *how* and *if,* by diverting *how* into *if* and demolishing the *if* using an argument based on *how*. It is crucial to make this distinction between these two categories of *how* and *if*. This is the main problem with the argument against teleology, initially concocted by Hume and why it is utterly baseless and as such is a non-argument, which has been accepted blindly over the centuries.

However, the Humean argument can be debunked from the various other angles. It is further argued by Hume and his followers that to move from the human world where there is always a designer or a maker for every man-made artefact to a meta-human world of nature and Creator of nature is to indulge in fallacy. Those who argue against the existence of such an Intelligence say that nature has no purpose written on it. We can say that aeroplanes have a purpose because human beings make aeroplanes for a specific purpose, but how can we presume the same for nature? There is no causal link between the human experience and the conclusion that there is a God.

In the first place, this pseudo-argument which surprisingly has been taken seriously post-Hume does not really pose any challenge for the teleological argument. Why on earth can one not derive the conclusion that, for example, the Swordbill hummingbird's extra long beak is for gaining access to nectar inside equally deep flowers. In fact, every single thing in nature has been similarly designed for one or multiple purposes, and further, the interconnectivity between all the animate and inanimate designed objects must necessarily imply not only a particular purpose but a universal purpose. That is because, in such an interconnective and multi-purpose system: "every part not only exists by *means* of the other parts, but is thought as existing *for the sake of* the others and the whole"[46]. Therefore, it is the functioning of each part that maintains the sustenance of the whole of the system. We shall discuss this in more detail in the next chapter.

For the sake of argument, if we grant Hume's premise, could such a conclusion be built upon this premise? To say that one cannot make a certain conclusion about the world we live in as an inference from human experience is to posit a distinction or a boundary between human experience and the system as a whole. Now we take it as a truism that as between the two conclusions the logically valid one is that which follows as a necessary conclusion in rational discourse, or is supported by solid evidence. In this case, the distinction sought to be introduced into the discussion, namely, that one cannot reason from human experience to the system as a whole, is neither rationally necessary nor supported by the evidence. Since the evidence supports no distinction between human experience and the system as a whole, it follows that the inference from our experience about the system as a whole is a valid one and thus the conclusion that this world was made by a skilled Being is only a logical result of untainted rational discourse.

That there is indeed no distinction between human experience and the system as a whole, is evinced by the possibility of evolution. Evolution, rather than destroying, further corroborates teleology. In fact, the teleological approach reinforces the possibility of the evolution because human designs, through cybernetics and robotic systems, are verging on automated and self-replicating machines, not unlike theorized evolutionary mechanisms. If, there was

---

[46]. Kant, Immanuel. (1951), *Critique of Judgement,* p. 220.

The Certainty of Human Knowledge

indeed such a distinction between human experience and the system as a whole, then human beings could not, at least from the conceptual perspective, be moving in synthetic designs towards the methodology of the design in nature, as realized by the theory of evolution, which is supposed to have debunked the design argument. Indeed, it is an obvious fact of life that the human synthetic design of objects has borrowed heavily from nature in terms of ideas, structure and function, and as we gain greater knowledge of the mechanics of things, we have the potential to come closer to natural designs in terms of processes as well.

When one realizes the possibility of evolution as the mechanism for development and that a Singular Originator has certainly created life and developed it somehow, perhaps through the process of evolution, then one also realizes that life may have been written as a program (to use an analogy) and that the Originator, in this case, is not a God of the gaps who intervenes every now and then to fix problems in nature. One does not, with this conception of a Creator, believe in a created system in which 'skyhooks' (imaginary supportive constructs) are introduced to miraculously operate the laws in the universe at the intermittent whims of the Creator to get things going. The real miracle lies in the intelligence with which the processes have been designed, which display the transformative power of cause and effect relationships and the unification of all the laws, which prove the singularity of the Creator. Given all the evidence that surrounds us, how then, could one be so adamant as to deny such a blatantly obvious fact of an infinite Intelligence as being the Creator? What could be the purpose behind such an obtuse denial? As the American educator J.B. Emerson neatly puts it: "Nature is too thin a screen; the glory of the One breaks in everywhere."

Teleology in Question: Purpose versus Randomness

Another bit of major confusion which tends to distort the perspective regarding the issue of the existence of God is the notion of randomness as opposed to purposeful development. As the brief discussion on evolution earlier highlights, the processes in nature are not random but based on laws. Indeed, genetics is not random but is based on precise rules which we are constantly fathoming. What are the laws or rules which govern the genes, though? Brian Goodwin, a pre-eminent theoretical biologist, who is dedicated to discover the basis of biological transformations, gives an analogy:

> Split a bar magnet in two. You find you have two complete fields. The north-south polarity reasserts itself with each magnet, and if you subdivide it the process continues–fields have this quasi-holistic quality.
>
> The parallel with what happens in cell division is very revealing. Cells divide into two in a way which is typical to all organisms, and you can discern polarity just as you can in bar magnets.[47]

Cell division is regulated geometrically only up to a certain stage after which other forces start predominating. There are the basic and fundamental field processes which then seem to be modified by genes much as the spiral formed in a draining bathtub yields altered shapes upon one placing one's finger in the water (the finger being analogous to the gene, and the shape of the water to the fundamental field processes)[48]. Furthermore, theoretical biologist Stuart Kauffman, in his recent book *The Origins of Order: Self-Organization and Selection in Evolution* has investigated the dynamic results of basic rules that govern the functions of units that he has used as representation of genes. Kauffman's

---

[47]. As cited by Hitching, Francis (1982), in *The Neck of the Giraffe*, p. 167.

[48]. Ibid., p. 167.

The Certainty of Human Knowledge

research indicates that the interaction and networking between genes operating on simple principles, together as an ensemble, leads to emergent order which is characterized by maintenance, reproductive and regenerative functions. Kauffman has discovered, from such modelling, that a square root relationship between gene number and mean cycle length exists.[49]

This being the case, even if natural selection is being posited as a mechanism, it must have, as its basis *law* because genetics is not in reality divorced from the other forces which operate in the universe. Indeed, no chaos exists anywhere — only various levels of order. No randomness exists behind the levels of complexity — only various levels of ignorance.

The other fact is that it is undeniable that animals are well adapted to their niches and that in every age this has been the case. The notion of adaptation is, indeed, the paramount question in evolutionary theory. As evolutionist Nile Eldredge comments:

> In contrast, the focus of this book is on the original (and still very much central) question of evolutionary biology: the explanation of phenotypic diversity and the design apparent in nature (the adaptive "fit" of organisms to their environments) approached through analysis of the biotic and physical environmental context of such change.[50]

One can note the inescapable teleology in the preceding passage. Adaptation implies design and design implies a designer which implies an Intelligence. Indeed, the issue of

---

[49]. Kauffman, S.A. (1993). *Origins of Order: Self-Organization and Selection in Evolution,* p. 482-483.

[50]. Eldredge, Niles. (1989), *Macro-Evolutionary Dynamics,* p. 10.

adaptation (best fit) is surfacing in the speculation of the development of a complex phenomenon such as flight. Even if random biological evolution has indeed occurred, it is a misperception that animals in bygone epochs were not well adapted to their niches. Contemporary theorists themselves are now realizing this:

> Bock (1979) has criticized Simpson's (original 1944) model of quantum evolution because, in common with saltational models, it involves no intermediate *stable* taxa with organisms successfully adapted to a niche somewhere between the starting and end points of the transformational series under analysis. To Bock (1979), all steps in such a macroevolutionary sequence are adaptive and under the control of directional natural selection; his model obviously contrasts with Simpson's initial formulation of an inadaptive (and preadaptive, a concept Bock endorses) phase.[51]

This means that if directional evolution did occur, it was based on the balance — there was no randomness about it. It was proceeding in such a way so as to create the emergence of mammals and hence human beings. There was even a perspicuous plan behind the extinctions! Interestingly enough, even those who believe in chance and natural selection such as David M. Raup, a statistical palaeontologist and expert on extinction studies, concludes the following:

> [If extinctions did not occur] many of the innovations in evolution, such as new body plans or modes of life, would probably not appear. The result would be a slowing of evolution and an approach to some sort of steady-state condition. According to this

---

[51]. Ibid., p. 38.

The Certainty of Human Knowledge

view, the principal role of extinction in evolution is to eliminate species and thereby reduce biodiversity so that space–ecological and geographic–is available for innovation....

NASA and the other agencies around the world that search for extraterrestrial life– especially intelligent life–have recognized the importance of extinction in evolution. Twenty years ago, we thought that stable planetary environments would be best for evolution of advanced life. Now NASA is thinking explicitly in terms of planets with enough environmental disturbance to cause extinction and thereby to promote speciation.[52]

On this issue, Niles Eldredge similarly concludes that:

Mass extinctions are cross-genealogical and occur without regard for the stage of accrual complex adaptations within single lineages. Mass extinctions commonly eliminate complex adaptations and reset the ecological, hence evolutionary, clock. Thus, without mass extinctions, more elaborate complex adaptations would likely accrue, but, on the other hand, truly novel adaptations–the sort that mark large-scale taxic differences, and the usual stuff of "macroevolution" — would be correspondingly even more rare in

---

[52]. Raup, David M. (1991), *Extinction: Bad Genes or Bad Luck?*, pp. 187-188.

phylogenetic history than they appear to have been.[53]

The concept of Intelligence is yet inescapable from even another direction — that is, from the concept of "preadaptation":

> ...Simpson invoked allometrically enlarged molars in grazing horses as a preadaptation; once the molars became sufficiently enlarged, they were suitable to be used in grazing, and selection then began rapidly to drive some horse lineages up the steep gradient of the grazing adaptive peak.[54]

The author, realizing that preadaptation implies teleology states:

> ...the term "preadaption" in evolutionary biology has often suffered from an almost mystical sense of premonitory [preplanned], directional change, as if future evolutionary modifications are somehow anticipated by earlier stages of phenotypic transformation. By choosing such clear examples–in which utterly "co-opted" functions are so starkly different from previous functions — Gould and Vrba (1982) clarify the distinction between current utility and mode of historical development.[55]

If something is preadaptive (or predesigned, according to the chance-based evolutionists own definition for adaptation) and

---

[53]. Eldredge, Niles. (1989), *Macro-Evolutionary Dynamics,* p. 210.

[54]. Ibid., p. 50.

[55]. Ibid., p. 51.

The Certainty of Human Knowledge

premonitory (monitor beforehand) then one cannot escape the singular meaning and singular implication of such notions. When, for example, one claims that if it is sub-zero degrees Celsius, the conditions must be present to "freeze pure water", where sub-zero degrees Celsius can only have one concomitant outcome — to "freeze" the pure water — there can be no other interpretation as to what is the outcome of freezing pure water. Language and cause and effect are integrally coupled in such discourses and their meanings are clear. Similarly, the concept of *pre*adaptation, far from carrying any mystical baggage, by necessity, requires foresight, preplanning, pre-preparation and premonitoring, not only in the theoretical scenario, but also 'out there', in concrete physical set-up. Indeed, if preplanning or premonitoring does not imply preadapatation and vice versa, then it is just as if to use an analogy, a 'scientist' expects that it is possible that proteins will not always be made up of amino acids; proteins imply amino acids just as preadaptation implies preplanning. Furthermore, inanimate matter and processes do not and cannot have the capacity to create in terms of adaptive structures and environments. It is not difficult to see, therefore, that such inconsistent thinking is itself mystical not rational, occultistic not scientific and downright paganistic. The paganistic aspect creeps in because such notions of preadaptation without a mind behind them, would imply that matter and processes possess intelligence, which they clearly do not. Indeed, it is these kinds of views which are, in this sense, almost mystical and not those of one who ascribes to a singular Intelligence as the Preadaptor of all things.

However, for argument sake, let us weaken our case, and use the 'proof by contradiction' argument taking what we would consider a primitive view, by siding with those who ascribe things to chance. Even those who believe in randomness know very well that randomness is constrained between limits and that there are the 'laws of statistics'. Modern chaos theory attests to this fact very well. As Jack

From Facts to Values

Cohen, a reproductive biologist and Ian Stewart, mathematician point out:

> Statistics is just one way for a system to collapse the chaos of its fine structure and develop a reliable large-scale feature. Other kinds of feature can crystallize out from underlying chaos–numbers, shapes, patterns of repetitive behaviour. Many of those features have their own intricate internal structure (for example, the Mandelbrot set) which is quite different from the underlying rules that generated the feature in the first place. The intricacy of the Mandelbrot set bears no obvious relation to the simplicity of the process that produces it. The rules for making a Mandelbrot set are dynamic; the internal intricacies are geometric. That's why we describe it as a complicated simplicity; there's no contradiction.[56]

They further on state that:

> Fine structure, be it patterned or chaotic, implies features. Even a system with no obvious features would possess the feature "featureless"; it's a Catch-22. Features arise because rules at one level of interpretation "simplexify" or "complicify" to give features one level higher.[57]

Randomness, as it is understood by the present scientific community does not and cannot imply the non-existence of some form of creative agency for the universe. Randomness

---

[56]. Cohen, Jack & Stewart, Ian. (1994), *The Collapse of Chaos: Discovering Simplicity in a Complex World,* p. 234.

[57]. Ibid., pp. 433-434.

The Certainty of Human Knowledge

has bearing only on the nature or attributes of such an agency, not such an agencies existence. This is because if something is only partially random, then it is also partially organized non-randomly with respect to its structure and because of this, the organizational process and limits of randomness cannot be ultimately governed from within; they must, on the contrary, be so governed from without. In other words, the limits have to be set from the outside, by an outsider. From this, if the believers in chance still wish to remain logical, they have to concede that there is some type of intelligence that has created the universe. The only question then remains in respect of the nature and attributes of that intelligence. That such an intelligence certainly exists, they must indeed conclude, even if they completely neglect the fact of the existence of the balance in nature and the possibility of directed evolution.

The critique of natural selection as the evolutionary mechanism was discussed earlier. It is only one of many which shows its grave shortcomings. We strongly believe that within the next fifty years, if not earlier, natural selection will go the way of Freud's theory of psychoanalysis, yielding some insights but having a wholly untenable foundation, made obsolete. The type of biology that will be needed to understand how evolution has occurred based on laws integrated with the wider aspects of science such as physics and chemistry, as Brian Goodwin states:

> ... my hope is that the diversity of living forms–or at least their essential features–can be accounted for by a relatively small number of generative rules or laws ["as a result of patterns and directions at the atomic or molecular level"]. It's too soon to start trying to explain how a bear changed into a

whale. We need to know the laws that make form possible in the first place.[58]

Evidence is fast moving towards the convergence of the disclosure of an Intelligence, as opposed to Chance, and a sublime purpose, rather than blind and vicious randomness. Stephen Jay Gould, and indeed many of those who have agnostic and atheistic sentiments feel that the design argument is antiquated as it leaves out the element of chance; nature being based on natural selection is a devilish and cruel scheme of survival of the fittest, powered by impersonal random forces.[59] However, as it has been illustrated already, natural selection at best is only a theory, not a fact. If Gould's punctuated equilibrium is a mechanism for natural selection, and at the same time is also regarded by him as a theory, then so is natural selection itself a theory, by force of logic. However, Gould deals with natural selection as if it were a fact.

Now if it were realized that there is purposeful activity in evolution, though not necessarily of the Lamarkian kind, then one would see a purposeful and meaningful designer behind creation. The question which emerges, however, is one of efficiency. Indeed the efficiency of the process can only be known once we know how evolution is occurring. But even if we take the criticism of those who opine chance, that is, those who criticize the extinction of creatures, one must realize that efficiency itself is a function of purpose and purpose is a function of order. There may be a hierarchy of purposes, the purpose on the lower rung of the ladder serving and being constrained by that at the higher level. Looking at the results of the whole picture — the highest rung of the

---

[58]. Hitching, Francis. (1982), *The Neck of the Giraffe,* p. 165.

[59]. Gould, Stephen Jay. (1990), "Darwin and Paley Meet the Invisible Hand", *Natural History,* pp. 8-16.

ladder — the universe appears to be pursuing an indescribably successful intention, in having been based on the balance and in the creation of entities such as human beings (and perhaps other human-like entities on other conceivable planets) who can either make or break the balance. To achieve the state where human beings have emerged in this manner from the Big Bang, would necessitate the *planned* extinction and development of species leading up to man, the details of which one may only speculate about at this point, but which must be deterministic (as evinced by the arguments in this book). Yet what justification do we have for a view which places the human being on the pedestal of most of sentient creation? This question hinges on the issue of the global purpose of the universe itself. In fact the British philosopher Ayer, raises this point when he comments that "the fact that ends are pursued and sometimes attained within a system is not a proof that the system as a whole is directed towards any end. What needs to be shown is that the entire universe presents the appearance of a teleological system."[60] Ayer concludes that no one has been able to show this.

Let us tackle this issue head on: From a discussion of the dynamic balance with which the universe has been shown to have been designed (which forms the major topic of the next chapter) one can see that the universe is an integrated dynamically balanced whole and that it has been purposely designed with free-willed creatures such as human beings in mind to see if they will uphold the balance. One of the most quantitatively stunning examples of this is the following:

> Hoyle made a remarkable prediction: in the course of an intensive study of stellar nucleosynthesis he realized that unless [the reactions] proceeded *resonantly* the yield of

---

[60]. Ayer, A.J. (1982), *The Central Questions of Philosophy*, p. 219.

> carbon would be negligible. There would be neither carbon, nor carbon-based life in the Universe. The evident presence of carbon and the product of carbon chemistry led Hoyle to predict that [the set of equations] *must* be resonant with the vital resonance level of the C^{12} nucleus lying near ~7.7 MeV. This prediction was soon verified by experiment ... with the expected properties lying at 7.656±0.008 MeV. ...[confirming] an Anthropic Principle prediction.
>
> However, this is not the end of the story. ...Had the O^{16} level lain just above that of $C^{12}+He^4$, carbon would have been rapidly removed by alpha capture...
>
> Hoyle realized that this remarkable chain of coincidences — the unusual longevity of beryllium, the existence of an advantageous resonance level in C^{12} and the non-existence of a disadvantageous level of O^{16} — were necessary, and remarkably fine-tuned, conditions for our own existence and indeed the existence of any carbon-based life in the Universe.[61]

This clearly demonstrates that the Universe had been preplanned, right from the very beginning for the emergence of carbon-based life and was not developing in an erratic chance based manner. Barrow and Tipler, in their voluminous book *The Anthropic Cosmological Principle*, then pose the following question:

> Although a small change in ... resonance levels in C^{12} and O^{16}, might so alter the rate of cosmological or stellar evolution that life

---

[61]. Barrow, John D. & Tipler, Frank J. (1986), *The Anthropic Cosmological Principle*, pp. 252-253.

could not evolve, how do we know that compensatory changes could not be made in the values of other constants to recreate a set of favourable conditions?[62]

After some mathematical gymnastics, the two physicists conclude that: "If the attractor at x^* is 'strange' then there may be many other similar sets in the λ_i parameter space. This might ensure that there were other permutations of the values of constants of Nature allowing life."[63] What the authors of this speculation forget is that even if there were compensating factors, they would have to be so comprised and integrated precisely that they would lead to carbon-based life. Therefore, one cannot escape the situation with a quick wave of the mathematical wand. This argument is similar to an erroneous argument of a person who says that: "Knowing a human language in general is indeed a complex phenomenon and to utter a particular statement in English, with a sensible meaning, is indeed a remarkable achievement; however, maybe if the same thing were said in another language it would not be so remarkable!"

The other point which Barrow and Tipler are missing is that they are dealing with constants in nature which are not only so precise, but may indeed be the only arrivable ones in our particular type of space or space-time. In other words, in our type of universe these constants may indeed be the only constants existable because our space-time itself is unique in the sense that it can only yield one set of particular constants because of its 'structure'. Indeed, another set of constants might exist in a totally other universe which has totally other properties than our own — but that is a totally other universe — not the one in which we reside! And if we did reside in that other hypothetical universe we would be faced with the same

---

[62]. Ibid., p. 254.

[63]. Ibid., p. 255.

set of questions as to the remarkableness of the existence of the constants in *that* universe.

Statistical Fallacy

Those who attempt to deny an Intelligence behind design try to hide behind the transparent mantle of chance. The word chance has come to be misused considerably. In fact, chance is a mathematical concept related to the probability of an event. For example, the probability of getting "heads" in a coin-toss is 50%, or one half. This is because a coin has two sides, and hence there are only two possible outcomes and each is equally likely. In simple terms, we can say that the probability of an event occurring, P, is defined as the number of ways of achieving the desired event(s) divided by the number of ways of achieving all possible events. In this case, the number of desired events is one (heads), and there are two possible events (heads and tails), which yields the ratio 1/2 or 50%. How about the probability of getting a six in the throw of a dice. We can get a six in one way and there are six possible outcomes; therefore, the probability would be 1/6 or 16.7%. If we threw two dice expecting two sixes, we would only get this event happening once in about 36 attempts, because its probability is 1/36. This is because there are thirty-six possible outcomes, and only one way of getting the desired outcome. As the total number of outcomes (the denominator in the equation above) increases, the probability decreases and the event becomes less likely. The probability of getting seven with a single die is therefore zero (because it is impossible) and the probability of getting a number between one and six, inclusive, is one (because it is certain). As stated earlier, for practical purposes, events with probability less than on in 10^{50} are considered impossible by the mathematicians, because their likelihood of occurrence within a reasonable time-frame is negligible. Applying these concepts to a physical phenomenon, consider the odds against producing 25,000 enzymes by chance in the absence of any intelligent laws governing chemical reactions.

The Certainty of Human Knowledge

Assuming that each enzyme is a simple one made up of only 100 amino acids, the probability of producing the 25,000 enzymes works out to be one chance in $10^{2,825,000}$. Actually, the probability is considerably slimmer, because most enzymes are more complex than the proto-typical enzyme of 100 amino acids that we have considered.

For a comparison we may examine the probability of pulling out 10 cards in consecutive order (for example, pulling them out like this: *ace* followed by 2, 3, ..., 10) from a stack of 10 cards. This works out to be one chance in 3.6 million or 3.6×10^6. Now suppose we wish to calculate how many cards we would have to pull out in succession like this to equal the probability of one in $10^{2,825,000}$ as calculated above, in order to gain a physical understanding of this probability. This number works out to be more than 500,000 cards, a stack at least several hundred feet high. The calculation for this is a follows: We wish to solve the following equation for n:

$$n! = 10^{2,825,000}$$

Applying Stirling's approximation to n!, we have:

$$n! = \sqrt{2n\pi}\left(\frac{n}{e}\right)^n\left(1+\frac{1}{12n}\right) = 10^{2,825,000}$$

By taking logarithms on both sides and then iterating for *n*, we arrive at $n = 500,000$.

The probability of producing those 25,000 enzymes from *scratch* is the product of the probabilities of producing them from amino acids times the probability of producing the amino acids from simpler molecules, down to the probability of producing the molecules themselves from quarks an so on, over time. The total probability goes from vanishing small to incalculably small. Even if biological evolution has occurred (i.e. that species have transformed into other species) this cumulative property of probabilities must apply. Given the incredibly small probability of producing 25,000 enzymes from scratch, we need more than pure chance to account for this. As Richard Milton elaborates:

From Facts to Values

If Paley's watch is the argument from design, then the Darwinian case might be called the argument from probability. What does it really amount to?

Suppose we have a highly improbable event such as a perfect deal in bridge, where each of the four players receives a complete suit of cards. The odds against this happening are billions of billions of billions to one. Let us assume that since being manufactured the cards have been used for 99 deals and on the 100th time the pack was shuffled, the perfect deal arose. Can we say that each of these previous shuffles, deals and plays of hands (number 1 for instance) was a cumulative event that ultimately contributed to the perfect deal? Can we reduce the ultimate odds against the perfect deal by attempting to spread them around more thinly between the intermediate steps? Not *afterwards*, note, when we know the result, but at the time each step is occurring?

The answer is no, we cannot. Like the supposedly evolving DNA, the cards have a memory in that the previous deals have contributed to their current order and the ultimate perfect deal. But being part way towards a perfect deal does not alter the odds on the ultimate deal, because some of the key random events determining the ultimate outcome have not yet taken place.[64]

The above analyses show that when one tries to circumvent the cumulative nature of probabilities over time, one falls into

---

[64]. Milton, Richard. (1992), *The Facts of Life: Shattering the Myth of Darwinism*, p. 144.

The Certainty of Human Knowledge

an elementary mistake, termed the 'statistical fallacy' by the geneticist, Francis Crick. This fallacy is apparent in arguments from biologists who try to lessen improbabilities by arguing that if a thing developed from A to B over millions of years, for instance, and that it is indeed improbable for something to have developed in one jump from A to B, if the probabilities are calculated along intermediate steps along the path from A to B, then one would not have to contend with such extremely low probabilities, or perhaps with only a few. Like the improbabilities cited by Penrose with respect to the unique origin of the universe, when one looks at biological examples, be they in space or time, one will not cease to be amazed at those who postulate the emergence of order by chance. As Bernd-Olaf Kuppers, the biophysical chemist relates:

> The human genome consists of about 10^9 nucleotides, and the number of combinatorially possible sequences attains the unimaginable size of $4^{1000 \text{ million}}$ $10^{600 \text{ million}}$. Even in the simple case of a bacterium, the genome consists of some 4×10^6 nucleotides, and the number of combinatorially possible sequences is $4^{4 \text{ million}}$ $10^{2.4 \text{ million}}$. The expectation probability for the nucleotide sequence of a bacterium is the thus so slight that not even the entire space of the universe would be enough to make the random synthesis of a bacterial genome probable. For example, the entire mass of the universe, expressed as a multiple of the mass of the hydrogen atom, amounts to about 10^{80} units. Even if all the matter in space consisted of DNA molecules of the structural complexity of the bacterial genome, with random sequences, then the chances of finding among them a bacterial genome or

From Facts to Values

something resembling one would still be completely negligible.[65]

Certainty and Quantum Mechanics

The confusion over the notion of probabilities and uncertainties has invaded the domain of observation in the area of physics, tending to erroneously foster a relativistic view of existence as opposed to determinism. According to the dominant view of Quantum Mechanics, the position and momentum of a particle are related in such a way that if you know one then you cannot know the other. It is erroneously concluded from this that the electron, for instance, does not have an actual location and momentum at a particular instant. This completely fallacious notion has been propagated by various physicists such as Bohr, in contrast to determinists such as Einstein and De Broglie. The notion can be seen to be false in several ways: Firstly, even if it is true that we cannot measure something or see something, it does not mean that it does not exist. The Copenhagen School was based on logical positivism which basically postulates that if one does not observe or measure something, then it does not exist. Secondly, if the electron has a measurable position, it has to have a momentum even though we cannot measure it. If it has a measurable velocity then it must have a position even if we cannot measure it. Thirdly, Quantum Mechanics cannot be the whole solution, even though it describes many things successfully. This is because we have come to realize, and increasingly so, that the basic laws in this universe must be integrated. The very fact that relativity and quantum mechanics are incommensurable at the present time, means that they are both incomplete, and a more embrasive and unitary explanation will be required at a higher level. At present, various approaches are being considered by a few

---

[65]. Kuppers, Bernd Olaf. (1990), *Information and the Origin of Life*, pp. 59-60.

The Certainty of Human Knowledge

scientists who believe that the universe is deterministic at all levels and probability is just a function of human ignorance. It is in this approach that true advancement lies. This, therefore, means that we may indeed be led to a deterministic solution for the quantum level, and even beyond that, as our knowledge advances.[66] Fourthly, if there is order and structure at the macro-level then how can there be indeterminacy at the micro-level, which is the basic building block for the macro-level. That is to say, why is there determinism at the macroscopic level, yet indeterminism at the submicroscopic level. There is a profound contradiction here for those who advocate indeterminism. Lastly, if we grant the indeterminists their conclusion, how is it that indeterminism is so well determined? This seems to be yet another example of *Nonsense* (Proposition 1).

Due to the indeterminate approach in quantum mechanics, the notion of indeterminacy has been transferred to areas in the social sciences as a subset of relativism. On the other hand, the adherents of mysticism have also jumped the band-wagon to 'prove' that the world is nothing but a grand illusion. There is the general notion, induced by mysticism and relativism that at the quantum level there is no determinism in the relationship between cause and effect and that there never can be, fundamentally, any certainty. Many others go even further and idiotically use such a notion as 'proof' that the universe is illusory, or that we generate 'reality' and many universes. However, it is often forgotten that whether we, as human beings, can or cannot determine something does not mean that it is not subject to cause and effect processes (deterministic laws). The reason many

---

[66]. Penrose, Roger. (1989), *The Emperor's New Mind*, pp. 232-299 & 359-371.

Bohm, David and Peat, David F. (1987), *Science, Order and Creativity: A Dramatic New Look at the Roots of Science and Life*, pp. 76-103.

scientists cling onto indeterminism to colour their world view is because they view things *anthropopsychically*, that is, they think that something is real or really exists only if human beings can measure it. To say the least, this is obviously incorrect, but such views as stated before are entrenched and held onto because of the educational system which is permeated by relativistic notions.

Is the Concept of 'God' a Placebo?

Often, when the notion of the Creator is brought into a scientific discussion, particularly in the context of teleology, some scientists and philosophers become apprehensive because of the past and present records of some dogmatic religious institutions. However, what is overlooked is not only the problematic defence of atheism with all its serious flaws and fallacies, but also the problematic refutation of theism. The fallacious approach to this issue arises from two faulty notions: 'God' and 'Belief'. These have both led to primitively worthless judgements. Let us first analyze the notion of 'God'.

The profound common mistake in any atheistic, theological, philosophical and scientific discussions involving the notion of God is to ignore that there are various concepts of God[67], just as there are various concepts of ethics and rights. There is the henotheistic concept, the polytheistic concept, the monotheistic concept, the trinitarian concept, the panpsychism concept, the pantheistic concept, the kathenotheistic concept, the anthropomorphic human-like concept, demi-god concept, the God-incarnate concept, the fatherly-figure concept, the goddess concept, the family god concept, warring god concept, the totemic god concept and so on. Proving the irrationality of a particular concept about

---

[67]. See Jordan, Michael. (1992), *The Encyclopedia of Gods*. Jordan provides approximately 2500 different names and concepts of 'divine deity' collected from different cultures and era.

The Certainty of Human Knowledge

God is not at all the same thing as refuting the existence of a rational concept of God, such as a Singular Intelligence as the *First Cause*, the *Uncaused Cause*, the *Immovable Mover*, the *Designer*, the *Originator*, and the *Creator* who is not subject to gender, plurality, culture, personification and time and space continuum.

Another barrier involved in belief in God as the Originator is the erroneous nature of 'belief' itself. There is an old atheistic adage, purporting that 'God' did not create man, but rather, man created 'God'. This idea has been around for at least a couple of centuries and was supported by many hotshot philosophers, sociologists, psychologists and anthropologists. Among them were Hume, Freud, Marx, Feuerbach and Nietzsche. Subsequently, many have been influenced into thinking that this idea is true, because it was pointed out by the above-mentioned array of clangourous philosophisers. This assertion holds that the concept of 'God', as a powerful deity, being responsible for creation of this vast universe, is merely wishful thinking. It is utterly a product of the human imagination. Man, a helpless mortal creature who is terrified by the forces of nature and hardships of life seeks emotional comfort, consolation and protection. Therefore, he invents 'God'. 'God' is man's oldest and the most urgent need for a strong supernatural and compassionate Being, residing in the wonderful imaginary world called heaven, who responds to the outcries of his troubled creatures in misery and misfortune. Thus, this imaginary concept of 'God' is merely the hope of the hopeless, a help for the helpless. In a nutshell, He is invented to be used as a means to a psychological end.

However, there are several serious flaws in this myopic outlook that are puzzling, not the least of which is how it could have been in vogue for all these years. The fallacy arises from the erroneous notion of 'Belief', which in turn has led to primitively counterproductive conclusions.

All of the above theoreticians basically argue that the concept of 'God' as such is a human fabrication, a form of placebo. A placebo is an unmedicated preparation, an inactive substance that has absolutely no physiological effect, but may effect the relief of pain in someone who is set-up to believe that he is actually being easily treated. Its psychological effect, however, solely depends on the person's expectations. The expectation is the causal factor and plays a decisive role in the treatment. But, a man who is sexually dysfunctional cannot benefit if he already knows that the 'medication' given to him is only TicTac. Consequently, this would obviously entail that no patient can prescribe himself a placebo. If there is no set-up involved, no amount of 'will' to believe can improve his condition. Similarly, a prospective and thoughtful individual, as well as a gullible fool, even in the most frightening and unfortunate circumstance, cannot take up a fraudulent belief and false hopes, based on a self-invented notion of God and paradise, when he knows better that the whole idea is illusory and mendaciously unfounded, simply due to its inherent dysfunctional nature. Illusions, myths, false hopes and manufactured reality will remain psychologically deceptive, so long as one mistakes them for truth. Once the truth is revealed, though, the placebo effect is no longer operative.

Consequently, a man in a total state of darkness, who denies reality is either a fool, crazy, confused or is knowingly following his selfish desires and vested interests. One cannot manufacture reality and then confidently believe it, just as one cannot knowingly give oneself a placebo pill and expect it to work. One could only accept it, but cannot truly believe it, because it is utterly impossible to believe a manufactured reality once it is realized that it is manufactured. Therefore, belief per se, can never produce conviction. No amount of staunch belief can produce facts. Belief and conviction are two distinct yet interconnected components. The latter is a concomitant result of the former. That is because, real belief — the result of conviction — can only arise out of understanding; understanding requires justification, justification requires proof, and proof demands evidence; evidence means digging something from reality. Belief

The Certainty of Human Knowledge

without evidence is nothing but self-hypnosis. It is submission to blindness. The security of conviction is that which arises from certainty, which in turn can only be realized, if and only if, one has used reason and examined the evidence yielding conclusions free from all types of inconsistencies. Only then, one can acquire tranquillity and peace of mind. Peace of mind is a product of this process. It comes only after there are no contradictions. It comes only when paradox and ambiguity are eliminated.

However, when we deal with the concept of God as unique, outside spacetime, indeed the very Originator of spacetime, such a placebo argument for every ideology collapses, because according to this non-anthropomorphic concept of God, this God may or may not answer man's prayer, all depending on His wisdom as to what is best for the individual. The Big Bang Originator concept of God is not like Superman or the Genie in the bottle, who answers to every demand that man makes. Therefore, the confirmatory belief in a cosmic Originator who is not subject to push-button demands, cannot be a placeboic belief, "an opiate for the masses", just as a prescribed placebo of the type in which an acknowledgement is made at the outset to the patient, that it may or may not cure him, has no effect and is no longer a placebo.

Furthermore, if we are dealing with a concept of God, within an ideology, where He may even respond to the prayer of the disloyal and the unbeliever, why should I then believe, when I too, equally have a chance of getting what I want if I am disloyal?

Knowledge: Its Integrated Nature

From the discussion in this chapter it is clear that the very same methodology which is used to become certain about something happening in this universe must be the same methodology as that which should be used to conclude with certainty that there must be a Singular Intelligence as defined in this book, who is responsible for origination. All legitimate proof and disproof must be based on the notion of consistency, which incorporates the process of using reason and evidence to eliminate that which does not make sense and that for which the probability or cumulative probability is zero or approaches zero.

Up to now, it has been shown that the methodology one uses to determine reality, be that whether a Singular Originator exists, or whether a homicide was committed, depends on exactly the same methodology. In this approach there is no separation between so-called secular and non-secular — this universe is an originated, integrated and interconnected system. It is only by using reason and the evidence, where the measure of reality is consistency, that does truth become distinguishable from falsehoods. Anyone connecting the totality of reality in this way is truly knowledgeable. Assuredly, any 'educational system' which would truly embark on a programme to enhance humankind would use this methodology and realize the integration between things in this universe and the nature of its origin. Any 'educational system' failing to realise and incorporate this approach would be doomed to failure in the establishment of a rational, sane and just society — a society in which its members have not cut themselves off from Reality. Humankind has caused increasing socio-environmental disorder at all levels, precisely because most individuals and societies have not been following this methodology.

The Certainty of Human Knowledge

Scientific Investigation and Ethics

Finally, it is befitting to discuss the social conditions and ethics of scientific investigation. Let us first start with social conditions which are so vital for the progression of science and the realization of Certainty.

In our present academic institutions and scientific circles, there is an increasing pressure on academia to publish more and more, with no genuine emphasis on the veracity of their findings. "Publish or Perish", as it is often heard. In this setting, many investigators search only for the sake of searching, not for the sake of finding. Already, some of them have even gone as far as faking data.

However, as it has already been established, the most important characteristic of the scientific methodology is its objectivity in seeking the truth and nothing but the truth! After all, the only thing that matters here, should be to reveal the unknown. Consequently, as pointed out by Cohen and Nagel[68] if our goal is set to unlock the secrets of nature, and we are aiming for reliance, "clarity and accuracy, order and consistency, security and cogency", and above all the absolute certainty in our actions and intellectual development, then we must no doubt resort to some criterion for fixing crucial priorities "whose efficacy in resolving problems is" truly independent of our wills, base desires, vested interest and external pressures. That is to say, a scientist must aim at discovering the truth, not at inventing it. His intention should not be focused on achieving fame. Nor should it be focused on winning the approval of his or her colleagues in order to obtain their support. Rather, it should only be for broadening human intellectual horizons — for discovering that which was not known before.

---

[68]. Cohen, Morris and Nagel, Ernest. (1934), *An Introduction to Logic and Scientific Method,* p. 195.

From Facts to Values

In the pursuit of certainty, scientific methodology is effective only so long as the proper prerequisites of ethical, political and social conditions are present. That is to say, science must continuously maintain its freedom and objectivity, and scientists must maintain their integrity. They should not seek to impose the desires and wishes of certain elite classes or organizations, or to develop a flux of things in a capricious and dubious manner. However, when humanity falls for alluring trappings, manifested in fabricated forms, as opposed to solid content, and indiscriminately proclaims every new baseless doctrine as the truth, then the exclusive devotion to truth becomes totally subordinated to a desire for supposedly elegant novel formulations.[69] In such an intellectually polluted environment, when priorities are mixed up, no genuine effort exists among scientists to reveal the secrets of the universe. There will only be competition among them for grant money, reputation and to be 'number one' in their respective fields. Consequently, in this atmosphere of misdirected goals, science inevitably shifts mainly towards the advancement of technology, constrictive economic development and mass production, often by any means necessary. This pattern of value-free science, for instance, can easily be observed in the continuous destruction of the environment and the alteration of natural design in order to stimulate the economy of certain classes, corporations or nations through scientific manipulations. The military-industrial complex is a chief instigator of such irresponsible science. Therefore, in many such cases, the goal for the search for truth and breakthrough becomes subverted to the search for profit, power and domination. Science as a means of enlightenment shifts to a means of empowerment and usurpation. Thus, this goal becomes the only motivating factor for pursuing investigations, research and writing. Science must always remain married to values, in order to avoid any

---

[69]. Ibid., p. 402.

The Certainty of Human Knowledge

deviation towards purely reductionistic, mechanistic, positivistic and opportunistic trends, lest it becomes impaired.

Yet, what can be said of the required relationships between ethics and scientific investigation would also be applicable to any other investigative discipline. Scientists are not the only ones who need to have ethical values. The whole of society needs a just moral code in order to function optimally in every branch. However, what is the basis of morality in society? Can there be Certainty in the moral, social, civil realms, just as there is in 'natural science'? What are the implications of fact and certainty? The next chapter attempts to dwell on these fundamental questions.

Chapter Three

The Equigenic Principle: The Foundation of an Absolute Value System

It seems surprising at first, but is none the less certain, that our reason does not draw its conclusions from Nature, but [erroneously] prescribes them to it.

Kant

The Usage of Facts

From the previous chapter, we can gather that it is not just the scientific community that must function according to certain moral principles, but any community. The global society needs rationally-based moral values in order to avoid descending into the cauldron of chaos and corruption. To say that an interconnected value system based on facts is urgently needed is an understatement. We have moved beyond the point of urgency. While this is being written, the world is facing indescribable horrors which are a cumulative result of the dissociation of humankind from a methodology which leads to epistemological absolutism and Certainty.

The pertinent question is: If Certainty is obtainable and facts establishable, what are its imperative and practical uses? Philosopher, Hilary Putnam states that:

> ... the only aim of science is to discover truth (besides pointing out that science has additional aims, which is of course true), is that *truth is not the bottom line:* truth itself gets its life from our criteria of rational acceptability, and these are what we must look at if we wish to discover the values which are really implicit in science.[70]

If that is the case, perhaps more than anything else, the establishment of facts with certainty would have a direct impact on human values and the concomitant behaviour — values in ethics, economic, social, civil, public and environmental policies — in short on everything that we do. Naturalist and ecological crusader, Thomas Berry states:

> The greatest single need at present is the completion of the story, as told in its physical dimensions by science, by the more integral

---

[70]. Putnam, Hilary. (1981), *Reason, Truth and History*, p. 130.

account that includes the numinous and consciousness dimensions of the emergent universe from its primordial moment. Once that is done, a meaningful universe, a functional cosmology, is available as a foundation for the total range of human activities in the ecological age.[71]

Certainly, a meaningful system should govern all human activities. However, what is that system? What should be the basis of our morality or system of values? Who or what determines it? Can ethical values also be universal, similar to the universality of the laws of physics? To say no, is as though we still believe that things are relative, which has already and unequivocally been proven to be otherwise. Furthermore, is the nature and methodology of human reasoning any different, in its fundamental respects, in the realm of the 'social' sciences than that of the 'natural' sciences? Can human values be divorced from determined facts? Or should they indeed be based on facts? There are some who seriously argue that a move from fact to value is fallacious. Yet, it seems rather strikingly absurd to think that there is a problem with building values on facts. Without facts no decisions can be made logically. From theories is derived probability, but truth or certainty is obtained only from facts. If values are not based on facts, then what should they be based on: Fantasies, dreams, whims, religions or social conventions?

The two commonly used sources of morality are religion and secularism (conventional systems), both of which are problematic, for none of them is purely subservient to discovered facts.

In the case of religious values, what constitutes as religion to begin with? We must consider that theology is not a universal science like biology, for any idiot can grab a piece of

---

[71]. Berry, Thomas. (1988), *The Dream of the Earth,* p. 120.

The Equigenic Principle

paper and pen and write what he would claim to be a divine revelation. If the notion of 'religion' is not universal, consequently, the values derived from 'religion' cannot possibly be universal. Thus, should society imbibe every nonsensical practice, simply because it is wrapped up with the notion of 'our religiously' obligatory rituals. If we allow such provisions then any action can be justified under the banner of a newly formed 'religion', denomination, or sect. Values based on religion are uncontrollable, syncretistic, arbitrary, dogmatic, ritualistic and culturally relative. Thus, we could never have any absolute and universal values to resolve societal conflicts, and could never match reality with map of reality based on thought constructs.

Under secularism, on the other hand, defined values are not independent from the interests, wishes and the desires of the value-makers. One of the major criticisms against secularism is its tendency to relax the codes of existing culturo-religious morality. To suit one's purpose, usually, all that is required is lobbying and getting enough consent. And that is exactly why conventionalism is so popular in secular societies. Under conventionalism, this permissive attitude and the lack of an absolute foundational criterion for judgement has led to a total disregard for the balance in the social web of society. On other hand, conventionalism could restrict moral codes to the other harsh extreme, such as in totalitarian states. Yet, in either case, there is no stability in either system. The extremism at both ends is bound to shatter into smithereens, given its due course of time. We shall examine the outcome of conventional values in much more detail later on, and show that the deficiencies of secularism and religionism cannot be found under an Absolute system.

As opposed to all other alternatives, values based on facts are inherent and universal. Such values are valid by nature, not by convention or by the authority of a so-called religious figure or King. Therefore, in order to have a truly valuable value system, all designated values ought to be founded on facts. For example, if it is scientifically determined that consumption of alcohol is detrimental to the individual and the society as a whole, then the inescapable value that is derived from this fact is: *"One must not drink, period."* There can be no 'but' here. Therefore, the practice of this decree is not due to authoritative compulsion, but rather due to a voluntary submission to the facts, derived from understanding. For the benefit of society, the state ought to implement factual values, educate the masses and punish the violators. This entails that the so-called scientific approach is wholly viable for setting up a universal standard for the 'moral' judgement of right and wrong.

Given these pertinent considerations, would it be possible to derive values from first principles: using our mind and the signs in the universe, endowments readily accessible to any human beings, anywhere on this planet, at any time? In this chapter, we shall argue in the affirmative, that this is the only secure approach. To establish this assertion, we shall attempt to develop a principle of what is commonly referred to as 'universal justice'[72] and rights based on factual knowledge of the physical laws of nature — a principle of 'absolute justice' for both the human and non-human inhabitants of global society.

Justice and Rights

The notion of justice and rights is one of the most predominant issues facing the whole of humanity today. In our age, there is perhaps more conflict on various issues than ever before. These conflicts always revolve around the question of 'rights'. All over the globe there are ongoing

---

[72]. Despite popular belief, terms commonly used such as 'universal justice', 'global justice' or 'absolute justice', technically speaking are tautological concepts similar to terms like 'hot fire', 'wet water' or 'green grass'. Justice must indeed be absolute and universal, otherwise it is not justice at all. Such adjectives added to justice are redundant.

The Equigenic Principle

debates on women's rights, minority rights, refugee rights, animal rights, language rights, fetus rights, civil rights, equal rights, gay rights, etc. In any society, the establishment of the flawless charter of rights is the most vital element not only for its survival, but also for its health and enhancement. Across the globe each society has taken a particular ideology — either explicitly or implicitly — as the core principle by which it goes about conducting its daily affairs. Most often, the ideology adhered to, serves as the foundation for every rule of conduct. All internal and external policies are set, based on the particular ideology being upheld. However, we must always keep in mind that, just as if we were to take the wrong train, every station we would get to, would be a wrong stop, similarly, if we adopt a wrong value system, every critical decision would be an erroneous one. Therefore, just as it is crucial to know which train we ought to take, so too, it is crucial to know which value system we ought to adhere to, in order to guarantee the fulfilment of everyone's rights. Yet, humankind has been swimming in a labyrinth of opposing value systems. Some of these are culturally based, others are conventional, and yet still there are some others which are merely justified by majority consent. One may wonder which one of these ideologies is the most optimal one. In fact, far from being optimal, all of these views lack a solid foundation. This is because the root of the issue of rights, which entails an undercurrent of the central questions, is often disregarded by the theoreticians of justice and rights who are merely theorizing on theories. The central questions surrounding the notion of rights, however, boils down to just one basic issue — *what is the basis of justice?* What model or foundation of justice are we to use in order to arrive at optimality in the flow of life, where justice is served for all? What is the measure of justice? How could we achieve justice? How would it be implemented? Indeed, how would we arrive at a globally optimal system to deal with all issues, be they judicial, environmental, political, social, economical, taxational and so on? Our much sought after model of justice should not only be able to deal with singular issues; it should also be able to handle all issues with integral dexterity. A universally optimal system can only be deemed to be so, if it is characterized by the possession of such properties.

In an optimal system, what should be the criteria for deciding upon a myriad issues? For example, how would we be able to establish whether a violation of one's right has occurred, when an individual, group or state interferes or neglects to do so by either allowing or disallowing a particular course of action? In other words, when could one ascertain whether one's individual or collective rights have been violated or deprived? These rights may range from being able to express ideas freely, being able to enter into any country, or being able to 'marry' a partner of the same sex, etc. For some others, the denial of all these 'rights' constitute 'rights'!

In order to resolve such questions, in this chapter, the optimal system of justice and human rights will be deduced based on the notions of *interconnectivity, consistency, universality, timelessness and the concomitant functionality*. The major emphasis of the chapter is on the criteria by which we should be able to determine justice and rights, in order to deconstruct and disprove erroneous notions and reconstruct human thought and society on a hopefully more saner path. This chapter is an attempt to move towards this direction.

The Equigenic Principle

The Problematic Nature of Conventional Rights and Systems of 'Justice' Built on a Relativistic Foundation

Many jurists, academics, political scientists, philosophers and states have tried to develop theories, charters, conventions, legislations and constitutions to establish justice and human rights. However, most of them have utterly failed to establish an absolute foundation of rights. Many of these exponents do not even bother to approach the issue of rights by building upon a justifiable foundation. Rather, they attempt to formulate rights upon the basis of the best possible consent. Nonetheless, the common denominator among all these ideas is their relative nature — the unforgivable sin. As it has already been established, rules which are based on relativism are faulty, fallible, fluctuatory and unproductive.

Relativism gives birth to 'conventionalism' and 'positivism'. Both are subject to the mores of the period. Under this system, for example, one decade's human rights violation becomes another decade's guaranteed human rights protection or vice versa. By examining various conventional theories of justice and rights, it is observable that they all suffer from this flaw. Take the example of the *European Convention on Human Rights* which was formulated in an era and locale where utilitarianism was the predominant ideology, a philosophy that greatly influenced the formulation of this Charter.[73] However, half a century later, as utilitarianism becomes outdated, no one today aiming at the root of the issue would argue for this ideology as being the very foundation of a universal human rights charter, since the doctrine is self-centred and narrow in its scope.[74] Although, portions of the utilitarian approach may be necessary to deal with justice, it is certainly not sufficient to establish universal justice. It fails: "(a) to take seriously the value of fairness; and

---

[73]. See Articles: 4 (b & c), 8, 10, 15, etc.

[74]. Rawls, John. (1971), *Theory of Justice*.

(b) it does not provide an adequate foundation for equal civil and political liberties."[75] This demonstrates that formulating theories of justice and rights based on the predominant human ideology of the era, without any absolute foundation, is like building a castle on sand — once the theory is disproven, the whole structure, built on its premises crumbles. This is solely because the ethical norms in relativistic spheres are all subject to change and modification. We have experienced this phenomenon in science as well. For instance, when what was once known to be a 'scientific fact' collapsed, all of its ramifications disintegrated. Let us, therefore, try to build rights on factual principles, not expandable or revisable theories.

Due to the use of relative standards for drafting a human rights charter, both the United Nations and the European Commission on Human Rights are obliged to constantly come up with new revisions and protocols to complete those deficiencies which are realized by the passage of time. Therefore, if it is granted that all these theories and charters of rights are relative, then we can never ascertain that there are absolute violations of human rights in a certain country in every single case. Conformity or violations against a relative charter must not be the measure of human rights. We can only go so far as to say that there is violation of, for instance, the United Nations Universal Declaration of Human Rights or the European Convention on Human Rights in that state which has agreed to abide by such specific charters. However, if we choose to measure human rights violations or compliance, according the UN charter, does this mean that there was no violation or compliance of human rights prior to the UN declaration of 1948 — that no human rights existed prior to this date? The answer is obvious.

---

[75]. Buchanan, Allan and Mathieu, Deborah (1986), "Philosophy and Justice", in the *Justice: Views from the Social Sciences*, edited by Ronald L. Cohn, p. 25.

The Equigenic Principle

One could, at this stage, pose the obvious question as to why these charters as a whole, or for the most part are relative? "To what extent is the notion of human rights an absolute or relative one? Are our views of human rights the product of our own culture?"[76] The answer, perhaps, is yes. It is due to the very fact that such rights are subject to the period, the geographic location and the prevalent cultural practices. For instance, it was only in this century in Europe, that women were given permission to vote. Prior to this, women in Europe had no voting rights, or rights to engage in any political activities whatsoever. Therefore, voting rights for women were purely based on conventional agreements. Needless to say, all conventional agreements could easily be reversed, once there would be enough consent against them.

Most conventional rights are based on dominance hierarchies and power relationships, usually proposed or structured by the academical or political elite. Political philosopher Bruce Ackerman states that:

> Rights are not the kinds of things that grow on trees — to be plucked, when ripe, by an invisible hand... *Rights talk presupposes only the conceptual possibility of an alternative way of regulating the struggle for power — one where claims to scarce resources are established through a patterned cultural activity* [italics are ours] in which the question of legitimacy is countered by an effort at justification.[77]

Hence, conventional rights are shaped by human socio-cultural values. Such ethical models arise out of the desire of

---

[76]. Higgins, Rosalyn. (1983), *The European Convention on Human Rights*, p. 539.

[77]. Ackerman, Bruce. (1980), *Social Justice in the Liberal State*, p. 5.

From Facts to Values

the members of a particular society to regulate individuals for particular goals, or for that which they perceive to be beneficial for either the elite or the society at large. Since there are so many different cultures and values in this world, it is therefore, not surprising that there are a wide variety of different and conflicting conventional rights. These temporally based conventional rights also emanate from and are characterized by insufficient knowledge — the knowledge that the elites possess up to the time of the formulation of such rights. Therefore, the products of their thoughts, embodied as rights, are inextricably bound by locality and age. Moreover, most systems of justice are framed to function within a specific territory. Any system of justice which can only work locally, and cannot be expanded universally is narrow in scope and inadequate. For example, when a crime is committed, the punishment may vary greatly, depending on which regional model of justice we may use, *even though the social environment is the same.* For instance, the punishment for homicide or abortion varies among states within the same country, such as in the United States. In another example, consider the various definitions and rights of a refugee by different international conventions. Such discrepancies "mean that a genuine refugee with full status in one part of the world would be considered ineligible and 'false' elsewhere."[78]

One of the major problematic characteristics of the laws founded on relative conventional charters is that there is often a visible dichotomy between the 'moral' and the 'legal'. For example, consider the United States policy on the public protection of refugees which stipulates: anyone who "knowingly conceals, harbours, or shields from detection... any alien... not lawfully entitled to enter or reside within the

---

[78]. Joly, Daniele & Nettleton, Clive & Poulton, Hugh. (1991), *Refugees: Asylum in Europe?* p. 15.

United States commits a federal crime."[79] However, in this respect many individuals, as well as many humanitarian organizations knowingly refuse to abide by this governmental policy, since they feel that it violates their moral values. In fact, there is a defiant underground movement in North America, known as the 'sanctuary movement', whose aim is to protect illegal refugees. Here then, we witness the case of a state law, which, quite apart from the threat of punishment, fails to persuade and penetrate the consciousness of its citizens. On the other hand, in many European societies the practice of prostitution, pornography, legalized gambling, sport hunting, euthanasia and the consumption of narcotics and alcohol have been legalized; yet many citizens still refuse to indulge in such activities despite their legalization and normalization in the public domain. In fact, both the 'moral' and the 'legal' are themselves considered relative concepts. Consequently, there is often a clash between these two contrasting relative categories, leaving the society in a state of utter dilemma and confusion. In actuality, the brute fact that the moral and legal often do not overlap, indicates that there is something drastically wrong somewhere. It could either be in the moral values of the ordinary citizens or in the criteria of judgement of the legislators, or perhaps even both. The above dichotomy undeniably exists in all manmade conventional principles of justice, be they utilitarianism, libertarianism, socialism, communitarianism and so on. Therefore, it is unsatisfying to attempt to establish a theory of justice on a nation's or state's notion of 'morality', since the field of moral criteria is also full of 'controversies' and 'dilemmas'. The contemporary

---

[79]. For specific details refer to 'The United States Immigration Reform and Control Act of 1986'.

For commentary see: Gerety, Tom. (1988), "Sanctuary: A Comment on the Ironic Relation Between Law and Morality", in *The New Asylum Seekers*, edited by David A. Martin, p. 158.

philosopher, Alan Gewirth who recognizes the problem of legal positivism, falls into this trap:

> ... the criterion for answering the question must not be legal or conventional but moral. For human rights to exist there must be valid moral criteria or principles that justify that all humans, qua humans, have the rights and hence also the correlated duties.[80]

This may be an excellent solution, if we already had established an absolute foundation for moral values. To establish this foundation, is to resolve all human dilemmas. What can be constituted as 'moral' in this day and age of prevalent relativism? When we cannot come up with a universal concept of rights, how can we can come up with universal concept of morality? In fact the latter is more complex and controversial than the former. The notion of rights is only one subset of societal moral issues. Thus, Gewirth's solution begs the question of foundation.

None of the above difficulties should exist in an 'absolute' charter of rights. However, the notion of 'absolute right' has different meanings for different philosophers. For example, Alan Gewirth defines absolute rights as:

> A right is absolute when it cannot be overridden in any circumstances, so that it can never be justifiably infringed and it must be fulfilled without any exceptions.[81]

The above concept of absolutism as such is not at all what is meant by 'absolute' in this book. Rather, what we are

---

[80]. Gewirth, Alan. (1981), "The Basis and Content of Human Rights", in the *Human Rights,* edited by J. Roland Pennock and John W. Chapman, p. 120.

[81]. Gewirth, Alan. (1984), "Are There Any Absolute Rights?", p. 92.

The Equigenic Principle

primarily interested in is: What constitutes a right as being absolute? It is crucial to examine the process which leads to something being designated as absolute. The aforementioned quote is the end-product of absoluteness; however, what is the process which leads to its absoluteness? How is it, that a given right is universally valid and must never be overridden? Gewirth's definition begs the question of absolute. Moreover, the fact that the 'absolute' right cannot be infringed may be conventionally agreed upon. It is also conventionally agreed as to which rights ought to be designated absolute, and which ones ought not to be. However, our definition of absolute rights is fundamentally different. Our concept of absolute refers to a universal set of rights which do not suffer from the vicissitudes of the age, or from the limited nature of human knowledge. These constitute a consistent set of rights that are not plagued by the discrepancies and dissimilarities between the categories of moral and moral, and, moral and legal. Such a set of laws, far from being influenced by our subjective cultural values, ought to shape our values and social norms. A set of inherent laws which applies neutrally and universally to all humans and non-humans, for all times, in all circumstances, just as the law of gravitation applies for all bodies, for all times, and in all circumstances. None of the international charters of rights do posses such characteristics. For example, the UN universal human rights charter is not like the universal law of conservation of matter and energy which existed from the beginning of the universe, for it is only a human construct which came into existence in 1948.

Indeed, is there any source from which such a universal set of rights could be extracted? Could there be a set of absolute rights from which all human actions could be measured to determine violation of or congruence with the absolute rights? If so, what could they be founded upon? Where do absolute rights emanate from?

In the journey towards the discovery of inherent, universal and absolute rights, a truly knowledgeable anti-dogmatic individual will not be swayed by rhetoric, eloquence, fashion,

From Facts to Values

peer pressure or "political correctness". Today's Bruno would look to the core of the issue, without special pleading and remain steadfast on that which is proven beyond any doubt to be the truth, no matter what is at stake.[82]

Using our faculty of the mind as discussed earlier and the given universe, let us ascertain what our proposed approach can yield. At the very outset, we must note that an absolute system must be based on an absolute foundation. Therefore, in this universe, what functions as absolute? What exists in this universe which is not subject to human fabrication or alteration? What is that which is independent of period and locality? What is out there which is inherently absolute in this context? What was playing an active role before the first human law makers emerged onto the scene? What had existed before the first homo sapiens stepped onto the face of this planet? ***Nature!*** Humankind, since its inception, has been subject to the laws of nature, long before even the establishment of the first civil society. In fact, it is the very same laws which have led to origination of human beings. Could we, therefore, develop a charter of justice based on natural laws? What is natural law in the first place? Is the concept of 'natural rights' derived from natural law valid? Or is it just another manmade imaginary construct, posing as something natural? No doubt, there are those who give their personal interests, preferences, values, desires and wishes much greater weight and priority, while pretending that it is nature which is doing all the insisting. These are the ones who use nature as a means to a specific end. We shall come back

---

[82]. It was Vaclav Havel, the former President of Czechoslovakia who once said: "...a single, seemingly powerless person who dares to cry out the word of truth and to stand behind it with all his person and all his life, ready to pay a high price, has, surprisingly, greater power, though formally disfranchised, than do thousands of anonymous voters."

The Equigenic Principle

to this point later on in the discussion. But first let us start with an analysis of the various views on this issue.

From Facts to Values

'Natural Rights' as Understood by Previous and Contemporary Philosophers

Various philosophers and legal experts have used the term 'natural rights' and argued for or against them. Aristotle, Spinoza, Hobbes, Locke, Bentham and Peter Hogg have different conceptions of 'natural rights'. However, in this chapter what is meant by 'natural rights' is completely different than what these thinkers have been referring to. For example, for Spinoza and Hobbes natural rights are derived from their erroneous perception of nature, where Spinoza, for instance, sees nature as merely being driven by power. As an example, he cited that a big fish eats a little fish by natural right, since it has the power to do so. From this, he extrapolates that nature has also conferred such dominating tendencies in humans which are based on desire and power. However, if one uses reason "as the wise man has sovereign right ... to live according to the laws of reason, so also the ignorant and foolish man has sovereign right to ... live according to laws of desire."[83] For Spinoza, the laws of desire are the laws of nature. Hence, if man wants to establish a beneficial society, he must move away from nature towards 'reason'. That is to say, if all people used 'reason' they would establish the best form of government, which, according to his assumptions would be democratic. In a democracy, "it is almost impossible that the majority of a people, especially if it is a large one, should agree in an irrational design. And, moreover, the basis and aim of a democracy is to avoid the desires as irrational and to bring men as far as possible under the control of reason, so that they may live in peace and harmony."[84] Spinoza's assertions in the light of historical reality are rather naive and presumptuous. For example, when

---

[83]. Spinoza, Baruch. (1951), *A Theological-Political Treatise,* Ch. 16.

[84]. Ibid., Ch. 16.

The Equigenic Principle

Britain was ruling India, and France ruling over Algeria, etc., there was not much hue and cry against colonialism and outright racism and oppression; rather the majority of the public blatantly supported the nationalistic domination overseas. Yet, these countries were deemed to be the paragons of large democracies. Is this, to quote Spinoza, a rational design? Is this a best form of government? One could, in fact, go further and question what Spinoza meant by reason? Reason does not sit like a disconnected idol in a vacuum, but rather, is situated in a global context, where that which matters in terms of relevancy is interconnected and not left out. Spinoza's notion of reason, in this respect, is counter-reason, leading to a deficient model for society. Furthermore, is Spinoza's model of nature as being based on power relations correct? 'Not at all' concluded by two contemporary philosophers, Robert Augros and George Stanciu, in their fascinating book *The New Biology: Discovering the Wisdom in Nature*. Augros and Stanciu have elegantly illustrated that far from erroneous Darwinian and Hobbesian concepts of nature as 'red in tooth and claw with ravine', there indeed exists harmony, balance, order and cooperation among flora and fauna in nature.[85] Consider the following symbiotic examples: many animals depend on each other for protection, food, transportation, and cleaning. On the African savannah, the baboon and the Thompson gazelle are always together. The gazelle profit from the keen vision of the baboons who can ascend trees for a lookout; the baboons, on the other hand benefit for the sensitive olfactory system of the gazelle. This 'cooperation' exists despite different predators for each of these two potential prey. There are countless other examples of mutualism and symbiotic behaviour. Spinoza, Hobbes and even Darwin lacked the vision to realize this and projected

---

[85]. Augros, Robert and Stanciu, George. (1988) *The New Biology: Discovering the Wisdom in Nature*, Chapters: 4, 5 & 7.

anthropocentric notions onto nature, tainting it with human notions of selfish power, greed and cutthroat competition. In reality the interactions among species are neither 'cooperative' nor 'competitive' — the evolutionists and ecologists all along have been barking up the wrong tree, in their *anthropocentric* conception of animal social behaviour. The principle which is involved here is much higher — it has to do with the smooth functioning and the preservation of the ecological balance and optimality, both spatially and temporally towards on overall goal. Given the misperceptions of Nature, it is, therefore, not surprising to see why their notions of 'natural rights' have encapsulated such bizarre and erroneous notions.

Take a modern definition of natural rights as defined by H.L.A. Hart, where he states:

> I have two reasons for describing the equal rights of all men to be free as a *natural* right; both of them were always emphasized by the classical theorists of natural rights. (1) This is one which all men have if they are capable of choice: they have it *qua* men and not only if they are members of some society or stand in some special relation to each other. (2) This right is not created or conferred by men's voluntary action; other moral rights are.[86]

In this quotation we cannot see any discussion as to where natural rights emanate from, but a mere reinstatement of the classical philosophers views flavoured up with the trappings of modern parlance. However, other contemporary philosophers attempted to redefine natural laws and have been influenced by the school of Hobbes and Locke. For example, political scientist Frederick Vaughan states that these two philosophers:

---

[86]. Hart, H.L.A. (1984), "Are There Any Natural Rights?", pp. 77-78.

The Equigenic Principle

> ... erected, in its stead, a *new natural law* that was founded on a new natural right. Hence, in place of Aristotle's conception of natural right (or natural justice), Hobbes founded a new natural law on the foundations of the new natural right of self-preservation.
>
> This new modern natural law shared nothing but the name with the old natural law. The new natural right of self-preservation (meaning comfortable self-preservation, not mere existence) was the basis for the new modern order of "possessive individualism" or modern capitalism. It rejected the theological aspects so essential to medieval or Scholastic natural law; it returned to the purely rational domain and posited the existence of a new natural law on the foundations of a new natural philosophy. The Biblical foundations of the old natural law were replaced by a rational account of man's first condition by nature — the state of nature.[87]

Once again these theoreticians have not delved into an analysis as to what are the sources of natural rights. In fact, the modern concept of natural rights as compared with the classical definition, is different only in degree, not in kind. It can never be substantiated that the sources of natural law is nature, by merely stating so. This statement is a mere tautology and does not yield new information.

---

[87]. Vaughan, Frederick. (1991), "On Being a Positivist: Does it Really Matter?", p. 407.

From Facts to Values

Natural Rights: "Nonsense upon Stilts"?

Jeremy Bentham who denounced natural rights as nonsense upon stilts was one of the strongest and the most hostile opponents of natural rights theory. For him, rights were an output of legal law. He believed that real rights emanate from real laws; but from imaginary laws, such as the "laws of nature", arise only imaginary rights. He explicitly stated:

> That which has no existence cannot be destroyed — that which cannot be destroyed cannot require anything to preserve it from destruction. Natural rights is simple nonsense: natural and imprescriptible rights, rhetorical nonsense, nonsense upon stilts.[88]

Similar to Plato, Austin and Hobbes, he also believed in the ultimate sovereignty of the legal institution of state. For him too, 'right is that which the government, being the stronger part of the political society, commands.' As he stated:

> Rights are, then, the fruits of the law, and of the law alone. There are no rights without law — no rights contrary to the law — no rights anterior to the law ... There are no other than legal rights; — no natural rights — no rights of man, anterior or superior to those created by the laws [legislative]. The assertion of such rights, absurd in logic, is pernicious in morals.[89]

Yet it is puzzling as to why anything other than the institution of legal rights by human beings is sheer nonsense, for, how can any rights, be they moral or natural, derive from legal

---

[88]. Bentham, Jeremy. (1843), *Anarchical Fallacies,* edited by Jeremy Waldron (1987), *Nonsense upon Stilts,* p. 53.

[89]. Bowring, John. (1962), *Pennomial Fragments, in the Works of Jeremy Bentham,* Vol. 3, p. 221.

rights? According to this view then, what would be the basis and the foundation of any legal rights? Legal laws must obviously have a foundation. For example, consider Bentham's views on animal welfare, which was far in advance of his time as compared to the whole of Europe. Bentham, unlike his German counterpart Immanuel Kant, tried to bring animals into the moral jurisdiction. He denounced popular recreational hunting, fishing and baiting, since such activities caused animals a great deal of pain and suffering. He even went as far as introducing new legislation in the British Parliament to protect animals from vivisection and other forms of cruelty. In response to the popular Cartesian notion of mind/body duality and the argument that animals have no soul, since they have no mind or the faculty of speech, he wrote in the *Introduction to the Principles of Morals and Legislation* that:

> The day may come when the rest of the animal creation may acquire those rights which never could have been withheld from them but by the hand of tyranny. ... a full-grown horse or dog is beyond comparison a more rational, as well as a more conversable animal, than an infant of a day, or a week or even a month old. But suppose the case were otherwise, what would it avail? *The question is not, can they reason? Nor, can they talk? But can they suffer? Why should the law refuse its protection to any sensitive being?* [italics are ours] ... The time will come when humanity will extend its mantle over everything which breathes...[90]

From the above passage we can gather that Bentham does not at all talk like a person who believes in the idea that the

---

[90]. Bentham, Jeremy. (1823), *Introduction to the Principles of Morals and Legislation*, Ch. 17.

sources of moral law and natural law ought to be the legal law. Rather, on the contrary he moves from the external world to the legal law. That is, his conclusion with respect to animal rights is exactly what a concerned naturalist would say. In fact, Bentham is moving from natural right to legal right, using cause (pain) and effect (suffering) as the guideline for the postulation of legal law. His position here betrays inconsistency because he is not anchored to a consistent standard by which to judge the moral nexus between things. The vital importance of non-contradiction in establishing the truth of any philosophy, has already been highlighted in the pervious chapter.

Moreover, Bentham does not establish as to what exactly are the valid sources of legal rights, which is the primary concern at the core of the issue of justice. Any legal legislation requires justification, and if justification ought to be based on legal law, then what are the sources of legal laws? This is indeed a classical example of a circular argument or a tautology, where the premise and the conclusion express the same proposition. Bentham states that "there is no law contrary to the legal law". But this proposition itself is a law, according to this scheme; therefore, he and his followers are all blindly begging the question by chasing their own tails (by self-refutation, it falls under Proposition 1).

Furthermore, when a conventional legal system is deficient or unjust, such as in the case of animal welfare he is quite helplessly forced to appeal to the external world of nature, in terms of pain and suffering which are biological responses. However, this contradicts his very own methodology of not going 'contrary' to the law — yet leading to another inconsistency. It is also interesting to note, as an aside, that Bentham's argumentation of positivistic law, based on pain and suffering has a strikingly moralistic flavour to it.

Moreover, consider this: if the only true law is the legal law, then one can suppose that when, generically speaking, Cain killed Abel, the act could not have been condemned, legally or morally, since after all there was no such a thing as moral law or natural law and there was no legal law prohibiting murder or manslaughter. Finally, if the legal right is the ultimate criterion, then how could we resolve the case in which two legal rights come into conflict with each other? It seems that Bentham's view is truly nonsense *without* stilts!

'Natural Law' and Mystical Movements

It is really a tragedy when things that are right are sometimes being defended or presented by the ignorant. Indeed, there is nothing more pathetic than when a mature judgement is adopted by an immature mind.

For instance, there is another political and 'spiritual' group of people in the West who use 'natural law' in their arguments on rights and the formulation of laws for society. Although the initial premise(s) of such groups may be valid, their conclusions do not follow from the premise(s). These groups mix sense with nonsense — the net result being multiple nonsense. The aim of a great many of such groups is the promotion of mysticism. However, in order to attract the audience of potential followers they use that which makes sense initially — the order, beauty, serenity and efficiency in the processes of the universe — as packaging or as a bait for items which lack any logical substance in a universe of cause and effect. For example, it is true that nothing in nature is wasted due to the natural recycling mechanisms and it is true that there are "no unemployed roses in nature". However, for instance, in order to resolve the unemployment problem in society — in other words the wastage of human potential — how would being able to master levitation or hopping around help as a governmental policy in the eradication of human mismanagement and corruption. Such a case is indeed a good example of those who use nature as a means to a specific dubious end and then pretend that it is nature which is doing all the insisting.

From Facts to Values

The Circular Dilemma of Positivism

Similar to Bentham, communitarian philosopher Howard Adelman defines rights as follows:

> There is no right independent of the communitarian base in which such rights are articulated.[91]

> Rights were set out to justify placing limits on state action, action which was to be dependent on citizen consent while allowing individuals to pursue their various goals unimpeded. State actions not based on consent of the governed were illegitimate.[92]

Adelman's definition is representative of a dominant view in the debate. This view, however, has a number of serious shortcomings. Aside from its relativistic connotation, Adelman is in a similar predicament as Bentham. Although, the content is different, the form of the argument is equally flawed. Adelman, too, begs the question with his tautological definition. The whole notion of lawful and unlawful, legal and illegal, rightful and unrightful, just and unjust, legitimate or illegitimate is but one set of concepts converging on a singular axis as a point of reference. The pertinent issue is: What makes something illegitimate, unjust, unlawful, illegal or unrightful in the first place? To determine one of the aforementioned, means determining the rest. Therefore, in attempting to define the point of reference for rights, it is futile to use an offshoot which implies an identical concept.[93] This

---

[91]. Adelman, Howard. (1992) "Justice, Immigration and Refugees", p. 9.

[92]. Ibid., p. 4.

[93]. Copi, Irving M. (1978), *Introduction to Logic,* Rule 2, pp. 155-156.

The Equigenic Principle

amounts to no more than a vacuous tautological fallacy. Perhaps the flaw in his argument could be better demonstrated if his definition were restated as such:

> ***Rights*** are set out to justify placing limits on state action, action which is to be dependent on citizen consent while allowing individuals to pursue their various goals unimpeded. State actions not based on consent of the governed are ***unrightful***.

In his approach to Justice, Immigration and Refugees, Adelman like others, takes the liberty of abstaining from the most crucial issue pertaining to justice — its *root*. However, it might be pointed out that the notion of foundations is not the issue in the above context. One may wonder, then, what is the real issue at hand? What is the use of a tautological definition after all? If a definition is circular then where is its foundation? Foundation implies that it supports a hierarchical structure in the argument not circularity, even if the word 'base' is used within the description of the circular argument.

Moreover, on what grounds do the wishes, consents, interests and goals of community become the norms and standards for determining rules and regulations? How are they justified and established as the determining criteria? On the contrary, the issue here should not at all be the wishes and desires of the people. And it is here, where Adelman misses the whole point. The ultimate concern here ought to be, to create a system that is harmoniously functional, where, for instance, the fewest number of crimes would be committed and the fewest number of people would have to be punished. What matters in policy-making is to examine whether the proposed system meets the basic needs of humanity as a whole; not only their material needs, but also their psychological needs. Is the society which is being looked after sick or healthy? To what extent does the system that is envisioned create a euphonious society, a society which is at peace with itself and nature. When harmony is not sought,

From Facts to Values

optimality is unobtainable, and injustice gradually permeates into every facet of life.

In refutation of positivistic laws based on community approval, we need to be reminded of the presumptuousness of individualism. According to individualism, the main goal of legislations ought to be to preserve the rights of individuals. To preserve means not only to allow, but also to accommodate the pursuit of each person's course of actions, whether that be abortion, euthanasia, suicide, taking hallucinogens and so on. Thus, the society is only a means by which to attain these goals and is never an end in itself. In fact, most societies aspire and promote individualism, which, in turn provides the grounds for the justification of one's personal decisions, according to one's ambitions and personal goals, irrespective of their social consequences. Just like an individualist who erroneously thinks he is living in a vacuum, and can always justify things merely because he feels like it, a communitarian thinks that one's community is living in a vacuum. Therefore, the community becomes the centre of the universe; everything else is there to accommodate its aspirations. The moon, the sun, the air, the law of gravity, the food-chain, the cycle of hydrology, the alternation of the four seasons, the passage of time, and so on, all exist to serve man's whims and desires. What is pathetically neglected in both cases is that we are all only an insignificant speck of dust in this vast universe. Consequently, the notion of 'me' or 'us' as the central issue in a debate which ultimately involves the welfare of the global family, particularly in the context of the totality of existence, is indeed pointless and extremely arrogant to say the least.

Adelman's communitarian position is indeed the remnant of the individualistic outlook in a collective form. An individualist always states: "I do what pleases me, the heck with everybody else", while communitarians state exactly the same thing, but the noun is plural, "we do what pleases us, the heck with everybody else". This outlook, no doubt, is a breeding ground for justification of pleasure principle.

The Equigenic Principle

Other positivists such as Peter Hogg take a position similar to that vacuously espoused by Adelman:

> The theory of legal positivism holds that law consists exclusively of "positive" law, meaning law that has been made by the law-making institutions of the state. Legal positivism denies the existence of a "natural law" that emanates from some source other than the law-making institutions of state.[94]

Philosopher L.A. Rollins:

> Real rights are those rights actually conferred and enforced by the laws of a State or the customs of a social group. Such rights are sometimes called "positive rights."[95]

Positivist, Maurice Cranston goes one step further:

> Positive rights are facts. They are what men actually have.[96]

But, how on earth can the customs of a social group become laws and further be treated as 'facts' — the only existing 'real rights'? This is something that only an intoxicated relativist can fathom! The transition of predominant social customs, from customs to facts, can only take place in a mind which is divorced from reality and is under some kind of illusion. If laws must be based on a positivistic system, derived from the social norms of the society, then what is all the fuss about the Holocaust, the nineteenth century slave trading, female

---

[94]. Hogg, Peter W. (1991), "On Being a Positivist: A Reply to Professor Vaughan", p. 412.

[95]. Rollins, L.A. (1983), *The Myth of Natural Rights*, p. 2.

[96]. Cranston, Maurice. (1979), "What Are Human Rights?", p. 17.

circumcision and a host of other similar atrocities. After all, in each case the state was acting according to its own positivistic interpretations, approved by social norms. It is indeed a wonder, as to why it is so difficult for so many to realize that whatever is or becoming customary in society is not necessarily propitious.

These pseudo-intellectual positivists are blind to tangible reality right in front of their very own eyes. It is exactly because of such a relativistic mentality and easy going attitude that humanity today is in a grave crisis. When we allow the everchanging norms of community to dictate our socio-political policies it leads to moral decay in society. Take the example of the judgement in the recent court case involving 'lap dancing' and its concomitantly abhorrent licentiousness in a Toronto strip joint, where the judge and the Provincial Attorney General summarily dismissed the charges by concluding that such activities "do not violate the moral standards of community". This pathetic verdict was based on laws founded on community's norms and customs.

It seems that, in a positivistic scheme, what is 'valid', is valid only by convention, not by its nature. However, if we merely define rights as those rules which have found their ways somehow into major instruments, constitutions, and conventions. "This may be pedagogically convenient, but it is hardly satisfactory intellectually. It assumes that no human rights exist outside of treaty law, and it ignores the important process of identifying what legal rights have come to be codified as human rights, and why?"[97]

As discussed previously, the fundamental problem with positivistic approach is that the whole system is just a matter of arbitrary construction. The best product it can possibly yield, cannot be better than its own logical construction, involving internal consistency throughout the system, as

---

[97]. Higgins, Rosalyn. (1983), *The European Convention on Human Rights*, p. 538.

The Equigenic Principle

advocated by Bruce Ackerman. As such, although, it may deal with internal consistency, it fails to consider the notion of external consistency. Positivism, in its highest form, cannot be independent of logic. Yet, all systems of logic cannot be independent of the rules within that system. Without such rules the system cannot be validated. Its validity solely depends on its own rules. All arguments for the validity of any positivistic systems are tautological. To illustrate this point, take the example of a dictionary, where every single word is defined according to another word within the same dictionary. The dictionary, therefore, is only internally valid, not externally. A definition given in a dictionary, may or may not agree with the definition given in another dictionary. The given definition may or may not even correspond with the reality of cause and effect. Therefore, just like a dictionary, rights set in a positivistic system are all human innovations and their justifications are based on its own internal system. This system may or may not have any relationships with the external reality of cause and effect.

A more relevant example can be seen in the defence policies of Turkish government towards Kurdish uprising. The Turkish government continuously refers to the PKK as bunch of outlaws. This simply boils down to: according to our constitutional laws you guys are outlaws. However, according to the Kurds, it is the Turks who are outlaws. According to Kurdish revolutionary laws the guerrillas are freedom fighters.

Brian Slattery, another Osgoode law professor who recognizes the circularity of positivism, would respond as such to positivistic definition of rights:

> If the standards of one legal system are chosen over those of another without reason given, the solution is *arbitrary*. If reasons are supplied, they must be founded on principles that transcend the competing legal systems involved, for to draw reasons just from one system or another would involve *circularity* and also *arbitrariness*. That is, the question of

> which system of law should govern cannot be resolved by reference to principles secreted by one of the competing systems without arbitrarily assuming the supremacy of that system, which is the very question to be resolved.[98]

Here is Frederick Vaughan, an opponent of positivism, in his own words:

> ..., unless we can justify those rights in more than the caprice of the passing moment, we are like the blind leading the blind.[99]

Finally, in dealing with positivism, what is dangerously fallacious is to measure rights prescribed in different human communities according to one's own system, as for instance, assuming that whatever America formulates as rights, is what the whole human race needs, seeks and ought to be given. Such a narrow outlook carries the underlying assumption that the West sets the standards for human rights. One common example, is the evaluation of women's rights in a comparative context. In the West, women's freedom is often measured in the most bizarre manner: Freedom, modernity and progression are viewed by how much skin a woman is expected and willing to reveal. There is rather a peculiar assumption at the very outset, that the more she takes-off her garments, the more she displays her private parts and the more she emphasizes on her sexuality in public, the more liberated she is, the more rights and freedoms she enjoys. Juxtaposing this Western perspective with other socio-cultural values, modesty then becomes a sign of ultra-regression. Thus, the more willingly an alien woman covers her body, the

---

[98]. Slattery, Brian. (1991), "Aboriginal Sovereignty and Imperial Claims", p. 691.

[99]. Vaughan, Frederick. (1991), "On Being a Positivist: Does it really matter?", pp. 408-409.

more she desexualizes herself for the public, then the more she is taken to be oppressed, suppressed, repressed and depressed. Basically, such egocentric convictions lead us to view others disparagingly, echoing beliefs such as "if they do not live like us, they are deprived and depraved." Indeed, how pathetic and naive can such ubiquitous and self-aggrandizing assumptions be. Consequently, such an erroneous attitude is not free from deleterious side-effects and violations of rights. For example, in the above case, it results in a significant subliminal societal discrimination against desexualized women in one way or another. Most often, recognitions and opportunities for women who cover and preserve themselves decreases, despite their qualifications, while recognitions and opportunities for women who present themselves as sexual objects increases, despite their possible lack of qualifications.

In conclusion, positivism falls into the category of a tautological theory, not solid fact. As we have pointed out, values ought to be established according to facts, not theories, for what is the merit of theoretical values, after all?

We can observe that the common property of all these attempts at describing natural law and positive law is that they suffer from the fallacy of begging the question. They all circumvent the foundational issue of rights. Thus, the opponents of natural rights take these arguments as definitive and assume by induction that natural rights have no ground in any legal scheme for humankind.

From Facts to Values

The Foundation of All Rights

In the previous section we observed how detached positivism is from external consistency. In this section, it will be argued that if we are to aim for external consistency, then internal consistency will automatically follow. Internal consistency is a subset of external consistency and external consistency means looking into the interrelationships in the causal panoply of the universe.

Human beings and all other living creatures inhabit a universe which is governed by physical laws. These laws are defined by cause and effect relationships, and are, therefore, inherent, absolute and universal. What is meant by cause and effect, is that every course of action is followed by its effects; in other words, for every action there is a network of concomitant reaction(s). The interconnectivity of the chain of events (cause and effect) is well analyzed by sociologists, political scientists, economists, physicists and ecologists in their respective fields.

In this world of interconnectivity, animals are dependent upon resources for sustenance. They are perfectly adapted to derive sustenance from nature. In fact, they are adapted to the extent that their biological structures and functions permit such sustaining interactions to take place. Animals' biological structures and functions are correlated with their niches. Their interaction is their behaviour which, in turn, is governed by rules and limits. These rules in turn establish a balance in nature. In nature, undeniably, there are pre-existing engrained rules, governing the behaviour of all living organisms, which in the dynamic interplay of life lead to omnidirectional balance and optimality. One example, among countless others on earth, to maintain such natural equilibrium is the novel usage of niches, according to time. Most habitats have two ecological communities, the daytime and the nighttime.[100] For

---

[100]. Augros, Robert and Stanciu, George. (1988), *The New Biology: Discovering the Wisdom in Nature*, p. 95.

The Equigenic Principle

instance, in tropical rainforests and prairies during the daytime, bees, butterflies, weasels, most lizards and birds are active. At sunset they rest and the night-shift takes over, which includes cockroaches, frogs, snails, moths, mice, bats, and owls. Moths, for example, "feed on white or pale yellow flowers that only open at night, thereby" leaving the flowers that only open during the daytime untouched. The latter flowers are used only by the day-shift creatures such as bees, wasps, butterflies and humming birds. Ecologist Charles Elton describes the temporally specialized usage of resources by day and night:

> Not only is one kind of animal replaced by another, but one kind of food chain is replaced by another, and certain niches which are unused by any animal during the day become occupied at night. The weaselbank vole industry is changed into a tawny owl-wood mouse industry. The woodpecker-ant connection has no equivalent at night, while the moth-nightjar or bat chain is almost unrepresented by day. In fact, one food-cycle is switched off and another starts up to take its place. With the dawn the whole thing is switched back again.[101]

This example vividly indicates that animal behaviour follows certain patterns, which lead to optimality in the preservation of the balance of nature. At this point one may ask: how does the so-called 'teleological presumption' creep in? As a rejoinder, one may well ask; would any alternatives other than the so-called teleological be feasible? Are the above

---

Gamlin, Linda. (1983), (ed.) *Nightwatch: The Natural World from Dusk to Dawn*.

[101]. Elton, Charles. (1968), *Animal Ecology*, p. 86.

From Facts to Values

ecological shifts the product of accident, or, were mutually conventional arrangements made among the various species that were involved, arranged by word of mouth? The above-mentioned citation is a clear example of the limits of the habitat usage which ensures the proper flow of the system leading to stability — one of the measures of the balance. These purposive rules and limits are not manmade but inherent in nature, and are indubitably teleological (goal-directed) in the context discussed.

There is a great deal of confusion concerning the issue of the balance of nature, where it is thought that, for instance, the extinction of species over the aeons undermines the notion of balance, let alone perfect adaptation, because it implies that when the environment changed, then some species were not adapted to it and could not cope. Many neo-Darwinian biologists presume that the balance was broken and they went extinct! The problem with this view is that it is rooted in the conception of the present state of nature as having been a result of evolution based on chance and randomness, where things happen by trial and error — where these notions are taken as the premise, rejecting a goal directed system (teleological). However, it should not be difficult for anyone to see that this universe has directionality, from its very emergence with the Big Bang to the present. The development of this universe is such that it is as if it were 'pursuing an intention'; this was candidly confessed, in fact, during the Eighth International Conference on the Origin of Life, held at Berkeley, California by the keynote speaker, Nobel Laureate George Wald of Harvard University. He was commenting on the growing realization that the parameters by which the universe has been arranged over time are so precise as to anticipate and be provisional for future lifeforms. One of these lifeforms is the unique species — homo sapiens. As has been noted even by the champions of randomness and chance in the areas of evolutionary biology, if the dinosaurs had not died out the mammals, and hence humans, as the 'dominating and pervasive' species would not have surfaced. Furthermore, in the introduction to *Mechanical*

The Equigenic Principle

Design of Organisms, the co-authors, zoologists and biologists, apologetically state that:

> The idea that biological materials and structures have functions implies that they are 'designed'; hence the book's title. We run into deep philosophical waters here, and we can do little but give a commonsense idea of what we mean. In our view structures can be said to be designed because they are adapted for particular functions. They are not merely appropriate for these functions, because that could happen by chance.[102]

The notion of the balance of nature, therefore, in reality has two components. The first is the component of stasis or stability to maintain the order. The second is the balancing of the relations by the elimination of one species after its having existed for some duration due to a change in the ecological order by, say, a change in the global weather pattern. Therefore, both the equilibrium states of stasis and the dynamical equilibrium states of possible evolution form one system in space and time functioning with directionality. That everything in nature and over time is perfectly adapted to the environment is a fact which cannot be justifiably denied. This has led to the notion of the Strong Anthropic Principle (SAP) as defined by cosmologists J.D. Barrow and F.J. Tipler as that which leads to "interpretations of a radical nature ... [such that] ... *There exists one possible Universe 'designed' with the goal of generating and sustaining 'observers'.*"[103] More concisely, they define (SAP) as: "The Universe must have

---

[102]. Wainwright, S.A., Biggs, W.D., Currey, J.D., Gosline, J.M. (1976), *Mechanical Design in Organisms,* p.1.

[103]. Barrow, John D. and Tipler, Frank J. (1986), *The Anthropic Cosmological Principle,* p. 22.

those properties which allow life to develop within it at some stage in its history."[104]

The whole panoramic panoply of cosmic development from the Big Bang to the galaxies, to the stellar systems to a once barren earth, to the final emergence of a blue planet, profuse with animated nature displays an intelligent process. In this scheme the human being is a part of nature, not apart from nature, and is governed by the very same set of universal laws. Although man is a part of nature, he may be able to impede the equilibrium of nature, due to his ability to choose. He causes harm by not connecting things the way they have been designed to be connected because of his ability to choose not to connect. This choice is a direct function of man's highly evolved brain-mind complex, which is far beyond that of any other creature on earth. The responsibility of man is indeed commensurate with the evolution of that cerebral capacity. Yet again, here we see a balance both in what nature has yielded for man as well as what man is expected to fulfil due to his potential. However, the difference between human beings and other organisms lies in the physiological structure and its correlated function, which includes the mental faculty — *the mind*. If animal behaviour is regulated by its structure and function, which is integrally coupled to the environment leading to the balance, then in principle, this scenario should also hold true for man; that is, man should likewise be integrally coupled to nature. In other words, if the rules in the animal kingdom ensure the global balance, by linkage to the way in which the animals have been adaptively designed, so too, in principle must be the rules which govern the human being. This is because the *particular* rules are derived from the same *general* laws which are applicable to all entities, from amoeba to man. These innate rules emanate from natural processes which are based

---

[104]. Ibid., p. 21.

The Equigenic Principle

on cause and effect relations which themselves naturally tend to preserve the equilibrium, if not impeded by human beings.

Social balance in animal communities is intrinsically and intricately connected to ecological balance. Similarly, social balance in human communities ideally ought to be linked to the balance of nature, if the total system is to remain in equilibrium. Unlike humans, animals do not violate the inherent rules, nor do they fall short of them. Human beings on the other hand, due to conventional rights and various other factors often do so, as the present state of the world clearly attests. In fact, all that is necessary for a global balance is that human beings follow such absolute, natural laws as derived from nature, commensurate with their natural physical and mental endowments.

The fact of balance in the universe as the basis of the absolute system of rights is most significant, because justice itself is a function of the balance. Anything that falls short of this, cannot be called justice, due to its incompleteness, disjointedness, inconsistency and localization — all leading to the cyclones of disaster through adverse side-effects. Justice is not embodied by capitalism, communism, socialism, conservatism, liberalism, utilitarianism, libertarianism, pluralism, positivism, conventionalism, communitarianism, totalitarianism, puritanism, contractarianism, relativism, humanism, mysticism, feminism, theocracy, democracy, oligarchy, nationalism, tribalism, or any other 'ism', because as already has been established, they are all human constructs and visionary ideologies, designed to serve the selfish interests of those who formulate them. Justice is only embodied by doing the right thing and doing the right thing means recognizing and acting in synchrony with the pre-eminency of the structural and functional balance of nature, by realizing how things should fit in within that very scheme, in order to maintain it for all the intervolved elements which comprise this universe.

From the above discussion, it is evident that all systems in nature are interlinked whether we are aware of the details of

From Facts to Values

the interlinkages or not. This is the way nature functions and this is the cause of its success in the profusion and diversity of life in the social or communal level in both animal and conceivable human communities, by what we could term as being absolute in content and scope. Any other man made convention system cannot be better than this system because this system is the system which maintains the balance, the equilibrium. Any other system, in fact which goes against this system, based on cause and effect relations, would be an unnatural system causing disequilibrium and harm. If the system is absolute then is complete and universal, and vice versa.

The Equigenic Principle

Take the case of termite colonies, where millions of termites live and interact together incessantly. Here is an example of interdependency of justice based on the balance. In such a dynamically efficient and harmonious society, every member follows the inherent natural laws prescribed to sustain the whole society. The efficacy of the society is no less precise than the interacting, interlocking components of a Swiss watch. Termites direct their daily activities by a complex system of government. Every single termite engages in its goal directed functions. No one violates any rules. There is no sexism, no egotism, no racism, no oppression, no fear of persecution or seeking of refuge to another colony for safety. There is no monopolization of the common resources. There is no deprivation of one's needs. No one neglects the obligations and duties; all work together as an efficient team for the needs of the entire colony. What indeed is the key to their unmitigated perennial stability and resilience? This colony is only one among many other animal communities serving to maintain themselves as well as the overall balance of the ecosystem on earth.

Does all of this mean that the human being should live like termites? When it comes to human society, is it appropriate to draw inferences indiscriminately from animal world? Obviously not. It is not always possible to make logical comparisons between human and animal communities. We ought to be aware of the use and misuse of analogies. All animal communities have their own set of rules of behaviour. What is natural behaviour for one species does not make the same behaviour natural for another species. This is because the particular rules are specifically geared according to structure and function of each species and these may vary significantly from species to species and more so from animal species to humans. For example, the species of lemming in Scandinavia naturally control their population by jumping into the lake, if their niche gets overpopulated. Does this mean the people in overpopulated China and India ought to follow the same strategy? In the case of lemmings, in order to produce overall stability and balance in the interconnected ecosystem, it is necessary that they do this as it is the optimal option. Lemmings naturally follow this behaviour as it comes from within, where they are instinctually drawn to this end just in order to preserve the balance. However, in the case of humans, overpopulation is not the real problem;[105] rather, it is the distribution of resources in terms of food and artificially bordered lands. Moreover, unlike lemmings the humans have an alternative to improve their situation. In fact, the lemmings throwing themselves into the lake is similar to them being eaten by predators. In this case, however, the lake acts as a predator in which they are actually eaten by the aquatic species. This process, is part of the predator-prey food web system which comprises the animal kingdom and which maintains stability and the particular niches that each species lives in. No human society collectively and instinctually would be drawn to this regulative animal function, since it is counter to the maintenance of balance. The whole exercise from an

---

[105]. Lappe, Frances Moore and Collins, Joseph. (1986), *World Hunger: The Twelve Myths*.

Belsey, Andrew. (1992), "World Poverty, Justice and Equality", p. 36.

From Facts to Values

anthropocentric perspective may seem like massive or insane suicide, but from nature's objective perspective it is an equilibrium producing action. The phenomenon, in principle is no different than a lion chasing, capturing and devouring a zebra.

Now do all of these mean that human beings should live like termites, lemmings or lions? In principle, yes we must — and by this it is meant submitting to the natural laws. The termites naturally flow with the structure of their environment. This environment is coupled to their own physical structures. The most important coupling between the human and his niche — which is the whole earth — is the usage of his mind and reason to recognize the connections between things in order that he maintain the balance instead of deviating from it. If any human being does not use his or her mind interconnectively then, that given faculty which is innately geared for critically observing, questioning, thinking, reasoning and recognizing the connections will be in violation of the same *principle of submission* which the termites are unconditionally geared for. The inevitable consequence will be: an erosion of equilibrium and stability, not only in human societies but also in the animal and ecological spheres. That is to say, like the termites' unconditional conformity in every endeavour of life, the human being, has to, in this case, *willingly* keep in mind that he must measure the consequences of his actions at the personal and social levels, in order to maintain the overall balance of the whole global family which he is only a part of. It is solely through the realization of the balances that would man be able to establish justice, and it is only through this kind of justice — the only *real* justice — that would man be able to live in overall peace, and hence, security. Nevertheless, there are many who think otherwise. Philosopher L.A. Rollins in his attack on natural law states:

> The difference is that laws made by government are enforced by the punishment of detected violators by the government

The Equigenic Principle

while natural laws are not enforced by the punishment of violators by nature.[106]

However, in this day and age, with the ever-increasing destruction of the environment, hardly any ecologist who would concur with Rollins' fragmented view. The lesson that nature has been teaching us all along, which man has been blatantly ignoring all along, is that, should we interfere with the laws of nature, should we neglect our duties towards nature, we shall suffer from its devastating consequences, especially once the repercussions gets out of control. The point here is that nature has its governing laws, as well as its own modes of punishment, some direct, whereas others subtly indirect. Problems arising from the phenomena of environmental refugees, greenhouse effect, acid rain, drought, endangered species are cases in point. The tragic monumental collapse of the Atlantic fisheries in Newfoundland, Canada, is a good example where nature retaliates against man the defiant. In fact, the superiority of nature's laws as compared with conventional governmental laws is that in nature all violations are detected and consequently recorded in the chain of cause and effect. But, as Rollins admits, in conventional systems many violations may go undetected and unpunished, and hence they cannot be deemed to be adequate systems of justice. Therefore, it clearly follows that, if humanity deviates from this natural state, it would be engulfed in a quagmire of abysmal injustices and social anarchies with only one question left: how much worse will it get? The American poet H.W. Longfellow realized that: "The laws of nature are just, but terrible. There is no weak mercy in them. Cause and consequence are inseparable and invevitable. The elements have no forbearance. The fire burns, the water drowns, the air consumes, the earth buries. And perhaps it would be well for

---

[106]. Rollins, L.A. (1983), *The Myth of Natural Rights*, p. 3.

our race if the punishment of crimes against the laws of man were as inevitable as the punishment of crimes against the laws of nature — were man as unerring in his judgements as nature."

At the societal level, let us consider the following example of humans defying the balanced laws of nature. In certain regions of India, many factors have contributed to severe economic hardships, including the lack of proper education. This has led the imprudent masses to develop the epidemic preference for the male child over the female child, where a boy is seen as an added source of income to the family, but a girl is perceived as an unproductive and costly consumer.[107] This erroneous attitude has consequently caused a widespread heinous practice of infanticide of the newborn female. This, in turn has prompted a disastrous imbalance of the male/female ratio in the region[108] and has consequently led to many other sociological, economical and ecological crises, which have then generated many violations of justice and human rights and vice versa through feedback effects. This example demonstrates a clear point: That is, injustice breeds injustice in the chain of cause and effect. Therefore, in order to prevent the harmful aftermath of an occurrence of injustice at the end, or anywhere along the chain of events, we ought to take the proper first step. That is allowing the series of events to grow naturally towards the appropriate direction, in order to maintain the balance. Only the

---

[107]. Anderson, John Ward and Moore, Molly. (1993), "Murdered at Birth–for Being Female".

Thor Dahlburg, John. (1994), "Where killing baby girls 'is no big sin'".

[108]. According to "*Let Her Die*", a joint 1994 BBC & CBC television documentary, it is believed that currently India is in shortage of approximately 25,000,000 females, the approximate population of Canada.

The Equigenic Principle

realization of the above, would then guarantee complete justice throughout the entire chain of events. All other issues, such as the inherent natural right of baby girls to life becomes secondary.

By inherent natural rights what is meant is not that which the classical, modern and contemporary political philosophers have held. This distinction is most crucial. Natural rights as described in this section are founded on the equilibrium of nature alone. Such rights can be termed as **equigenic rights,** having their origin in the nature's equilibrium. Equigenic rights are not only founded upon, but are also realized through, demanded by, and have their origination in the ubiquitous balance of nature. This is what makes them truly absolute, in the non-conventional sense. A lack of understanding and application of this natural perspective is what has caused all the untold devastation throughout the ages, in all parts of the world. Humankind has indeed ignored the equigenic rights of a great many of the integral animate and inanimate components of the cosmos by deviating from nature's web of dynamic equilibrium.[109] The problems that we are facing today are, in fact, symptomatic of this deviation.

The Equigenic Principle resolves the fact and value issue, since facts are determinable and the notion of value or good becomes precisely definable and achievable as being based upon the balance of nature and the structural and functional processes that comprise the whole. One would be able to use the Equigenic Principle as a point of reference for what is good, and good would be deemed as having a physicalistic

---

[109]. It is interesting to note that in this sense the Equigenic Principle recapitulates the Strong Anthropic Principle, in the sense that the very structures in the universe have been designed to a very precise degree so that carbon based life in general and specifically human life should emerge to maintain the balance, at a most complex level.

property[110] or a natural property — not something conceptually abstract, but empirically embedded, confirmable and realizable.

The neglect of the notion of the balance has indeed led to a problematic obfuscation of the issues as volumes and volumes have been written over the years with no apparent resolution. To draw upon an analogy, once the geocentric theory was being espoused, it led to the creation of epicycles to explain retrograde motion. The system became more and more complex (epicycles within epicycles) in order to explain discrepancies. However, realizing that the sun was at the centre, all of these problems were resolved in one grand stroke. Similarly, by realizing the Equigenic Principle one automatically resolves such issues, towards creating a society which is integrated in thought and in practice, with itself as well as with the rest of nature. One not only realizes that values are not relative and subjective, but are absolute and objective. One can then assist society to move towards an optimal condition with respect to all the facets of life.

Let us discuss some of the conventional aberrations arising from disequilibrium and their adverse consequences and how the Equigenic Principle can resolve these issues. The key thing in each proposed solution is that the values derived for resolving matters are based on the argument from design, the preservation of the balance, and cause and effect relationships. In other words, all proposed values are factualized.

---

[110]. Putnam, Hilary. (1981), *Reason, Truth and History,* pp. 205-211.

The Equigenic Principle

Nationhood and Racism

Like the rest of nature, all human beings have emanated from a single source, as homo sapiens, and due to our sameness in this respect we cannot differentiate from each other in terms of innate superiority or inferiority. Everyone is entitled to the same equigenic rights. We are all cast from the same mould and are also interdependent on each other in the intricate web of life. This is easily detectable in the animal kingdom, where the various organisms interact interdependently.

Animals are not going their own ways, following their own invented laws; rather they follow the given pattern inscribed in nature itself. All species behave according to their equigenic rights. For humans, the realization of natural laws on all levels, is diametrically opposed to the concept of the human's own manufactured notions of rights derived by social conventions. In fact, social conventions and consensus must be in complete congruence with natural universal laws in order for the whole system to function beneficently; for if man-made conventions traverse against the natural flow of the universal laws, they cause crippling dysfunctionalities and deviations, ultimately leading to an inevitable collapse of the integral systems of society.

For example, consider the man-made concepts of nationhood, citizenship, ethnic membership and artificial borders. All of these concepts are human constructs, arising from resource manipulations and ultimately leading to power struggles and confrontation. The seventeenth century British philosopher, John Locke, said:

> But I moreover affirm, that all men are naturally in that state ['state of nature'] and remain so, till by their own consents they

make themselves members of some politic society.[111]

In fact, nation states are modern inventions. They arise when resource exploitation becomes competitive. As Edward Said succinctly puts it: Borders are fabrications of empires.[112] These empires may be large or small, from a tiny country to a superpower. The proliferation of such borders is due to the perceived need for maintenance or change in power structures, where usually only the internal or external elite are the prime beneficiaries The current examples of regionalism in world are cases in point. The above concepts are a gross violation of the Equigenic Principle, which do not exist in the state of nature in any such anthropocentric form. Nationalism and nations territorial boundaries are meaningless in nature's realm. No monarch butterfly, wild goose, or caribou, for instance, requires travelling documents when they migrate from one continent to another, passing through countless forests, rivers and mountains. All interspecies or intraspecies 'power' differences that exist in the animal world are related to differences in design, given the organisms particular function. Any perceived power differences among animals are a means to an end — *the end being balance and optimality.* This would mean that if there are territorial boundaries for a pack of wild dogs or for an individual bird, such boundaries do not extend beyond their required needs in order to preserve every species' equigenic integrity. For example, a bird may claim a tree to be its private property but may never claim a forest as its personal possession. In the state of nature, territorial boundaries serve to maintain resilience and stability in the ecosystem. The end and the means lie along the same path.

---

[111]. Locke, John. (1963), *The Treatise of Civil Government*, Book II, Ch., 2, Sec. 15.

[112]. Said, Edward W. (1993), *Culture and Imperialism.*

The Equigenic Principle

However, in the case of humans, since by nature's constitution, they all have the same basic compositional frames, there can be no grounds for the denial of any basic necessities and rights which might arise from artificial power differences created by human hands. It is usually some of these kinds of power differences or one person or group having 'an edge' over another, which is then misused by creating boundaries or nations through artificial amplification of the differences. These differences serve as excuses for creating those very same boundaries or nations. This, however, goes counter to the natural system, for in the state of nature, any power differentials are automatically utilized for the preservation of optimality, not for the selfishness and greed of participants involved. Such rapacious motivations would indeed be retrogressive. In fact, it is these misused differences which lead to nationhood and discord, rather than cooperation and unity. Communitarian, Michael Walzer asserts:

> Men and women without membership anywhere are stateless persons... Statelessness is a condition of infinite danger.[113]

Although this may be true in our present fragmented nationalistic philosophy, such as for the Palestinians and the Kurds, however, the notion of 'state' based on a narrow concept of community is in itself a substantial condition of infinite danger. It leads to monopolization of resources and consequently creates the externalization of one group by another. Justice is always in jeopardy when one group is externalized. This is indeed evident in Walter's writings as he admits: "..., but no one on the outside has a right to be

---

[113]. Walzer, Michael. (1983), *Spheres of Justice: A Defence of Pluralism and Equality*, pp. 31-32.

inside."[114] Membership is exclusive to insiders. Further, he adds that:

> We who are already members do the choosing, in accordance with our own understanding of what membership means in our community and of what sort of a community we want to have. Membership as a social good is constituted by our understanding; its value is fixed by our work and conversation; and then we are in charge (who else could be in charge?) of its distribution. But we don't distribute it among ourselves; it is already ours.[115]

Yes, of course, is this not what nationalism and communitarianism all about — the monopolization and control of natural resources by one egocentric group? Then, how are we going to resolve the serious problems stemming from communitarian approach? For example, take the case of the River Nile passing through three neighbouring republics of Egypt, Sudan and Ethiopia, where each republic deems itself as being apart from the rest of the socio-ecological community, rather than being a part of it. Each of these communitarian states is involved in the development of tunnel vision projects for the welfare of its own populace, without due regard for other human beings and the ecology outside its respective borders. This common example illustrates the severe lack of an understanding of viable approach pertaining to the so-called 'global justice'.

That is not to say that there is no value attached to nationalism. Nationalism can be useful only in the context of defence of a group against foreign domination and oppression. In order to mobilize its citizens to stand up as a

---

[114]. Ibid., p. 32.

[115]. Ibid., p. 32.

The Equigenic Principle

cohesive group offering resistance. It should be stressed that by giving this example, nationalism is not being exonerated by any means. What is being pointed out — to give the devil his due — is that aspect of nationalism which is worthwhile. The differences in ethnic communities could be used positively to enhance the richness in human knowledge and understanding, not for despising one another. In any other context nationalism leads to cultural chauvinism.

One of the greatest hazards to peace, security, equality, freedom, brotherhood and sisterhood, justice and the respect of human rights is the imprudent dichotomy between 'self' and 'others', between 'us' and 'them', to see oneself as being distinct from the rest of humanity. Although, such a dichotomy can be erected by various means and for various ends, the outcome is always the same. It leads to the creation of volatile, insensible nationalistic and patriotic emotions, which in turn proceed to the xenophobic and psychological development of hatred and the dehumanization and demonization of 'them' by 'us' and vice-versa. 'Us' is always good, 'them' is always wicked; 'us' is always noble, 'them' is always despicable, 'us' is always benevolent, 'them' is always cruel; 'us' is always peaceful, 'them' is always violent; 'us' is always civilized, 'them' is always barbaric; 'us' is always faithful, 'them' is always infidel. The crime of 'them' is by virtue of birth: not to be born among 'us'.

It is indeed the ethnocentric nature of ethnic groups and their exclusive sense of 'community' that often ignites and fans the flames of mutual and impersonal hostility. Consequently, the social politics of marginalization are entirely predictable: intense oppression and deprivation create extreme discontentment within sectors of the regional and global society. Under these pressures, normal social chemistry is altered and coercive exclusionistic ideologies begin to displace healthy inclusive ones. Reason and moderation evaporate, irrationality prevails. Historically, the 'us' verses 'them' dualism has been a major cause of confrontation, hostility and bloodshed, leading to artificial divisions among the human race. What is even more pathetic is that the notion of distinct community is often being imposed upon by outsiders. Many states have been created or separated primarily due to this ubiquitous attitude, insidiously implanted by colonialist, imperialist and expansionist policy of divide and conquer. A quick glance at the modern history of the Indian sub-continent, Africa and the Middle East attests to this assertion, in which, by the emergence of the nation-state concept, and subsequently, by the externalization of 'them' by 'us', conflicts and the greatest violations of human rights have occurred. Once, nationality and state membership is perceived as 'sacred' privilege , then citizens ('us'), become willingly prepared to make sacrifice, usually by offering their own lives or performing the 'sacred act' of killing 'them' to save the nation.[116] Under such a feeble psychological frame mind, one's affinity towards justice, peace, humanity and truth is, therefore, replaced by an affinity to flags and anthems. "I am proud of being X, Y or whatever", is often heard from nationalists. Yet, it is strikingly puzzling, as to how we miss the obvious fact that, whether we happen to be anglo or negro, oriental or caucasian, male or female, tall or short, red hair or bald, beautiful or not beautiful, is completely independent from our wills. What makes me to be what I am, is due to circumstances all beyond my control. Then, what is it there for 'us' to be proud of, and for 'them' to be ashamed of, when we had absolutely nothing to do with it? Consequently, in this atmosphere of pent-up emotion, nationalism turns into nothing more than brutal racism and fascism. Nazi Germany and the formation of the Zionist state of Israel are cases in point.

Therefore, considering the above and given the model of nature, it is in man's best interest to avoid positivism and follow the natural system, in which he must totally submit

---

[116]. Durkheim, Emile. (1951), *Suicide: A Study in Sociology*, see "Altruistic Suicide", pp. 217-240.

The Equigenic Principle

only to the natural laws — the laws which are not relative, but indisputably universal and absolute.

Following this system, one could instantaneously envision that the man-made problems of nationalism and communitarianism can be totally eradicated in one stroke — problems that are never encountered in the animal kingdom. From this, one can also realize that the concomitant problem of racism is eliminated. In fact, the associated artificial concept of racism does not even arise in an individual with such a wholesome outlook, for one would regard the whole of humankind, with all its diversities, as a single family. Blacks or whites, Arabs or Jews, Serbs or Bosnians are all just a part of the lavish mosaic of human species. One would understand that the diversities and specializations are there to strengthen, enhance and complement the sustenance of the entirety of humanity. One would consequentially also realize that people ought to see each other solely as human beings, not as a pile of physical attributes with 'cultural' and 'ethnical' baggages. One would realize with pristine clarity that there is no basis in the natural differences for inequities and destruction to be meted out upon one another — whatsoever. In short, it all comes down to male and female human beings spread across the globe, where colour, language and physique is nothing but a state of nature.

Consequently, the problem of restricted immigration will not even arise once we begin to recognize and respect each other as human beings, all entitled to the equal equigenic rights and privileges. The question of who gets in ('state membership') becomes ludicrous. Any free individual has the natural right to choose and become the resident of any region of the world the moment he or she steps into that land with the intention to live there. This freedom is no different than when people within the same 'state' or city have the right to choose freely as to where to live. There would be no differences between rights and privileges of an indigenous resident with a new settler. We can see from this that just as animals are constrained to move only to the extent that they

From Facts to Values

do not perturb the balance, so too, should man be able to choose to travel or live wherever desired, so long as the overall balance is not broken. The whole earth would be one's 'country'. In fact, one's only community would not only be the planet earth, but rather everything that is encompassed by existence in this universe, would be regarded as part of the cosmic community. The tree, the moon, the sun, the insects, etc. The understanding of this concept alone would eliminate all environmental, racial, and refugee related problems. In order to practically transform global society to submit to this vision, education is required on a massive scale. This education's primary function would be to encourage each individual to think for himself or herself and to avoid dogma in the pursuit of knowledge as defined previously. This would entail a reflection on nature itself, to realize how it has been designed — to come to a realization of equigenic rights. It would obviate the need for a hierarchical structure in society from which irrational dogmas are issued to indoctrinate the masses into believing in conventional systems or that there is no way out of the vortex of conventionalism. This is not a naive and simplistic call for a lovey-dovey, let's 'get-together-as-one' air-headed view of unity. It is not simplistic because the focus is not on unity per se, but on the purity of intentions, thoughts and actions which are consistent with each other. True unity can only be a concomitant product of purity. This purity emanates from an intellectual search for the root of the socio-ecological problems that beset us, which is realized through communication, commitment and understanding. This can only be achieved if there is honesty and an element of concern from within — where the connections between things are not covered. The internalization of all this, through the examination of the externality of nature would eventually become a collective effort and embrace the totality of nature, including within the nucleus of its orbit, other human beings, animals and ecology. As a result of this process, in contrast to conventionally based systems, which are artificially imposed on the masses from without, a society which functions on the Equigenic Principle would be distinguished by the resonation

The Equigenic Principle

of a concern to uphold equigenic laws, arising willingly and eagerly from within each individual without coercion.

To achieve viable unity as the necessary outcome of purity, humankind has to be in total voluntary submission to the laws of nature. Once submission has been actualized, both at the mental and actional level, once we submit to the laws of nature by the abandonment of unequigenical human conventions, then universal prosperity based on the balance is assured. However, if we engage ourselves in the opposite direction, by ignoring the Equigenic Principle and follow human desires, wrapped up with the encumbering garments of conventional laws, then failure in all its apocalyptic senses becomes inevitable.

From Facts to Values

Justice in the Distribution of Resources

The United Nations Universal Declaration of Human Rights supports that every individual human being on the face of this planet is entitled to freedom, liberty and security. The charter states that: no one shall be held in slavery or servitude; no one should be subject to cruel, inhuman or degrading treatment; no one should be subject to exile and to forced migration. Everyone has the right to free choice of employment, to just and favourable conditions of work; everyone has the right to a decent standard of living, adequate enough for the health and well-being of himself and his family, including food, clothing, housing and medical care. Every mother and newborn is entitled to special care and assistance.[117] In addition to the U.N. charter, there are other regional conventional charters of rights such as the *American Convention on Human Rights*, the *European Convention on Human Rights* and the *African Charter on Human and Peoples' Rights* and so on, which with great degrees of similarities promote the same rights for everyone within their jurisdiction. Furthermore, Article One in both the *International Covenant on Economic, Social and Cultural Rights* and the *International Covenant on Civil and Political Rights* asserts that everyone has the right to freely set up their natural wealth and resources. It clearly emphasizes that under no circumstances can people be deprived of their own means of sustenance. However, despite the blessings offered by various international organizations in theory, in practice there are enormous instances of violations in each of the articles mentioned above, impeded by the very institutions which have constructed these rights. What has gone wrong? Why have these charters failed to fulfil their aspirations? The states which once perceived the vital need for human rights' conventions and have participated in drafting, endorsing and implementing diverse human rights' charters have indeed become the ones who are responsible for the very violations

---

[117]. Articles: 1, 2, 3, 4, 9, 23, 25.

of most of these articles. Renowned historian Peter Nobel states:

> The economic conditions in many countries in the Third World and particularly in Africa are such as to deprive their inhabitants of many human rights. Further, some programmes for economic change or development have themselves resulted in violations of human rights and fundamental freedoms for these inhabitants.[118]

There is no doubt that the devastation of the economic, social and ecological environment is directly a result of numerous ill-designed governmental and corporate policies, where economic 'growth' is completely divorced from socio-ecological reality. In fact, some of the worst polluters are the state-owned industries and the state regulators. Thus, the economic and environmental disasters that can easily be predicted and prevented are often accelerated. What is often taken very lightly is that the environmental degradation of the past decades is a secondary consequence of poor developmental projects, where in each case 'global justice' is knowingly disregarded. Here, there is a colossal economic discrepancy at work, between the industrial nations of the North and the so-called 'Third World' nations of the South. This gap leads to an extreme poverty in the South, where even one's basic needs are not meet, while the other group is engaging in an orgy of consumption.[119] In her writings, Susan

---

[118]. Nobel, Peter. (1987), *Refugees and Development in Africa*. pp. 48-49.

[119]. George, Susan. (1977), *How the other Half Dies: The Real Reasons for World Hunger*.
George, Susan. (1978), *Feeding the Few: Corporate Control of Food*.

From Facts to Values

George, argues that poverty is not a scourge, but a scandal. The West is responsible for such disasters, and deliberately uses the food crisis to its own economic and political advantage. Jon Bennett states:

> If human poverty and hunger are so persistent, their causes must be found in the institutions, policies and ideologies which serve to widen the gap between rich and poor. People die of hunger because they are poor, because they cannot afford to buy what food is available. They lack access to basic resources. In short, they are powerless within a system of injustice.[120]

Chronic poverty is not caused by some haphazard, random chain of events. It is undoubtedly characteristic of a deficient system, where there is an unjust and exploitive economic relationship between the powerless 'underdeveloped' countries of the South, and the powerful industrial countries of the capitalist North.[121] The unceasing poverty is result of an anthropocentric oppression of nature and interhuman oppression of the 'Third World'. For example, 80% of the resources of the world are being consumed by the 20% of its population in the North. Many exploitative governmental policies of the North that involved over-fishing, deforestation, desertification, dumping industrial waste onto somebody else's backyard and other ill-designed developmental projects such as building large dams, highways, strip-mining have

---

George, Susan. (1984), *Ill Fares the Land: Essays on food, hunger and power.*

[120]. Bennett, Jon. (1987), *The Hunger Machine: The Politics of Food*, p. 13.

[121]. Neilsen, Kai. (1992), "Global Justice, Capitalism and the Third World".

The Equigenic Principle

caused global warming, pollution (air, water, land), land erosion, acid rain, salinization and so on. Consequently, this has resulted in numerous disasters such as diseases, famines, environmental refugees (forced migration) in the South. The North is getting rich at the expense of others dying in the South.

Indeed, the hypocrisy of various international and national bodies in resolving world problems is becoming clear even to those who are shortsighted. For instance, the industrial nations who are economically and militarily powerful are continuously exploiting the weaker nations, while at the same time pretending to be charitable. They often give with one hand, but take ten times more with other hand. The most notorious case, for example, is putting a country in debt — charging them with interest which they clearly cannot afford to pay. Consequently, the indebted country is obliged to sell out all its national resources at the cheapest price. Moreover, the industrial countries provide the 'Third World' countries with the kind of aid, which makes the country utterly dependent on them for capital, equipment and expertise. In return, they demand salaries that are paid in the West, in countries where the cost of living and earning is far less than in the West. In many cases, the 'experts' provided are mediocre, who cannot get a job in their own home country. Harrel-Bond points out to a case of typical linguistic mental oppression: "Why is it that when non-white foreigners work in the UK, they are 'migrant workers', but when the British get jobs in Africa they are 'experts'?"[122]

We hardly see any substantial projects which can make them self-sufficient or may improve the infrastructure of the country, such as productive agricultural and industrial projects. Often, directly or indirectly, they end up being the losers. As one economist has calculated, for every dollar that

---

[122]. Harrel-Bond, B. E. (1986), *Imposing Aid: Emergency Assistance to Refugees*, p. 67.

From Facts to Values

United States gave in aid to West Africa, it received back $2.54,[123] a net profit of 154%. So much for the 'humanitarian' and foreign 'aid' approach!

Some other NGOs such as World Vision have a hidden agenda for their 'humanitarian' activities in the poor countries. These groups approach hungry people with grains of wheat in one hand and the Bible in the other hand, preying on the vulnerability of helpless starving nations. It seems that their intention is not primarily set to help without any expectation, but rather, they have some vested interests in such projects.

What is said here, is just to suggest that if our intention is truly set to help, then we must get to the root of the problem. Yet, despite the sincerity of many individuals involved, all that has been offered in the past few decades by the international NGOs is a fragmented and partial approach. According to Harrel-Bond, the aid strategy is not effective. It will never eradicate inequality. The promotion of the foreign aid strategy is similar to attempts to fight AIDS by promoting condoms — a futile band-aid approach. In essence, the old saying that if you give a hungry man a fish, you have fed him once, but if you teach him how to fish, you have fed him for rest of his life truly applies here, but tragically has been ignored in most cases. What is needed here, is justice, not a handout. Charity and aid cannot change unjust structures, because injustice and inequalities are structural and have solid foundations. The economic misery of the 'Third World' nations are the result of centuries of exploitation, subjugation and piracy by the blood-sucking imperialist and neo-imperialist powers who have robbed all their resources in the first place, but are now acting like 'Mr. Nice Guy', the benefactors of 'underdevelopment'. Frantz Fanon states:

---

[123]. Abubaker, Ahmad. (1989), *Africa and the Challenge of Development: Acquiescence and Dependency Versus Freedom and Development*, pp. 91-100.

The Equigenic Principle

> For centuries the [Western] capitalists have behaved in the underdeveloped world like nothing more than war criminals. Deportations, massacres, forced labour, and slavery have been the main methods used by [Western capitalists] to increase its wealth, its gold or diamond reserves, and to establish its power.[124]

These Western forces operate like the MAFIA. In fact, they are worse than the MAFIA, for they would annihilate in broad daylight any movement resisting their nefarious objectives. They use elimination tactics through, first formulating their own self-serving version of international laws, and then by enforcing those laws by military power or economic sanctions. These tactics are also often accompanied by manipulation of public opinion on the immeasurable crimes committed. Noam Chomsky narrates that St. Augustine tells the story of a pirate captured by Alexander the Great, who asked him "how he dares molest the sea." "How dare you molest the whole world?" the pirate replied: "because I do it with a little ship only, I am called a thief; you, doing it with a great navy, are called an Emperor."[125]

To abolish poverty sincerely, through a healthy development, requires justice and fair income distribution. In many of the impoverished countries, where there are people suffering from malnutrition and deadly diseases, there is a huge gap between rich and poor. While so many are living in absolute poverty, the aristocrats are living in palatial luxury. While hundreds of thousands of people are starving to death, millions of dollars are being transferred to the foreign banks

---

[124]. Fanon, Frantz. (1961), *The Wretched of the Earth*, p. 101.

[125]. Chomsky, Noam. (1990), *Pirates & Emperors: International Terrorism in the Real World*, p. 1.

by their corrupt rulers. These rulers are nothing but foreign puppets, who propel the economy of other countries, while the economy of their own country is starving for capital. The former Shah of Iran, Ferdinand Marcos of the Philippine and Somoza of Nicaragua are just a few cases in point.

In the distribution of resources, no human's model even comes close to nature's inbuilt principle of justice. Nature's economy is based on an inherent law of efficiency and perfect conservation. We can observe this perfection in practice as opposed in theory. A glance at the interspecies and intraspecies interactions, reinforces the thesis that an absolute universal principle of justice must in essence be based on perfect balance. For example, consider the ecological fact that in any natural undisturbed ecosystem, the ratio between predator species and prey trophic species approaches one to one.[126] A perfect balance. In fact, if this ratio be anything other than one, one species can eradicate the other species in a short period of time, leading to a total destruction of the ecological web. Ecologist Stuart L. Pimm states:

> While there may exist global processes that could offset the catastrophic loss of species we are now experiencing, they are surely extremely slow. For example, from 50% to 100% of the vertebrate species have been lost from some Pacific islands in the past ten to one hundred years. I know of no evolutionary biologist who thinks speciation could restore the original diversity within less than ten millennia.[127]

---

[126]. Orians, Gordon H. (1972), "The Strategy of the Niche", in *The Marvel of Animal Behaviour*, pp. 168-189.
Cohen, Joel E. (1989), "Big Fish, Little Fish: The search for patterns in predator-prey relationships", p. 41.

[127]. Pimm, Stuart. (1991), *Balance of Nature*, pp. 5-6.

The Equigenic Principle

Human beings have the capacity not to follow the basic natural laws, and become the catalysts for devastation. For example, due to man's over-fishing, the oceans of the earth are literally getting depleted, causing many other species, who equally have the same equigenic rights to these resources, to starve and altogether perish. This in turn causes other human communities to suffer.

In addition, unlike humans, non-human predators do not practice senseless killing. According to Desmond Morris, a contemporary British anthropologist and zoologist, in the animal kingdom killings are done according to a unique contract, a contract between prey and predator, which is based on the law of "kill only for food, and eat only when hungry".[128] It is exactly due to this contract that a herd of zebra has no fear of lions in sight, since they know that the lions have just consumed their meal. Unlike lions, man's lifestyle and various governmental policies of overconsumption are indeed in gross violation of this natural contract, breaching the rights of other human communities and other species. Thereby, causing disastrous ecological problems on the global level. Moreover, many mammals such as seals have an inborn self-regulating mechanism to control their populations for ecological stability. This mechanism is based on the availability of food,[129] thereby ensuring the conservation of the balance and a fair distribution of resources.

These examples demonstrate that all of the global resources belong to the entire earth's inhabitants, not to a particular species nor to a particular race or nation. It also demonstrates that selfishness, greed and piracy are not the practices of nature. Yet, in human societies, there are often cases where a nation, a family or even a single individual

---

[128]. Morris, Desmond. (1990), *The Animal Contract: Sharing the Plane,* p. 10.

[129]. Bergman, Charles. (1990), *Wild Echo,* pp. 18-19.

claims undivided ownership of particular resources for themselves, far in excess of their needs, violating nature's own law of distribution. As a result of this blatant disregard for the equitable distribution of wealth people of many regions are deprived of their most fundamental needs, while there should be no deprivation in the natural state of world.

The rational realization of the 'global justice', the only real justice, demands the ultimate realization of global family of all sentient and non-sentient entities. If imbibed within the consciousness of every human being, it would transform all thoughts, behaviour and actions towards caring concern for the welfare of the entirety of existence — a concern devoid of even a modicum of selfishness. This world view would eliminate a possessive communitarian outlook towards global commons, which is the cause of most socio-environmental dilemmas. By eliminating nationhood, statehood, citizenship and the narrow concept of communitarianism, the distribution of resources in which nature's model is set-up does indeed become feasible. All of the earth's resources become universalized, just as in some nations all resources have been nationalized. This change cannot be brought about in its entirety if nation states continue to exist, in which there will be a monopolization of resources — where policies will not be enacted to equalize the distribution by sending it where it is needed most; however if the whole earth community is considered to be like one body where the foundational idea of where rights emanate from is understood, then we would start to see the effects of justice based on the balance of nature. In such a system, profit-maximization and competition by any means, especially by the means of 'might equals right' would be non-existent because it would be understood that the goal is the enhancement of life to maintain that balance. Everyone who participates or is in legitimate dire straits, through no fault of their own, should have access to surplus profit, because with such an interconnected outlook it would be appreciated that in such a system the natural resources are to be universalized for overall stability of the earth's population; this would ensure

The Equigenic Principle

that an elite class does not emerge in any region, by eliminating the ascendancy of a hierarchical political system. In fact, in such a system a hierarchy would not be conceivable because all humans would be deemed equal.

As far as the distribution of resources go, we human beings have the tendency to become obsessively distracted by rivalry for worldly gain until we reach our graves. We often become so obsessed by consumption and acquisition, that we tend to ignore the fundamental and inescapable fact, that we live on this earth only for a short while; once we depart from this earthly abode we shall return no more, and when we do depart, we can take with us nothing of that which we have been accumulating. Soon we shall turn to a pile of bones — bones to dust, dust to dust, under the dust to lie, the ultimate distribution in this universe.

From Facts to Values

Justice, Gender and Nature

Men and women are the complementary components of a larger whole. In a healthy society, there would never be any separation or competition among the sexes, since their existence would be fully dependent upon one another. However, in the last few decades, society has been witness to a strong competition and rivalry between the sexes in all spheres. This senseless adversarial attitude has not been without its pernicious side-effects. Psychologist, Abraham Maslow elegantly elaborates that:

> As always, dichotomizing pathologizes (and pathology dichotomizes). Isolating two interrelated parts of a whole from each other, parts that need each other, parts that are truly "parts" and not wholes, distorts them both, sickens and contaminates them. Ultimately, it even makes them non-viable. ... When men and women disappear into two separated, isolated worlds, both sexes becomes corrupted and pathologized. ...they need each other in order to be themselves.[130]

Indeed the battle of the sexes has pathologized and inverted human society. In many ways, women have become like men and men have become like women, corrupting the natural order of things.

The Equigenic Principle, has already been used to reject racism and nationalism. The same logic can also be used to debunk sexism. There are no differences between the sexes, in the sense of their intrinsic worth. However, the notion of justice and equality, when it comes to male and female roles in society, as well as in family, is often confused with the notion of *sameness*.

---

[130]. Maslow, Abraham (1984), *Religions, Values and Peak-Experiences.* p. 13.

The Equigenic Principle

> Justice in general then neither is, nor implies equality. Although like cases are to be treated alike, different cases are to be treated differently, and justice requires that we be neither discriminatory nor undiscriminating in our response to individual cases.[131]

Some women's groups, active in fighting for equal rights for women, seek the same conventional rights that are held by men in every feature of life. It is an irony that a movement which identifies itself as 'feminism' advocates giving up feminine qualities and encourages manly behaviour for women on the road to emancipation and success — a rather peculiar idea of liberation from that which is perceived to be the dominating constraint of male arrogance. Tragically, some feminist groups attempt to beat men at their own games, the very same games that led to the cause of the problems in the first place. Consequently, inappropriate behaviours that were once considered inconceivable for men to perform, these days not only do not bring about any shame or disgrace to women, but are viewed as widely acceptable norms. These behaviours range from the use of profanity in one's speech and manner to nakedness and promiscuity. It seems that, for instance, in terms of socio-ethical values, the erroneous concept of 'moral' equality has come to establish and promote 'immoral' equality between sexes, all under the banner of liberation and modernization.

The chaos here is the result of the mistaken belief that there are no differences between men and women, and hence, that the rights held by both sexes must be identical. However, using the frame of reference of nature presented in this chapter, based on the functionality and optimality of cause and effect relationships, these relationships dictate that if there are differences in design, then there are differences in function, and if there are differences in function, then there

---

[131]. Lucas, L.R. (1980), *On Justice*, p. 177.

From Facts to Values

are differences in behaviour. These differences confer complementarity within the total scheme, where the question of superior or inferior becomes ridiculous at best. For example, in order to consume steak one needs both fork and knife to facilitate the act of eating efficiently. Which one is superior — the fork or the knife? This means that, naturally, there are differences in the role of men and women in society as well as in the family, if the goal is fixed and pre-set on optimality, social balance and alleviation of social and psychological dissonance. This also means that the sexes must have different positions in some spheres of life. Therefore, while equal rights are absolutely endowed to both men and women by natural law, this does not necessarily mean that these rights must be *identical* in every single instance. There would be differences in the laws which confer those rights.

There are many examples of the differences, both mental and physical, which will not be discussed here due to the intensity of the nature/nurture debate. However, we may cite one primarily physical example to illustrate distinct differences between men and women which would lead to their optimal role in family and society. This area of discussion is well established as a fact and is, therefore, unchallengeable. It concerns the interrelationship between a newborn infant and the mother. For example, if the primary responsibility for taking care of newborn children is given to women, it is due to the natural outcome of female biological functions, since men are not equipped to perform this task. This law is universal among all mammals in nature, whether conventional democratic systems wish to outrule such commonsensical notions or not. The female's breast, like the rest of her anatomy, is a miracle of adaptation for a multi-purpose function. This single qualitative difference alone, is what makes a newborn baby dependent on the mother. Researcher Marie Messenger, who recommends breastfeeding as opposed to any other alternatives, rejects the practice of bottlefeeding, since "the proportions of these ingredients [in mother's milk] adjust themselves over time to suit the changing needs of the baby and this cannot happen with an artificially prepared formula. As we do not yet know *all* the ingredients of breast milk, the artificial formula manufacturers cannot ensure that their formulas contain all the components necessary for healthy feeding and growth, and since breast milk has evolved to suit a human baby's needs, we can be reasonably sure that it has everything in it that this human creature needs."[132] Consequently, there is a reduced risk in breastfed babies from gastroenteritis, exposure to pathogens in the environment, fatal diarrhoeal diseases and other dangerous digestive illnesses, simply because "breast milk contains substances that act to protect against infection inside the baby's system and prevent dangerous bacteria from flourishing in the baby's digestive tract. Breast milk also helps to protect babies from [acute] respiratory infections and from infectious diseases that the mother has had or has been immunized against."[133] She further adds that:

> The presence of protective antibodies in human milk is possibly the most important single difference between breast milk and cows' milk formulas. Cows' milk, as delivered by the cow to the calf, does have protective substances of its own — but processing destroys them.
>
> The immunoglobulins (immuno — immunity to infection; and globulin — protein in animal tissue) are very special proteins which carry the antibodies to protect the baby from illnesses against which the mother has built up an immunity. When the baby is

---

[132]. Messenger, Maire. (1984), *The Breastfeeding Book*, pp. 27-28.

[133]. Ibid., p. 10.

older, he can manufacture his own antibodies after immunization or infection. But during these first vulnerable months breast milk protects him, particularly against the dangerous illnesses such as whooping cough, *E. coli* gastroenteritis and influenza. For example, one of these anti-infective proteins — lactoferrin — helps to kill off bacteria by denying them the iron they need for growth. Lactoferrin is destroyed by boiling and processing so bottlefed babies miss out on this advantage.[134]

Furthermore, on the same subject she adds:

> When the newborn infant, with her vulnerable system, is fed on food not designed for her, an allergic reaction can be set up. For example, cow's milk formula contains twice as much protein as human milk and it is 'foreign' protein. The baby's system is vulnerable to proteins that are intended for different species, and it is believed that being given such proteins in the early days of life can set up an allergic reaction, or sensitization, which causes babies to develop unpleasant allergies. People with allergies in their immediate family, such as asthma, eczema or food 'disagreements', are advised to give their babies only breast milk.
>
> People who were breastfed as infants are less prone later in life to heart disease and complaints of the digestive tract. Breast babies are also less likely to be overweight than bottlefed babies and they are unlikely to

---

[134]. Ibid., p. 29.

> suffer from a form of tooth decay in very young children known as bottle caries which is usually the result of feeding the baby with bottles of sweet liquids. Their sucking mechanism too is different from that of bottlefed babies and is harder work. This may contribute to healthy jaw development; certain abnormalities of the mouth and jaw are rarer in children who were breastfed.[135]

It is exactly because of the above mentioned facts that the UNICEF is widely promoting the practice of breastfeeding in the 'third world' countries, in order to reduce infant mortality rates.

Some other studies suggest that the breast-fed babies are likely to be more intelligent than the bottle-fed babies.[136] That is due to the higher concentrations of erythrocyte docosahexaenoic acid in the mother's milk. The brain-enhancing fatty acid DHA in mother's milk is essential for mental agility and development which is absent in the formula. It is also found that breast milk produces large quantities of the gonadotropin-releasing hormone (GnRH), which is said to aid the development of a newborn's brain.

Moreover, breastfeeding benefits are mutual, since the mother is also a rich beneficiary in a lucrative symbiotic interaction. One immediate benefit is that: "Breast-feeding helps restore the mother's body to normal after childbirth. During feedings, the muscles of the uterus are working, and this helps the reproductive organs return to their normal

---

[135]. Ibid., p. 10.

[136]. Makrides, M.; Neumann, M.A.; Byard, R.W.; Gibson, Bob; Simmer, Karen. (1994), "Fatty acid composition of brain, retina, and erythrocytes in breast- and formula-fed infants".

position more quickly."[137] Some of the long term benefits are, for example, breastfeeding dramatically reduces the risk of breast cancer.[138] Incidentally, according to some other studies such as the one done by epidemiologist, Suzanne Haynes at the U.S. National Cancer Institute, the rate of breast cancer is much higher among lesbians than normal childbearing women.[139] The similar cancerous pattern is also observed

---

[137]. Bonnet, Monique & Bonnet Gerard (1984), *Feeding Your Baby*, p. 4.

[138]. Keun-Young Yoo et al. (1992), "Independent Protective Effect of Lactation against Breast Cancer: a Case-Control Study in Japan".
Layde, Peter M. et al (1989), "The Independent Associations of Parity, Age at First Full Term Pregnancy, and Duration of Breastfeeding with the Risk of Breast Cancer".
MacMahon, B. et al. (1970), "Age at First Birth and Breast Cancer Risk".
McTiernan, Anne and David B. Thomas (1986), "Evidence for a Protective Effect of Lactation on Risk of Breast Cancer in risk of breast cancer in young women".Young Women".
Newcomb, Polly A. et al. (1994), "Lactation and a Reduced Risk of Premenopausal Breast Cancer".
Ray, Colette and Michael Baum (1985), *Psychological Aspects of Early Breast Cancer*.
United Kingdom National Case-Control Study Group (1993), "Breast feeding and risk of breast cancer in young women".

[139]. Raeburn, Paul. (1993), "Breast-Cancer Risk Higher for Lesbians", The Globe and Mail, Friday, February 5, 1993.

The Equigenic Principle

among Catholic nuns who remain celibate all their life.[140] In addition, women who have breastfed are less likely to suffer from ovarian cancer and osteoporosis in later age.

The lesson to be learned from this example is that within nature there are laws which preserve optimality and perfection, through direct and sometimes subtle processes manifesting themselves. In fact, they often preempt the imagination and notions of even the best of human scientists who would be compared as rather primitive in comparison to the technology of nature.

From the above-cited example alone, it can be ascertained that societal structure must be engineered to meet the needs of mother and child, and that societal provisions designed taking these factors into consideration would obviously lead to further ramifications in the interrelated spheres of the social structure at large. This does not mean that the "the mother's place is solely at home", but that society would be so designed as to facilitate and accommodate various aspirations of both sexes without neglecting those needs which are crucial for healthy biological and mental development.

These examples illustrate that it is the biology and psychology of men and women which should dictate their respective roles in society, thereby defining rights. However, it is the conventionally based society, which detrimentally misconstrues biology and psychology, due to an enslavement to its shortsighted vested interests. The rights given to men and women based on a system of natural laws would treat all men and women as dignified human beings. As such, they would each have two kinds of rights: exclusive rights and identical rights, depending on the context. Identical rights mean that in many situations the rights for both men and women would be exactly the same, such as voting rights, the

---

[140]. "The Breast Care Test", A PBS documentary on breast cancer, 1993.

From Facts to Values

right to work, etc. Exclusive rights, are those rights given to the sexes which are compatible with their needs and function; consequently, they may not be identical, such as holidays for maternity leave given to female employees. Does the fact that men are not afforded this allowance constitute a violation of their basic rights? On the other hand, under some circumstances men are tolerated to work, walk around, and swim topless; yet such rights cannot be granted to women under any circumstances. In summary, it can be stated that the total value of exclusive rights plus identical rights, for both men and women are equal and that these two kinds of rights together sum-up to form equigenic rights.

The Equigenic Principle

Animal Rights Under Equigenic Principle

Thanks to conventionalism, we humans have given ourselves the autonomous authority to override animals and nature for the fulfilment of our egocentric whims. We have categorized ourselves as the chosen species, despite the fact that animals existed long before even the first homo-sapiens ever set foot on the earth. Today thousands of animals of all kinds are being brutally sentenced to deprivation and extinction, due to the insensitive activities of humankind. Indeed, the very ecosystems which serve as the basis of life are being devastated as never before. Yet, in this atmosphere, although there is a great deal of 'lovey-dovey mumbo-jumbo' about 'saving the planet', it appears that more than such sentiment is going to be necessary to make amends. An attitudinal shift is required so that our attentions are translated into the performance of the most useful kinds of actions possible. Sincere emotional concern is not sufficient. What needs to be examined is our attitude towards how we ought to relate to nature as human beings. Indeed, what is needed is the realization of a globally beneficial and integrated worldview.

In the debate surrounding the issue of animal rights, both the opponents, and even many of the proponents of animal welfare, assume that no absolute intrinsic rights exist which are capable of bringing animals into the moral fold. They hold that the whole concept of rights originates in the minds of human beings. They presume, that these rights are not absolute, but rather, arbitrary. According to this view, all rights extendible to animals, by humans, are determined by vested interests and socio-cultural factors. For example, naturalist, John Livingston states: "The difficulty inherent in these discussions arises in great measure from the failure to acknowledge that concepts of rights in human social environments which are built on dominance hierarchies or other forms of *power relationships*."[141] This is a representative view stemming from the assumption that *all* rights are relative and there is no absolute foundation or such thing as inherent rights. Livingston elsewhere states:

> Nonhuman nature cannot fit any ethical model, because ethical models are human abstract constructions designed to serve the humans who constructed them. An ethical model arises out of the interest of the human society to which it is seen to be useful. Ethical models are tools of social management, part of the technological prothesis. They are human-specific, and society-specific. They are not designed to serve the interests of other human societies, much less nonhuman societies.[142]

Livingston's view is a good example of tunnel visioned dogma in the form of incomplete thought. His argument is like stating that if my calculator works only up to eight digits, how would I be able to calculate the distance between the earth and Pluto? While, it is true that all popular and well-known theories of justice and charters of rights are man-made, this does not preclude the possibility of the existence of inherent, absolute rights. Here, is a typical example of academic pseudo-intellectual wrestling in action. In this debate, theories and concepts which are relative are treated as absolute in the sense of the be all and end all of higher human thinking. Conversely, that which is truly absolute, such as the Equigenic Principle, is not even recognized, let alone credited.

---

[141]. Livingston, John (1984), "Rightness or Right?", p. 309.

[142]. Livingston, John (1986), "Ethics as Prosthetics", in the *Environmental Ethics: Philosophical and Policy Perspectives*, edited by Philip P. Hanson, pp. 71-72.

The Equigenic Principle

Philosopher and supporter of animal welfare, Peter Singer in his book *Animal Liberation*, completely avoids getting embroiled into philosophical 'controversies' about nature of rights. He does not at all attribute rights to animals due to such naive misconceptions regarding the foundation of rights. Instead, to resolve the issue, he proposes that the basic moral principle of equality necessarily compels us to extend equal consideration to non-humans. Singer states:

> It is an implication of this principle of equality that our concern for others and our readiness to consider their interests ought not to depend on what they are like or on what abilities they may possess. ... the basic element–the taking into account of the interests of the being, whatever those interests may be–must, according to the principle of equality, be extended to all beings, black or white, masculine or feminine, human or non-human.[143]

Thus, according to Singer the human oppression of animals is not viewed as a violation of animal rights, but as 'speciesism' — defined as an attitude or prejudice which favours the interests of members of one's own species, as against members of other species. He formulates a concept similar to 'sexism'.

However, what needs to be pointed out is that the very assumption, that the source of all rights is an institution of human beings, is in itself fallacious: it is indeed, just another anthropocentric notion as to where rights emanate from. In fact, this premise is a prime example of a faulty argument known as the 'fallacy of dubious assumption' or 'fallacy of problematic premise.' This fallacy surfaces when the foundation of one's argument is based on a premise or on a set of premises which are not validated and are open to

---

[143]. Singer, Peter (1990), *Animal Liberation*, p. 5.

question. Therefore, what we should ask in the first place is: Is it indeed legitimate to assume that *all* rights are conventional?

John Locke, the seventeenth century thinker was among those over the centuries who noticed this erroneous form of argumentation. Locke was to some extent close to the Equigenic Principle. He argued for 'natural rights' discoverable by reason, as opposed to those imposed by the changing institutions of social convention. He asserted that the state of nature is the state of liberty, not of license, and that therefore, the state of nature has the 'law of nature' to govern it.[144] These laws are absolute and independent of governmental legislation. This led to the view that the rights derived from a recognition of these laws, are neither relative nor the products of human convention: everything is unnatural about the captivity of wild animals, just as everything is natural about their inborn freedom in the state of nature.

In the natural domain, when the relationship between members of the same species and coexisting participants is examined, we realize that within interspecies' and intraspecies' interactions, there is a prevalence of rights associated with their behavioural patterns. Many mammals, birds and even some fish are highly territorial as they explicitly mark off the extent of their boundaries. In the event that the markings are missed, any unwelcome visitors would be immediately chased out. The defence of a territory does not usually involve fighting. Most often, for example, the invader respects the displays of a resident bird's vociferous squawks or threat displays. Such communicative objections are usually sufficient to cause the invader to withdraw peacefully. The explicit unwritten right here is tantamount to: THIS IS MY TREE — KEEP OFF! Another example, is of hyenas abruptly terminating the chase of a promising prey animal as soon as

---

[144]. Locke, John. (1963), *The Treatise of Civil Government,* Book II, Ch., 2, Sec., 6.

The Equigenic Principle

they reach the border of neighbouring hyena territory, even though no other predators are in sight.[145]

Some mammals such as the dominant bull elephant seal, and the sea lion, are highly possessive of the females in their polygynous entourage. The dominant male fights off any rival male who approaches his females, making sure that the intruder understands that he alone has the right to mate with the females.[146] The message being conveyed in this case, is equivalent to: STAY AWAY FROM MY RELATIONS! It can also be observed, that in some specific instances, hyenas and wild dogs give up their hard earned kill without even putting up a fight, as soon as a lion approaches the carcass. There is a social ranking among the various species which have gathered while the lions feast. When they have consumed enough, the attendant species proceed one by one in a specific order towards the remaining flesh. The sequential order of approach is as follows: firstly the hyenas, followed by the wild dogs, then the jackals and lastly, the vultures. All of this suggests the existence of well established relational ranking among species: the lions appear to have a priority in this instance at least, over the meal, than their ravenous audience.[147]

---

[145]. Kruuk, Hans (1972), *The Spotted Hyena: A Study of Predation and Social Behaviour*. According to this author, " ... there is at least the strong suggestion that some 20% of hunting failures in Ngorongoro are caused by hyena social reasons — that is, the presence of clan boundaries.", p. 160.

[146]. Attenborough, David. (1990), *The Trials of Life*. An example of this incident is captured on film under the BBC television series entitled: The Trials of Life.

[147]. Suzuki, David. (1991), *Running for their Lives*.
Page, George. (1991), *Horse Tigers*.

From Facts to Values

Competition or Cooperation?

There are various perspectives in ethology, on whether there is cooperation or competition among animals. Some of those who posit that animal interactions are all purely cooperative state that because the above-cited examples of animal behaviour are mistakenly held as being competitive, it is then assumed that rights automatically exist. Such cooperationists feel that when the proponents of competition theory refer to such observations, they are anthropocentrically equating rights with competition, because competition in human society entails mights, so too it must be the case in animal communities. In fact, some of these 'radical cooperationists', hold that there is no actual competition among wild animals, and that therefore, one cannot even talk about rights when it comes to the wilderness.

Although the above-mentioned observations may not be sufficient to conclude the presence of competition among species, they are nonetheless an indication of territorial ownership. Whether the behavioural patterns exhibit competition or cooperation is, in fact, absolutely irrelevant here, since even in the case of cooperation, there are some associated constraints. After all, cooperation does not exclude respect for mutual ownership. Indeed, we cannot escape the fact that cooperation itself includes the fulfilment of the respective functions contractually or verbally assigned to mutually cooperating parties. This fulfilment is an expectant right of the mutually opposite members of the same cooperative unit.

Animals, in actuality, appear to be engaged in more than our simplistic anthropocentric notions of either "cooperation or competition". Each species conducts itself by rules, within myriad 'infrastructures' and dwellings which are optimally suited to their own particular needs.[148] Animal species also

---

[148]. Hansell, Michael H. (1984), *Animal Architecture and Building Behaviour.*

The Equigenic Principle

engage in various forms of communication,[149] in what could best be described as communities.[150] In order to flourish, any community, be it human or non-human requires a set of regulatory principles based on natural law, which ensure the collective stability of social order taken as an ensemble. Indeed, examples of such animal behaviour are profuse.

The All-Embrasive Feature of Equigenic Rights

By reflecting on the expanding Universe, and the diversity of lifeforms within it, we can certainly observe a panoramic display of remarkable order and consistency. Such harmonious order is maintained throughout, by the structure of the extremely delicate balances in the physical universe, as for instance in the ecological realm of existence, where plants and animals have been made to be ingeniously adapted to their respective niches. There is indeed a fragile equilibrium within nature's economy; even a minute change would disrupt the balances in this dynamically interrelated scheme of existence.

Consider a notorious case of human folly, which occurred in Australia. Not too long ago, a famous movie star appeared a number of times on camera, wearing an outfit made of snake skin. As a result of this blatant exposition, the outfit became the prevailing fashion of the day. To keep up with an increasing market demand, the suppliers raided the bushes, killing as many snakes as possible, not realizing that the snake has a function in the food web. It preys on rats. Since the inherent property of this physical universe rules that every cause is followed by effects, and that for every action there is

---

[149]. Bright, Michael. (1984), *Animal Language*.

[150]. Giller, Paul S. (1984), *Community Structure and Niche*.
Forsyth, Adrian. (1989), "Togetherness: The Logic of the Herd", *Equinox*, pp. 48-57.

From Facts to Values

a concomitant reaction, the subsequent callous mass slaughter of snakes, resulted in an explosion in rat population. The prairies were destroyed, as the multitudinous rats consumed all their favourite crops. This culminated in a man-made food shortage in parts of Australia and further led to increased habitat destruction through the continuation of ecosystemical dislocations. These were induced by none other than a network of cause and effect interdependencies. The example just cited, is not simply an isolated case; indeed, the world is plagued at present by the elimination or reduction of many species, interconnected to the precious web of life by similar or worse catastrophes.

In fact, this disastrous episode, graphically reveals that in order to maintain the balances in nature, the snake has the inherent right to remain unmolested and free in its natural setting. This right is not derived by an arbitrary or selected social convention; rather, it is the snake's natural right, as defined by the universality of cause and effect relations, manifested in the equilibrium producing checks and balances within the countless structures and processes in the universe. In fact, in some cases the Equigenic Principle would dictate that the animal in question should have more rights than the human, in order for the system to move toward the restoration of the natural balance. For example, if the human and the animal shared a common food resource and there was a shortage of supply, the animal would have precedence over the human, in the consumption of that resource, for the human would have many alternatives, whereas the animal would be tightly bound by its niche.

With this kind of an overview, it is observable that it should not be humans who should be inventing these rights. Rather, it should be we, who should recognize these unique rights, by observing the interrelationships within the processes inherent in the universe on earth. We should therefore choose to intraconnect these discoveries within the communities in nature, be those communities human or non-human, as naturally integral components of already pre-existing universal

The Equigenic Principle

laws. In a sense then, it is nature which projects the realization of these rights onto the sense of the human, if the human is observant of those very balances in nature in the first place, and it is this which is the equigenic right.

The realization of Equigenic Principle on all levels, then, is diametrically opposed to the concept of the human's own manufactured notions of rights derived by social convention. In fact, social conventions must be in complete congruence with natural universal laws in order for the whole system to function beneficently. For if man-made conventions traverse against the natural flow of the universal laws, they cause crippling dysfunctionalities which ultimately lead to an inevitable collapse of the integral systems of life. For example, take the case of governmental policies regarding deforestation: clear cutting in the Amazon and elsewhere around the world, has led to the death of forests, destroying their roles as the harbingers and maintainers of the crucial life support systems of our biosphere. The fact is, that not much regard had been paid to their complex ecological characteristics. Now, more attention, though certainly not enough, is indeed being paid due to a 'clear cut' realization of the adverse effects of such devastating conventional policies on the various creatures and their ecological niches. Any disruption in these natural orders is not only harmful for florae and faunae, but also devastating for man. After all, man is not apart from nature, but a part of nature.

From Facts to Values

The Parameters of Freedom in Nature

It has been established that the concept of rights other than equigenic rights is a human construct. This, therefore, entails that the *parameters* of rights other than equigenic rights also devolve into human constructs. In fact, the parameters of freedom under conventionalism are as fluctuatory as its foundation. Therefore, to resolve the second long debated controversy as to what would be the extension of human rights, it is necessary to, once again appeal to the absolute — natural law.

Freedom is one of the inherent and inseparable properties of nature. In fact, freedom and nature are synonymous and often interchangeable. Being free means following natural laws. Since everything in nature follows the natural laws, then everything within it is 'free'. Everything free in the following sense: a tree is free to grow and bear fruit, a flower is free to blossom, wild animals are free to reproduce, the grass is free to flutter in the wind, the river is free to wind its way through the meadow, the clouds are free to move under the direction of the winds, the waves are free to undulate rhythmically, the rain is free to fall, the soil is free to soak water, the birds are free to sing, the earth is free to rotate, the sun is free to shine, and the universe is free to expand. All of these freedoms are there to maintain healthy growth and overall equilibrium unto *perfection*. Everything in nature is free to do that which is locally and globally best for the overall system. Yet within all these freedoms, there are 'limits'. As writer, G.K. Chesterton once remarked: "The moment you step into the world of facts, you step into the world of limits. You can free things from alien or accidental laws, but not from the laws of their own nature." *This is because of the fact that the laws which ensure the balance, by their very features, impose certain constraints to prevent any deviations and imbalances from arising.* These constraints make the entire universe what it is — a flawless interlocking system in dynamic equipoise. These constraints are the very keys which interlock the various components of the universe

The Equigenic Principle

for sound development and functioning. The 'limits' are there merely to preserve and enhance the entire system without which there would be no ordered system and indeed no system or universe in the first place.

However, human beings unlike any other entities in nature have an added component — they possess the 'freedom to choose'. For man, being truly free, means surveying and exploring the options rationally, fulfilling one's role in consonance with freedom of nature, by maintaining the overall balance of this system. Therefore, if this universe consists of interconnections in the natural world of process and structures then any rational thought which perceives those interconnections must also be aligned with those very processes. That is to say, any rational thinking individual who fully grasps the reality of cause and effect relationships will not impede these natural processes by means of following narrow ambitions and desires which would tend to go counter to the these processes by interconnecting those things which do not fit together structurally and functionally. In nature, to be free is to be enslaved by none, but the physical laws in this originated universe. 'Not going counter' is the limit or constraint realized. This limit is part of the natural laws, facilitating the harmonious kenesis of nature and humanity. It is not a human artifice but an *actuality of nature* ascertained. Since such a rational individual will be flowing integrally with the processes of nature in thought and action as part of the overall balanced network of interactions — both ecological and social — this individual would, like nature, be truly free. His or her thoughts would be receptacles for the very patterns of nature. Any concepts contrary to the natural laws would be foreign to the constitution of his or her independent natural thinking.

However, in libertarian societies, freedom is interpreted as emancipation from any socio-ethical norms and obligations. Here, to be free means to take a fast ride on the pleasure principle, never mind the consequences. Let us analyze freedom under libertarian scheme when it comes to

From Facts to Values

human actions by taking a particular case — homosexuality. For example, if, by majority vote, one is allowed and entitled to 'marry' somebody of the same sex, a disruption of the naturally designed processes based on cause and effect relationships would clearly follow. These actions would indubitably lead to harm and imbalances for both the individuals involved, and the society at large. For instance, if a certain fraction of the male population of the society were to 'marry' or have 'relationship' with members of the same sex, firstly, on the individual level, the susceptibility of contracting particular infectious or communicable diseases associated with these activities will increase and get out of control. "We are dealing with something that is expanding out of control," said Dr. June Osborn, the chair of American National Commission on Aids, in the Eighth International AIDS Conference in Amsterdam during the summer of 1992.[151] Mark Harrington, a member of New York City-based Treatment Action Group, bluntly summarized that: "It is clear we are losing the battle. We have one class of drugs that slows AIDS down by two or three years, and then people go on and die."[152] This is not to say that homosexuality is the only cause of Aids epidemic — however, it is one of the major causes on its own, and in its indirect influence in causing the other major and minor causes through the chain of cause and effect. It is indeed at the root of the tree upon which the branchlike ramifications of the other causes and effects have proliferated.

Furthermore, on the societal level, it would leave the opposite sex spouseless, leading to a disruption in population growth, gender balance and male/ female ratio, (i.e remember the example of India). Allowing such unnatural

---

[151]. Gorman, Christine. (1992), "Invincible Aids", *Time*, p. 19.

[152]. Ibid., p. 19.

The Equigenic Principle

proclivities would be in violation of the natural rights of the neglected sexes and other members in society, in one form or another. However, at the very basic level, by looking into nature's design it is clear that these tendencies are incongruent with the natural processes, and cannot therefore be granted as rights, as social conventions could allow, and as some have now begun to allow and encourage. The tendencies are unnatural, firstly, because if a community was comprised of homosexuals, this community would not last long enough to see its next generation. In this case, a primary biological principle is being violated — reproduction and the propagation of the species, something that the future of human race unconditionally depends on. Considering this factor alone is enough to establish that homosexuality is not natural. Thus, the case is closed. It is fitting to quote Mao Tse-Tung who once remarked: "The only standard by which truth can be assessed is its practical results."

Secondly, one cannot dispute the fact that the human body is not designed to engage in homosexual activity — there is a great deal of precaution required in homosexual sexual activity to combat tissue rupture and consequent diseases. The mucous membrane that lines the opening of the rectum and the bowel area is very delicate. It tears off easily, if slightly stretched. Furthermore, in case of rupture, it fails to heal properly and with the normal rapidity of lesions as the rest of the body. If this happens, it can easily lead to serious infections, haemorrhoids, abscesses, peritonitis and anal fissures.

Sue Johanson, a Canadian sex educator and a well known supporter of homosexuality and everything else, while approving homosexuality as being natural is obliged to acknowledge the above complications[153]. Surprisingly, she explicitly admits that "rectum is not designed for penetration

---

[153]. Johanson, Sue. (1995), *Sex, Sex and More Sex: 101 Questions and Answers,* pp. 21-23.

by any hard object."[154] Elsewhere she concludes: "I realize that the Gay community and many others will be upset with me appearing to over-react to the risks, but the risks are real, and you are entitled to know what you are getting into."[155]

If the above details are considered, then one is obliged to ask: what biological evidence could be stronger than the fact that human body is not designed to function in homosexual activity? What could top this blatant evidence? All to the contrary, it seems that both human body and mind are designed solely for a heterosexual contact. There is nothing higher than this truth. The biological evidence to support this assertion is overwhelming. Take the natural physiological process involved in human sexual response. "Distinctly different, but complementary, physiological changes occur in both sexes to prepare the unaroused individual for coitus. These changes are not limited to the genital area. Sexual stimulation elicits neurological, vascular, muscular and hormonal reactions which affect the functioning of the entire body".[156] Once the male has reached the arousal level, the penis gets erected. This change for the male is usually instantaneous. The penis is consequently ready for penetration. The vagina in the sexually unstimulated state is tight and dry. Upon the proper stimulation, the inner lips of the vagina enlarge dramatically (vasocongestion), it further expands and lubricates itself to accommodate the

---

[154]. Ibid, p. 21.

[155]. See her pamphlet on "Anal Sex" released by Rogers Cable and Sunday Nights Sex Show, Rock Radio Network.

[156]. Singer Kaplan, Helen. (1974), *The New Sex Therapy*, p. 5.

The Equigenic Principle

penetration.[157] The vagina lubrication has also the quality of sterilizing the penis. In addition, it not only makes the penetration of penis easier, it also helps neutralizing the vaginal canal, which tends to be acidic while at rest.

> The acid-base balance in the vagina is delicately held in the 3.5-4.0 pH range (below 7 is acidic, above 7 is alkaline). Lubrication over sufficient periods of time, approximately 30 minutes, will increase the pH toward the neutral range of 7. The sperm is in the seminal fluid of the male are maximally mobile in a neutral pH. Seminal fluid, in combination with vaginal lubrication, neutralizes the otherwise acidic environment of the vaginal and enhances sperm mobility.[158]

Further on, "the uterus may raise up, so that it does not interfere with the deep penetration of penis."[159] Gerald D. Coleman concludes:

> Importantly, observations of the vagina during orgasm confirm that it is much more than just a "passive receptacle" for the penis. It is an active participant in coitus, and

---

[157]. Masters, William H. and Johnson, Virginia E. and Kolodny Robert C. (1982), *Human Sexuality*, pp. 30-39, 56-63.

[158]. Cori Baill and John Money, (1980), "Physiological Aspects of Female Sexual Development", in the *Women's Sexual Development: Explorations of Inner Space,* p. 70.

[159]. Winchester, A.M. (1973), *The Nature of Human Sexuality*, p. 79.

capable of enveloping and stimulating the penis to a climax.[160]

However, what Coleman neglects to touch is that, the climax is indeed mutual for both parties involved in the act, not just for the male. The point here is, that copulation between a man and a woman mechanically makes sense, while in a homosexual sex it does not. Intercourse is indeed an intriguing goal-directed process which is non-existent in homosexual as well as heterosexual so-called anal sex. There can be no denial of the fact that the bodies of both gay men and lesbians who emphasize on their homosexuality are designed for a heterosexual intercourse, both in terms of rationale and function.

Now, other than one's desire, what biological evidence is there to support that homosexuality is intrinsically natural? Let us not have a one-sided debate; let the burden of proof be on the shoulder of those who make such claims. Is there any argument in this universe which supports that it is natural for a man to be in lust with another man, and a woman with another woman? If so, what is the proof? Why would they not bring their proof, if they are indeed so truthful? An appeal to pity and sheer desires does not constitute as proof or justification.

From the Equigenic Principle it can be conclusively realized that so-called homosexuality is unnatural, and therefore would not be granted the rights bestowed to 'straight' society. Consequently, it is highly ludicrous to embark on program to prove that it is natural. For example, if it is mathematically proven that the shortest distance in Euclidean space is a straight line, then it would be idiotic to waste grant money, time and effort to try to prove that it is otherwise.

---

[160]. Coleman, Gerald D. (1992), *Human Sexuality: An All-embracing Gift*, p. 154.

The Equigenic Principle

The modern argument attempting to support homosexuality comes from some pseudo-scientific research, which alludes to the differences in the brain size of 'homosexuals' as compared to 'heterosexuals'. However, the most common fallacies in these studies is the mistaking of correlation for causation.[161] For example, a frequent error is to design an experiment which does not follow from the hypothesis being investigated. If a study wanted to establish a link between smoking and liver disease, for instance, it would have to eliminate competing causes for liver disease such as drinking. Otherwise a simple correlation between smoking and liver disease would be totally inconclusive. "That is, simply from knowing that two variables are correlated, we cannot establish what causal relation, if any, holds between them."[162] Correlation does not necessarily imply causation.

Besides, for the sake of argument, even if it is established by rigorous experimentation that the homosexual brain is in some way different from the heterosexual brain, these differences cannot be taken to necessarily imply that homosexuality is hereditary. It is known that behaviour also affects the brain; therefore, it is possible that these differences were caused by behaviour. One has to avoid the *post hoc fallacy*, that is, when relationship between two variables is discovered, but it is not known "for sure which of the variables is the cause and which the effect."[163]

Other research errors which could cast doubt on the outcome of an experiment can be seen in poor sample sizes,

---

[161]. Giere, Ronald N. (1984), *Understanding Scientific Reasoning,* pp. 187-190.

[162]. Miller, Scott A. (1987), *Developmental Research Methods*, p. 78.

[163]. Huff, Darrell. (1954), *How to lie with statistics,* p. 89.

the questionable reliability and validity of the methodology of experimentation, etc.,[164] and above all, not to mention the experimenter's inadvertent biases, especially if he or she happens to be a homosexual and 'gay activist'.[165]

Wayne R. Dynes, a specialized researcher in area of homosexuality, believes that it is "simplistic to attribute homosexual behaviour simply to [mere] biological factors."[166] What one ought to initially prove is, whether there are any determining connection between genes and human social behaviour? As it happens, the whole notion of connecting behaviour with genes has been discredited.[167] The basic error in such studies like that of Bailey & Pillard (1991) and Whitam, et al. (1993)[168], which involves sets of identical and fraternal male twins, is that they fail to account for other possible

---

[164]. Number of such studies are used in an article titled "The Gay Science of Genes and Brains", *The Economist*, December 5, 1992. Also see: LeVay, Simon. (1991), "A difference in hypothalamic structure between heterosexual and homosexual men", *Science*, August 30.

[165]. Most studies cited to support homosexuality as natural are conducted by homosexual researchers such as those investigated by Simon LeVay who is a self-proclaim homosexual.

[166]. Dynes, Wayne R. (1987), *Homosexuality: A Research Guide*, p. 732.

[167]. Horgan, John. (1993), "Eugenics Revisited", *Scientific American*, pp. 122-131.

[168]. Bailey, J.M. & Pillard R.C. (1991), "A Genetic Study of Male Sexual Orientation".
Whitam, F.L. et al. (1993), "Homosexual Orientation in Twins: a report on 61 pairs and three triplet sets".

competing factors arising from the social environment. Another glaring defect is that they fail to account for the fact that not all the identical and fraternal twins were homosexuals. Some of the twins were homosexual-heterosexual pairs. Nevertheless, the fact that they were identical (monozygotic) means that they had exactly the same gene-set. Therefore, if homosexuality is truly hereditary, one would expect both identical twins to be homosexual in 100% of the cases. Moreover, the fact that there is a higher concordance of homosexuality among identical twins could be the result of being raised close to each other, perhaps more closely than fraternal twins. One has to examine the homosexual tendency of identical twins that are raised apart, in order to eliminate the environmental factors, and to bring more evidence to bear on the issue.

Finally, one can also ask, if homosexuality is an inborn biological phenomena, then, why is it that there are many homosexuals who have reverted to heterosexuality? For example, the Masters and Johnson study shows that 79.1% homosexuals immediately switched to heterosexuality following their rehabilitation treatments, and 71.6% went to some relapses, however, managed to rehabilitate after a number of years[169]. Needless to say both figures of 79.1% and 71.6% are statistically significant numbers. This re-conversion indicates that the origin of homosexuality cannot be due to some genetic or biological factors and homosexuality is not a static dispositional trait like one's skin colour or gender.

Another attempt to argue that homosexuality is natural comes by drawing faulty analogies from the animal world. Proponents of homosexuality stress that if homosexual behaviour can be found to exist among animals, it would be natural for humans also. Notwithstanding the fact that there

---

[169]. Schwartz, Mark F. & Masters, William H. (1984), "The Masters and Johnson Treatment Program for Dissatisfied Homosexual Men".

From Facts to Values

are no rigorous and conclusive studies that prove this assertion as a matter of fact, there is an invalid assumption at the root of this claim. To begin with, the whole concept of 'gender preference' or 'sexual orientation' is a *gay-made* invention; it has no place in the natural world. Nature is free from human personification. Besides, suppose that this wishful thinking turns out to be true — so what? It is not possible to make one-to-one logical comparisons between human and animal behaviour. Each animal species has its own system of behaviour. What constitutes natural behaviour for one species is not necessarily natural for another, let alone for human beings. For example, most animals, after they defecate and urinate lick themselves as a mechanism for keeping themselves clean, while most humans would consider this extremely abhorrent and intolerable. At least the person who would insist on the naturalness and validity of the first claim, is not likely to accept the second claim.

The problem with the so-called 'sexual orientation' argument is that there are all kinds of perverted dysfunctional sexual activities and mental disorders that can equally be justified based on one's 'sexual orientation'. However, there is no doubt that no legislature will permit such activities to be protected in society (at least not yet). For example, there are many individuals with paraphiliastic tendencies to perform bestiality, sadomasochism and flagellation, paedophilia, necrophilia (sex with dead bodies), transvestism or transsexualism, bisexualism, fetishism, autoerotism, autogynephilia, asphyxia, voyeurism, exhibitionism, nymphomania, satyriasis, sexual cannibalism or even incest and rape. If denying equigenic rights to homosexuals based on the nonsensical imaginary notion of 'sexual orientation' is considered discriminatory and 'unconstitutional' then it follows that the existing legislations and criminal code with respect to these other activities should also be deemed 'unconstitutional' and discriminatory. That is to say, all arguments raised in defence of such activities ought to be accepted if a person simply claims that he or she is born that way and this is his or her God given 'sexual orientation' to have sex with animals or with young children. Therefore, under conventionalism on what possible grounds could the above-cited examples be considered as being deviations with pathological disorders, whereas homosexuality would be viewed as part of healthy human sexuality? It seems that wherever the cut-off point is set to be, it is just arbitrary and artificial.

To make a case for defense of homosexuality, all arguments ought to be based on clear facts, not baseless nonsensical theories. Wayne R. Dynes, acknowledges that:

> It is true that some studies seeking to demonstrate biological foundations of homosexual behaviour have been poorly designed and tendentious, but future work may be more convincing.[170]

Thus, when there is no argument, one is obliged to appeal to extenuation. Richard D. Mohr who is considered a 'gay activist' argues:

> When "nature" is taken in technical rather than ordinary usages, it looks like the notion also will not ground a charge of homosexual immorality. When unnatural means "by artifice" or "made by man," one need only point out that virtually everything that is good about life is unnatural in this sense, that one feature that distinguishes people from most other animals is people's ability to make over the world to meet their needs and desires, and that people's well-being depends upon these departures from nature. On this understanding of the natural and people's

---

[170]. Dynes, Wayne R. (1987), *Homosexuality: A Research Guide*, p. 732.

nature, homosexuality is perfectly unobjectable.[171]

Here is Jeremy Bentham's utilitarian attempt to justify homosexuality:

> As to any primary mischief, it is evident that it produces no pain in anyone. On the contrary it produces pleasure, and that a pleasure which, by their perverted taste, is by this supposition preferred to that pleasure which is in general reputed the greatest. The partners are both willing.[172]

Can claims based on pleasure constitute philosophical and legal arguments? Do these statements in any way prove the naturalness of homosexuality? If Mohr, Bentham or anybody else wishes to establish the naturalness of homosexuality, they had better come up with something other than mere desires. The crucial point of this book is that an individual who recognizes the Equigenic Principle would have already realized that the satisfaction of one's personal desires should not be the criterion of the do's and don'ts. In fact, once the notion of 'desire' becomes the 'be all' and 'end all' of every action, then everything under the sun would be justifiable based on whims. No lines could be drawn anywhere, leading to conflict, chaos and a total collapse of society which is presently well underway. In diametrical contrast, unlike the termites' humble submission, the arrogance of humankind sometimes reaches to the degree that, rather than us conforming to the laws of nature, we want all the physical laws of universe conform to our paltry and insatiable desires.

---

[171]. Mohr, Richard D. (1988), *Gay Justice: A Study of Ethics, Society and Law*, p. 35.

[172]. Bentham, Jeremy. (1973), "An Essay on "Paederasty", in the *Philosophy of Sex,* edited by Robert Baker and Frederick Elliston, p. 355.

The Equigenic Principle

As mentioned by Immanuel Kant: "It seems surprising at first, but is none the less certain, that our reason does not draw its conclusions from Nature, but prescribes them to it." Therefore, it should be no wonder as to why the state of the world is as it is today, when our behaviour, values, socio-political policies are all governed by pleasure principle.

While those who refute homosexuality are often labelled dogmatic or close-minded, and those who support it are considered open-minded, it is indeed fitting to ask: Who is truly dogmatic here? Is it the one who bases things on evidence, or, is it the one who follows desires and denies numerous self-evident facts? Just as in the Dark Ages, when the Church was unable to counter Bruno's rational arguments, and resorted to the use of unsubstantiated terms, completely devoid of logic and substance, in denigrating individuals or groups, many present day institutions in the New Dark Ages have also resorted to such a linguistically imposed mental oppression. And just as in the Dark Ages, when the Church labelled Bruno a 'heretic' and his 'crime' a 'heresy', so too, in the New Dark Ages new baseless terminologies such as 'heterosexism', 'homophobic' and 'homophobia' have been invented for attacking today's Brunos, all of which are bogus *gay-made* concepts, designed to have an upper-hand. Psychologically, people have a great aversion to being labelled with terms that have a negative import. No one would wish to be stigmatized as being 'phobic'. No one wants to have this negative title bestowed upon him or her, especially when it is often closely associated with some outlooks which are real, justifiably anti-social and dysfunctional such as anti-black, anti-semitic, anti-women, anti-refugee etc. This insidious attempt is used to disadvantage the other side at the very outset, by placing a negative label on them. The strategy implies that whoever does not have a supportive view on homosexuality is sick. However, this type of stigmatization in essence, is a typical textbook case of cheap *ad hominem* attack and name calling, devoid of any substantiative arguments. In order to better expose the 'phobia strategy', suppose that one believes that the doctrine of vegetarianism is unjustified on the merit that it lacks a logical foundation. Consequently, its promotion may be more harmful to the balance of the ecosystem. Can such an individual be labelled as having 'vegephobia'? Moreover, how on earth can an attack on *vegetarianism* be considered as being a personal attack on *vegetarians*, or be constituted as 'spreading hate-literature'? Yet, such assumptions and charges are always made as soon as one attempts to disagree with homosexuality as being natural.

In addition, if the 'phobia strategy' is valid and one is 'homophobic' by rejecting homosexuality, due to its lack of justification, then could it not be equally argued that the one who rejects the naturalness of 'traditional' family structure is 'heterophobic'? In many ways, opposition to homosexuality is depicted as backward and discriminatory. A documented case of this insidious approach of subtle indoctrination can be seen in the definition of homophobia given in the "*Sexual Orientation: Focus on Homosexuality, Lesbianism and Homophobia*",[173] a resource guide for teachers in Toronto secondary schools. It is by the usage of such subtle control mechanisms that are things in society inverted: what is natural by nature's function-cum-structure design is made to look like an option, and what is truly unnatural is made to appear natural. By the usage of these linguistic impositions, 'rights' are pushed through into acceptance by various boisterous lobby groups and institutions. As it has been established above, however, these rights have no basis in the way nature functions, from which all rights ought to be derived. In the approach which goes against reason, the abnormal is normalized by rampant notions of relativism. The basis of 'rights', through such a subliminal forms of mental

---

[173]. *Sexual Orientation: Focus on Homosexuality, Lesbianism and Homophobia,* A Resource Guide for Teachers of Health Education in Secondary Schools, Prepared by Toronto Board of Education, (1992), p. 3.

The Equigenic Principle

oppression leads to nothing but physical and mental desecration.

Now, let us discuss the issue of justice related to a specific case involving 'homosexuals rights'. Consider the frequent case of a person leaving his homeland, to seek refugee status in another country because he is not allowed to practice the sexually misdirected lifestyle, given that, the above reasons are encapsulated in the constitution of the country of origin. Would this be equivalent to granting refugee status to someone fearing severe torture and death, akin to the innocent victims of death camps, particularly when the host countries treat 'membership' as a 'scarce' commodity, and put limits on the number of refugees admitted? If so, what is the basis of justice here? There are many cases in the western countries, where asylum is often granted evenly without any differentiation. In fact, the numbers keep rising. The problem seems to be that we often treat every shout for asylum with equal validity and priority, without considering the whole issue.

In the above case, there are no grounds for asylum under Equigenic Principle. In fact, under the equigenic principle we can see that the mentioned lifestyle is detrimental to balance of nature; therefore, it ought to be treated as a violation. This would mean that, the action taken against such individuals would be prosecution, not persecution.[174] The prosecution of individuals involved is justified, *so long as* it is done, firstly by authorized officials, not by mobs and thugs. Secondly, the punishment must be proportional to the crime committed.

---

[174]. The UNHCR *Handbook on Procedures and Criteria for Determining Refugee Status*, states: "Persecution must be distinguished from punishment for a common law offense. Persons fleeing from prosecution or punishment for such an offense are not normally refugees. It should be recalled that a refugee is a victim–or potential victim–of injustice, not a fugitive from justice." Paragraph 53, p. 15.

From Facts to Values

Thirdly, the mode of punishment must contribute to discipline the individual and to the eradication of the crime at large, and therefore should be designed for that effect only. Fourthly, prosecution has to be done within the system which, far from encouraging such a lifestyle, is, on the contrary, discouraging it. This would mean that no one should be punished by the law, if a state fails to set-up a system which has such pre-conditions in place already.

Homosexuality is considered a 'contentious issue' in our time and its inclusion as an unnatural activity is based on a violation of Equigenic Principle as stated above, not on a dogmatic bias, as preached by fire and brimstone sermons, in which a 'believer' is supposed to be wary of thunderbolts from on high.

Finally, contrary to the radical libertarian belief which is opposed to any social, legal and political restraints on an individual's activities, human behaviour must be constrained as set by the laws of nature. In fact, the concept of limitless and absolute freedom is not only detrimental to human society as described above, but is also self-refuting and defeating for those who advocate it. For example, if we are to foster a society in which everyone is free to do as he or she wishes, then one member of society ought not to be denied the 'right' and the absolute freedom to remove the freedom of another member, such as the right of the advocator of absolute freedom, otherwise he or she is not really free. Obviously, such principles cannot be allowed for these apparent reasons. This means, that we are bound to draw the line somewhere. This is something which is agreed upon by the least radical of libertarians. They, too, state that rights given to individuals are not absolutely unlimited but are subject to some limitations. Therefore, we are once again compelled to go back to our initial questions: Where, and what should be the criteria for our decisions? What is the best decision?

In the earlier section, with the establishment of the Equigenic Principle, it was shown that in order to maintain the

The Equigenic Principle

balance, man must interconnect things to see how they fit together, just as animals themselves naturally function to maintain the balance in the construction of their dwellings, in their interactions etc. From this, it can be realized that denying the opportunity to 'interconnect things', to reason and to gain knowledge, or, conversely, allowing ignorance in the sense of letting people misconnect things, is the greatest violation of the Equigenic Principle. It is the greatest violation because it is due to such misconnections that do all the other imbalances arise. A state or society which operates in such a dysfunctional manner will indeed, therefore, cause disruption on earth, land, water and air, by the hands of human beings.

Boundaries of Civil Rights Under the Equigenic Principle

Freedom of thought allows for interconnectivity as discussed throughout this presentation. However, thought gives rise to public expression! What then ought to be the parameters of 'freedom of expression' if we are to establish equigenic rights? Take three hypothetical cases. Firstly, a historian who wishes to express his questionable view on some historical events, or challenge well cherished 'beliefs'. Should he be allowed to write and deliver lectures? Secondly, a scientist who advocates a racial superiority classification system. Thirdly, should state allow publications of pornographic materials? The key question here is: How would a system of rights based on the foundation of laws of nature deal with these and other similar issues?

In the first and second case, a man should be allowed to express his views so long as he can back them up with clear-cut, undisputed evidence. What is required from him, is to present the facts not myths. Here we see that the notion of proof is very much associated with the 'freedom of speech' because proof has to do with the truthfulness of the claim. Freedom of speech must be directly connected to the veracity of the claim. As far as racism is concerned, in a state operating on the Equigenic Principle, where racism has already been realized to be an aberrational and false idea, society would not allow its propagation by any means. However, if an individual, in all sincerity with no hidden dubious agenda, is under the impression that a particular race is superior to others, then this individual will be allowed to express his views, provided he brings conclusive proofs and backing. His sincerity, in this respect, can be determined by his reaction to the evidence. Obviously, since there is no support for racial views, such an individual's disclosure would enable society to educate him towards the right path, which would open up his thinking to the integrative aspects of knowledge and humanity and help to maintain overall societal stability. For such an individual, this erroneous view would be realized as being incorrect once reminded of the evidence.

In the third case any actions which would jeopardize the balance in the social and environmental arena would be prohibited. Under such a constitution, if something is proven to be detrimental, it cannot be allowed to be propagated. Pornography is nothing but a form of poisonous perceptual pollution. It completely disregards the integrity of both women and men, by projecting women as sex objects and men as sexual predators. Pornography is not at all a medium for expression, but a means for exploitation of human weaknesses. As such, the production and distribution of pornographic material disrupts the optimality and stability of family and society. This can easily be determined from cause and effect relationships and from the behaviour of those who are exposed to pornography, besides, not to mention its close associations with other concomitant criminal activities which it fosters.[175] Therefore, it should be banned completely. In

---

[175]. Potter, Gary W. (1989), "The Retail Pornography Industry and the Operation of Vice", *Journal of Deviant Behaviour,* pp. 233-251.

Pornography and Sexual Violence: Evidence of the Links, (1988).

The Equigenic Principle

neither case, is the prohibition an arbitrary decision. Furthermore, the responsibility to establish institutions or to counsel wayward individuals to use their reason and to base their views on proof should fall squarely on the society. This would create social conditions which would not tolerate pornography or racism and create preconditions which would not become the breeding grounds for the propagation and feelings for such ideas and activities.

In general, we can observe that the concept of so-called unlimited freedom in an ad hoc or artificially disciplined system, where almost any whim allowed is hollow, and the proposal of constraints as determined by the laws of cause and effect is the only efficient and realistic alternative.

Jatkola, Barbara. (1981), *Violence Against Women in Five Erotic Magazines.*

Russell, Diana E.H. (1993), *Making Violence Sexy: Feminist Views on Pornography.*

Valverde, Mariana. (1985), *Sex, Power and Pleasure.*

From Facts to Values

"Is–Ought" dilemma?

In 1739, David Hume offered a counter argument against natural law which has been used by positivists ever since[176]. However, despite the fact that the debate has already been clearly resolved,[177] it is still continuously being used[178]. According to this view establishing rights by appealing to nature is a form of 'naturalistic fallacy', to deduce values from facts or more precisely a move from 'Is' to 'Ought'. Hume stated that a fact cannot establish the truth of a normative proposition. To draw normative inferences from nature is to confuse fact and value. Thus, it denies the possibility of deriving an 'Ought' from 'Is'. The question is: is there any distinction between 'Is' and 'Ought'? Or 'Is' is 'Ought'.

To respond to this question, let us examine the nature of logic, reasoning and the 'ought'. Logic is a matter of construction. It has a premise, a middle term and a conclusion. Therefore, something is logical, if there is a necessary relationship between its premise, its middle term and its conclusion. However, since the premise and the middle term of a logical construction are assertions that precede the "logical" conclusion, and since it is a necessary relationship between the premise and the middle term which gives rise to a necessary conclusion, it follows that what is logical or illogical is a matter of mere assertions with its validity totally dependent on the consensus of those in discourse. A conclusion is deemed "logical" only because participants agree that the premise and the middle term (the

---

[176]. Hume, David. (1896), *A Treatise of Human Nature*. III, i.1.

[177]. Gewirth, Alan. (1982), *Human Rights: Essays on Justification and Applications*, Ch. 3.

[178]. Hogg, Peter. (1990), "On Being a Positivist: A Reply".

The Equigenic Principle

assertions) of a proposition have a necessary relationship. Where people disagree as to the premise of an argument or a proposition, they will not agree as to the "logic" of its conclusion. Internally, logic becomes a matter of consensus. Take the example of:

P_1 All cows have legs.
P_2 X is a cow.
_____

Therefore, X has legs.

The above proposition is logically valid, according to canons of logic. However, this is logically valid only because we agree that X is a cow and agree that all cows have legs. Once we dispute X's 'cowness' or the validity of the "all cows have legs", the 'logic' of the above construction disappears and the conclusion one gets becomes a matter of taste. In the same vein, if we agree on a nonsensical premise, and agree that there is a necessary relationship between the middle term and the premise, then the nonsensical conclusion follows and we have a logically sound construction, such as:

P_1 All cows have two heads.
P_2 X is a cow.
_____

Therefore, X has two heads.

The point of all this is that logic is not an Olympian point of reference dispensing validity. Logic, internally (as in the dictionary example) depends on the consensus of those in discourse. As such, it follows that the 'illogicality' or 'logicality' of a proposition is neither 'true' nor 'false', but agreeable or disagreeable. Agreement of course depends on one's experiences and desires, and as such is necessarily limited. There is no such thing as 'logic' which is independently meaningful in itself. As a matter of construction, 'logic' is never outside of cause and effect relationships, and as such is inseparable from the logician and the rest of the universe. Thus, to talk about logic or reason as if it were a being that sits

From Facts to Values

somewhere as a point of reference is to confuse the nature of human discourse.

Let us look for 'logic' or 'reason' and ask whether this sentence is valid! I am logic. I am reason. And if I am my experiences and my aspirations, then what is 'logical' or 'illogical' is simply a matter of my experiences and aspirations. When we agree that a certain proposition is 'logical' we do so only because we agree that the proposition in question is consistent with our experiences and goals. Where we differ in experience and in goals with regards to a certain proposition, its 'illogicality' or 'logicality' becomes a mere matter of taste. Thus, blanket statements such as: "It is fallacious to move from 'is' to 'ought'". Or, "one cannot derive an 'ought' from an 'is'", have nothing to do with 'logic' but are themselves fallacious, in so far as they betray an ignorance of the nature of human discourse. What are the premises of such propositions, are they empirically verifiable, or are they the necessary conclusions from human experience? If they are not, then who said that these propositions are valid?

The ultimate question in 'logic' is not whether something is logical or illogical, but the question is whether a certain proposition accords with one's experience and goals. All else is a waste of time. Now to the 'ought' propositions:

Knowledge of the 'is' + goal of the subject = the 'ought'.

The 'is', in any way one takes it, is never static. It is continually unfolding its potential. Or should we say, the potential is continually unfolding the 'is'. The 'is' of life includes the 'ought' of death and the 'is' of time includes the 'ought' of change. Of course, we and our fancies are included in time and life and are, therefore, subject to the is-ought continuum. In human discourse, the 'ought' follows the 'is' as a necessary relationship between relevant things. For example, the law with regards to motor vehicles is that vehicles coming from opposite directions ought not drive on the same side of the road. That is simply because we recognize that vehicles coming from opposite directions have

The Equigenic Principle

a certain relationship to each other. As a matter of our experience, we recognize that bodies which travel on the same line from opposite directions exhibit a potential for chaos, delays and accidents. Now the goal of our society is to avoid these things, so we rule that vehicles coming from opposite directions ought to drive on different sides of the road. This type of reasoning goes to the root of all normative propositions. All normative propositions are thus loaded heavily with the experience, the values and the goals of their proponents. In this sense then, so long as we have experiences and goals, we human beings cannot escape the normative. The 'is' is 'ought', but what 'ought' one derives from the 'is' depends on what relationship one recognizes and what goal one is trying to achieve. The supposed Is-Ought controversy is then a non-issue. It should not be analyzed in a vacuum, divorced from cause and effect relationships.

Finally, the naturalistic fallacy states that it is not possible to move from facts to values. Yet, it has already been demonstrated that by the use of the Equigenic Principle one can indeed easily move from facts to values because the Equigenic Principle rests on external consistency — checking one's statements with reference to the nature of Nature, of cause and effect. It is this which truly ought to be the Olympian point of reference. Besides, the naturalistic fallacy can also be refuted internally, since it too is a victim of the glasshouse syndrome. If it means that one cannot move from facts to values, then the statement: 'you cannot move from facts to values' must be a fact in order for it to have any functional value upon which to base an ethical value. If it is a fact, then let us take its advise and not make a value out of it. It seems then once again, the sceptic starts to chase down his own tail (Proposition 1). Thus, the so-called naturalistic fallacy is itself fallacious and inept, both internally and externally.

From Facts to Values

Is Democracy a Possible Alternative?

Democracy stands for the governmental institutionalization of enactments which express the actual will of those who are governed. It also carries with it, the concept of political equality. Everyone has an equal say as to how things have to be run. The underlying assumption here, is that democracy would allow the best to come up, that is the best possible consent so to speak. But, how is the quality of the so-called best possible consent to be measured? And how does a democratic system compare with the system based on the foundation of nature's laws as it has been discussed here in this book?

A democratic system has two major deficiencies which have been debunked in this chapter. The first is its conventional structure and the second is the way in which it is influenced by the people's desires and wishes. It perhaps requires no elaboration, that democracy and rationality are meaningless without each other. Indeed, choice without the rationality of evidence and logical consistency is a self-implosive construct. That is because, as has been illustrated earlier, when human conventional systems and rights go against the grain of the natural physical laws of the universe, they would end up disrupting the socio-ecological stability, thereby causing harm. Therefore, majority rule does not necessarily ensure that the so-called best choice is the optimal one — in particular, when the criteria for selection become the wishes and desires of the masses. In fact, such policies may indeed be a recipe for disaster, despite the fact that the whole nation is intoxicated by the illusion that they have achieved the ideal, enunciated by the phrase: "We have the freedom to choose," vacuously blurted out. William Penn who criticized the Western democratic system asserted that: "Let the People think they Govern and they will be

The Equigenic Principle

Governed."[179] Moshe Sober has this to say with regards to the Western style parliamentary elections: "Elections are mere multiple-choice exercises, allowing the voter to choose the entrenched party machine he least opposes."[180] Thus, it is exactly due to this faulty political system that those policies that are clearly counter to cause and effect relationships get passed into law and practised as 'rights'.

In reality, under the Western notions of democratic systems, where democracy is projected as being the highest system to have evolved, the supposed ideal of democracy itself — with all its above-mentioned deficiencies — is not even followed. In fact, in all of the so-called Western democratic states, which supposedly subscribe to such an 'ideal', there are entrenched elite classes that control both political and economic systems like parasites, in which policies that are truly beneficial and concurrent with natural laws, and rights are not followed for fear of going against their self-serving interests. However, since in these systems the most influential media itself is an invisible arm of the elite[181], it has induced the masses into believing that the democratic processes are not only the best and the only alternative, but that democracy is also being followed. Edward S. Herman and Noam Chomsky elaborate on this issue of elite control with respect to the media:

---

[179]. As quoted in Herman, Edward, S. (1992), *Beyond Hypocrisy*, p. 72.

[180]. Sober, Moshe. (1990), *Beyond the Jewish State: Confessions of a Former Zionist*, p. 33.

[181]. Herman, Edward S. and Chomsky, Noam. (1988), *Manufacturing Consent*.
Mander, Jerry. (1978), *Four Arguments for the Elimination of Television*, pp. 116-119.

From Facts to Values

> The elite domination of media and the marginalization of dissidents that results from the operation of these filters occurs so naturally that [even] media news people, frequently operating with complete integrity and goodwill are able to convince themselves that they choose and interpret the news "objectively" and on the basis of professional news values. Within the limits of the filter constraints they often are objective; the constraints are so powerful, and are built into the system in such a fundamental way, that alternative bases of news choices are hardly imaginable.[182]

On the issue of the 'freedom of expression', Chomsky states that:

> From a comparative perspective, the United States is unusual if not unique in its lack of restraints on freedom of expression. It is also unusual in the range and effectiveness of the methods employed to restrain freedom of thought. The two phenomena are related. Liberal democratic theorists have long observed that in a society where the voice of the people is heard, elite groups must ensure that that voice says the right things. The less the state is able to employ violence in defense of interests of elite groups that effectively dominate it, the more it becomes necessary to devise techniques of "manufacturing consent", in the words of

---

[182]. Herman, Edward S. and Chomsky, Noam. (1988), *Manufacturing Consent,* p. 2.

The Equigenic Principle

Walter Lippmann, over 60 years ago, or "engineering of consent",...[183]

These shortcomings of democracy and quasi-democracy can be easily realized by anyone not trapped by the system itself. Indeed, democracy, as such, is nothing but disguised hypocrisy. In contrast, those rights derived from the foundation of nature would facilitate optimal rights as they would not be subject to any of the above mentioned deficiencies or manipulations.

---

[183]. Chomsky, Noam. (1990), *Pirates & Emperors: International Terrorism in the Real World*, pp. 15-16.

From Facts to Values

Conclusion

All of the arguments that have been criticized in the second chapter have two things in common: they either they suffer from inherent contradictions, that is, they are either internally inconsistent, such as the self-referential arguments **(Prop. 1)** or they are externally inconsistent. This shows that inconsistency must be one of the major characteristics of falsehood. Consequently, if inconsistency is one of the characteristics of falsehood, then consistency must be one of the characteristics of the Truth. This point has also been consistently brought up in this presentation.

The arguments criticized in the third chapter are mostly theoretical **(Prop. 2)**. However, if by now, one still feels that the fundamental views presented in this book are not convincing, then the reader must show an inconsistency in the methodology used and defined at the outset. If no contradiction or flaw can be found in the methodology as well as in its application, then logically speaking, the conclusions must by necessity follow. One would, therefore, be led to the conclusion of the existence and implementation of equigenic rights as realizable ideals.

In a critique of any new views, proof or disproof of new concepts cannot be based on whether they are incongruent with the current so-called authoritative view. New discoveries cannot be discredited simply because a well-known figure held the opposite view. For example, if Aristotle, Spinoza or Jeremy Bentham had different views on natural rights, on what bases would any of their views falsify the view presented here? One can never disprove a theory by the usage of another theory; only a fact can disprove a theory, or a fact can disprove another claimed 'fact'. In this chapter, equigenic rights are claimed to be factual and not theoretical as has been endeavoured to illustrate. Hence, if, for example, one supports the classical notion of natural rights, then it must first be proven to be a fact, if the presentation in this book is measured against, for the express purpose of refutation. Moreover, if it is claimed, for instance, that Spinoza's notion of

The Equigenic Principle

natural rights is closer to the reality of this world, then the methodology used to establish such a claim must be first presented, examined and confirmed. The challenge is to offer a refutation by using facts and evidence, which if they are provided should gladly lead to abandonment of the position advocated in this book by its proponents in favour of the newly discovered facts. It must be remembered that consistency and non-contradiction, both external and internal are the key elements we have used to arrive at our conclusions upon the inspection of the greatest source of all — *the book of nature.*

In the last chapter, the foundation of absolute rights have been shown to be derived from nature. An obvious thought which comes to mind, however, is that so-called 'Mother Nature' is not in itself a conscious entity, thus, one could still pose the logical, legitimate and pertinent questions: What exactly is the real source of the originated laws and the natural rights derived from the Equigenic Principle? Does nature itself project the realization of rights onto the sense of man, if man is cognisant of the balances in the first place — the balances which are so intelligently structured in their equilibrating relations? What is undeniable is that all these rules and natural processes which lead to the dynamic balance, manifest a great deal of superior intelligence at work behind the scenes. The intelligence with which this entire universe appears to have been structured is so all-encompassing — in respect of the concordant functioning of the whole system — that it remains only logical and legitimate to question, as a corollary, whether the real and ultimate source of all absolute rights, as recognized by humans from the foundation of nature, could be the products of "Nature" or "Mother Nature". Such terms, in fact, stand for the personification of process, which is obviously an unconscious and imaginary entity. In contrast to this pedantic illogicality, does the omnipresent property of intelligence — that we can readily observe behind nature — emanate from an independent logic that was responsible for the origination of this universe of logical cause and effect interrelations? That is to say, could an entity encapsulating such logic, be the one who is the Author of equigenic rights?

In conclusion, if one utilizes the proposed criteria, it should pave way for clarity of thought, leading to the determination of the Truth. To discover the Truth — which is what Certainty stands for — requires an intellectual journey that each person has to make individually. One does not, however, have to return empty-handed. Indeed, truth is neither for one who does not strive earnestly, nor for the credulous who simply wants to 'believe'. It is for the objective questioner who strives to distinguish fact from fiction, the real from the illusory. If Reality is understood with Certainty, through the paramount measure of consistency, then it will naturally direct any questioner to understand further, the true nature of his or her role as a rational observer and participant within the reality of this universe. Yet, this journey cannot even begin if there is no element of concern from within, and one only exists to die without the Certainty.

Isaac Newton, as a renowned 'scientist', vigorously undertook this journey towards certainty. In his view of 'science', there was no exclusion of 'religion', and vice versa, in his view of 'religion', there was no exclusion of 'science'. Both pointed out to the same unavoidable conclusions. In his analysis of this vast universe, he regarded nature as the revelation of God and the study of it a form of worship. This is evinced by his description of the cosmos which alludes to the Creator: "This most beautiful system of the sun, planets, and comets, could only proceed from the counsel and dominion of an intelligent and powerful Being. And if the fixed stars are the centres of other like systems, these, being formed by the like wise counsel, must all be subject to the dominion of One... This Being governs all things, not as the soul of the world, but as Lord over all, ..."[184]. He categorically refuted

---

[184]. Newton, Isaac (1687). *Mathematical Principles of Natural Philosophy,* Vol. 2, Book III, Proposition XLII, General Scholium.

The Equigenic Principle

trinity and duality, concluding in pristine terms, that there is one and only one Singular Intelligence, who is the cosmic Originator of all that exists. This Originator is unique in real sense of the word. He alone is subject to worship by the whole of mankind.

> We are, therefore, to acknowledge one God, infinite, eternal, omnipresent, omniscient, omnipotent, the Creator of all things, most wise, most just, most good, most holy. We must love him, fear him, honour him, trust in him, pray to him, give him thanks, praise him, hallow his name, obey his commandments, and set times apart for his service,...[185]

Furthermore, Newton's concept of Originator did not carry any mystical baggages for he believed that by being in submission to this Creator, one must not ascribe to any intermediator.

> And these things we must do not to any mediators between Him and us, but to Him alone...[186]

In refutation of idolatry, atheism or 'godlessness', he says:

> Atheism is so senseless and odious to mankind that it never had so many professors. Can it be by accident that all birds, beasts, and men have their right side and left side alike shaped, (except in their

---

Also see: Thayer, H.S. (1953), *Newton's Philosophy of Nature: Selections from his Writings.*

[185]. A quotation from: *A Short Scheme of the True Religion,* as cited by Sir David Brewster, (1855), in *Memories of the Life, Writings, and Discourse of Sir Isaac Newton,* Vol. 2, p. 348.

[186]. Ibid., p. 348.

> bowels), and just two eyes and no more, on either side of the face, and just two ears on either side of the head, and a nose with two holes, and either two-fore legs, or two wings, or two arms on shoulders, and two legs on the hips and no more? Whence arises this uniformity in all their outward shapes but from the counsel of contrivance of an Author? ... Did blind chance know that there was light, and what was its refraction, and fit the eyes of all creatures, after the most curious manner, to make use of it? These and suchlike considerations, always have, and ever will prevail with mankind, to believe that there is a Being who made all things...[187]

The contemporary British scientist, Sir John Eccles, winner of the Noble prize for medicine in 1963, and American psychologist, Daniel Robinson, state: "We reject Darwinian, Freudian and Marxist explanations [of the totality of causal reality], for these as we have seen do not explain *any* notion, let alone ideas of transcendence. ... we, as noble and rational beings can give vent to the urgings of faith, not faith as the veil of ignorance, sloth, or fear, but faith as the state of mind vindicated by efforts of reason and common sense."[188]

The importance of the notion of Originator and its concomitant socio-political implications was also echoed by contemporary writer and politician, Vaclav Havel, in a speech given to an American audience:

> The first civilization to span the entire globe has a common destiny but something is missing. Man as an observer is becoming

---

[187]. Ibid., p. 347-348.

[188]. Eccles, John. & Robinson, D. N. (1985), *The Wonder of Being Human*, pp. 172-173.

The Equigenic Principle

> completely alienated from himself as a being [while] the crisis of transformation of science as the basis for the modern conception of the world [deepens]. Modern anthropocentrism has meant that the One who endowed man with his inalienable rights began to disappear from the world, to a place where public obligations no longer apply. The existence of a higher authority than man himself simply began to get in the way of [misguided and demented] human aspiration ... Politicians at international forums may reiterate a thousand times that the basis of a new world order must be universal respect for human rights. But this will mean nothing as long as this imperative does not derive from the miracle of Being ... Only someone who submits to the authority of the universal order and of creation can genuinely value himself and his neighbour and thus honour their rights ... Man can recognize liberty only if he does not forget the One who endowed him with it.[189]

If it is realized that there is indeed a system, in which there is no such separation and dichotomy between 'faith' and reason, 'science' and 'religion', then we will indeed be realize that "The highest wisdom has but one science — the science of explaining the whole creation and man's place in it", to

---

[189]. This speech was given at Independence Hall in Philadelphia, U.S.A, on July 4th, 1994. What is important to keep in mind is that submission to this One Creator has many implications, all of which ought to be observed in a consistent manner, not selectively where it suits one's interests. Submission is the translation of thoughts into actions, both being consistent with each other throughout.

From Facts to Values

quote Leo Tolstoy. If we utilize our reason, the greatest resource available to humankind, we should be able to discover a unified system in which no artificial distinctions are made, where knowledge is an integrated whole. The global reconstruction of society can only be realized once individuals start freely aligning themselves with this line of thinking. In order to purify our society and move towards the Certainty, we have to build a truly benefactory civilization based on cognisance of the Ultimate Reality — the singular Originator and Creator of the whole of existence.

Chapter Four

The 'New Humanism': Is It Really New?

The most successful tyranny is not the one that uses force to assure uniformity but the one that removes the awareness of other possibilities, the one that makes it seem inconceivable that other ways are viable, the one that removes the sense that there is an outside.

                                Allan Bloom

Consistency and the Concept of Revelation

This presentation has so far established a number of qualities to be the characteristics of the Absolute Truth with capital 'T'. In summary, the qualifications that are required from the 'new humanism' must be the following:

1) It must include a valid conception of Creator.

2) It must be an absolute, timeless, complete and unified system.

3) It must be a transcultural, transnational and universal world view.

4) It must involve reasoning, based on the full usage of the faculty of mind and not involve a leap of blind faith at any point.

5) Its message must be characterized by the notion of consistency: both internally and externally.

6) All of its laws must be based on cause and effect relationships, leading to and maintaining balance and optimality, encapsulated by the Equigenic Principle.

7) It must be a comprehensive package to include all spheres of life. There should be no artificial dichotomy between one sphere of knowledge and another.

Although most systems of thought claiming to be the Truth — particularly the purportedly holistic ideologies which encapsulate some notion of Creator(s) — do not employ most of the above criteria such as the methodology based on reason, evidence and consistency, and their associated concepts, it is thought by erroneous generalization, that *all* such doctrines do not employ reason as the foundational methodology. The assumption is that when it comes to the issues involving the notion of a Creator, it is all just a matter of personal faith. Although this description is well applicable to many such systems of thought, in an objective and comparative survey, it would be realized by an open investigation that it does not apply to all systems, as for example Islam. Islam is not a religion per se, like this 'ism' or that 'ism'. Islam is said to be the Absolute, immutable Truth with capital T. We have proven that Absolute Reality exists. Islam claims to be that Absolute Reality; therefore, one would follow it because it is the Absolute Reality. It becomes the Absolute Reality not because one has already chosen it to be so beforehand, but because of its omnidirectional proof-value. In other words, it has proven to be so by all the evidences. One must keep the distinction in mind that true Muslims do not claim that Islam is Absolute because it is their 'inherited or ancestral belief'. Their objective attitude is characterized and is uniquely distinguished by the Quranic attitude that if one were to show the Absolute other than Islam, then they will bow down to it, rather than to Islam, wholeheartedly.

The Quran claims to be a message from the Originator of the Big Bang and it possesses all the above mentioned characteristics. In the following section we shall scrutinize the veracity of this assertion.

Background Information

The word Quran, literally means a book to be read. The Quran is said to be a microcosm of the universe in form of paper and ink. It is regarded to be the direct and pristine communication from the single Originator, Creator, Sustainer and Cherisher of this universe to humankind. It is supposed to confirm that which is arrivable independently by the use of reason and sufficient information. The use of reason and evidence as the foundation of belief is an indication that Islam cannot be a dogmatic and authoritarian system as it is erroneously assumed. The laws mentioned in the Quran, which humans are supposed to follow, should lead to the optimality of sociological, political and ecological equilibrium as dictated by the use of reason. The Quranic rules of conduct are not arbitrary, but rather are wholly objective. For example, in Islam the consumption of alcohol is forbidden for humankind simply because it is sociologically and biologically harmful for humankind.[190] This is a proposition which is easily verifiable. The Quran states that in alcohol there is more harm than benefit — therefore, it clearly states that one must not even go near it. On the other hand, things such as fasting, daily prayer are required from mankind, because they are beneficial for mankind. Similarly, all laws in Islam, whether they deal with ecology or sociology are based on stimulus and response,[191] action and reaction, and cause and effect relationships.[192] In a holistic belief system there is no room for mythologies. It is precisely because of the abysmal track record of many dogmatic belief systems which are so replete with contradictions, that most people would assume that 'science' and all 'religions' except atheism are in conflict.

However, as it was indicated before there are various concepts of God, many of which are irrational and unsubstantiable. The Quranic description of God, not only is free from all erroneous notions, but also is in agreement with discovered facts. It is something which is more likely to appeal to the scientific mind than to a scholastic theologian. Allah, is described as the Singular Originator of this universe, the Creator of matter and energy, the *First Cause*, the *Uncaused cause*, the *Immovable Mover* — the Creator who is not subject to gender, plurality, culture and personification. Here are just a few verses which highlight these points:

---

[190]. *Special Report to the Congress on Alcohol and Health* (1981).
Oakley, Ray & Charles Ksir. (1993), *Drugs, Society and Human Behaviour*, Chs. 9 & 10.

[191]. Innate, not conditioned.

[192]. (Quran 7:157).

> *Say: Allah is the One God, God the Eternal, the Uncaused Cause of all beings. He[193] begets not, and neither is He begotten; and there is nothing that could be compared to Him.*[194]

Furthermore, the Quranic concept is universal and culture free:

> *All praise belongs to one God alone, the Cherisher and Sustainer of all worlds.*[195]

Simplicity, rationality, practicality and comprehensiveness are the main characteristics of Islamic laws. Unlike secular laws, Islamic laws are not based on arbitrary human, social or theological conventions. They are based on the physical reality of cause and effect relationships and are prescribed by none other than the Originator. The Quran explicitly states:

> *We[196] made for you a law, so follow it, and not the fancies of those who have no knowledge.*[197]

---

[193]. The quality of gender does not apply to this Intelligence (Allah). However, due to the limitations of the English language, for the purpose of communication, the masculine pronoun is used.

[194]. (Quran Ch: 112)

[195]. (Quran 1:2)

[196]. In the Quran, the word "We" is used to refer to the Originator of this universe in the grammatical first person. This usage is one of respect; no plurality is implied. Islam is purely monotheistic.

[197]. (Quran 45:18)

The New Humanism

> *Direct your face towards the proper belief for that is the nature created by God with which God has created humankind. There is no alteration in the creation of God; this is the right belief, yet most people do not know of it.[198]*

Convergence Between the Quran and the Equigenic Principle

Philosopher John Locke, like Newton believed in unitarianism as opposed to trinitrianism. He held that: "He that takes away reason to make way for revelation puts out the light of both, and does much the same as if he would persuade a man to put out his eyes the better to receive the remote light of an invisible star by a telescope." The methodology of reason is the common ground of both the Quran and the Equigenic Principle. In fact, as discussed earlier, both the Quran and the Equigenic Principle entirely correspond with each other. Precisely defined both the Quranic laws and the Equigenic Principle refer to the use of nature as the foundation of values realized when human beings, using reason (properly interconnecting things), recognize the balance in nature. The values realized as belonging and applied to any component of nature, are those which would help maintain the balance, or, without which, disequilibrium would necessarily ensue. Recognizing the balance entails recognizing the way things in the universe have been designed in terms of their structure and function and ultimately realizing the ultimate origins of the components including the universe as a whole. Recognizing the designs that facilitate the balance means simultaneously recognizing the extent and mode by which things ought to be used, or ought simply to be left alone as they naturally are. The Quranic laws which coincide in parallel with the Equigenic Principle are applicable to all the affairs of mankind, since man is an integral part of nature. As

---

[198]. (Quran 30:30)

such, the Quranic principles based on the Equigenic Principle are unifying principles by which human society ought to be structured and by which all animal societies are already naturally structured, in order to achieve the balance, which is the basis of all values leading to justice and concomitantly, the basis of peace. Since the Equigenic Principle is based on the absolute nature of cause and effect in the reality of this universe, it is not a relative, man-made principle but an absolute one, and, since it is based on the nature of the universe, it is the absolute foundation of values — the 'principal principle'.

In fact, any thought and related behavioural structure arrived at independently by observing one's surroundings which satisfies the seven criteria mentioned above would logically be coincident with both the Equigenic Principle and Islam. However, does the Quran meet the required standards of the Absolute Truth? Let us measure it with the seven established fundamental criteria mentioned above.

1) In a holistic belief system there is no room for mythologies. It is precisely because of the abysmal track record of many dogmatic belief systems which are so replete with contradictions, that most people would assume that 'science' and all 'religions' except atheism are in conflict. However, as it was indicated before there are various concepts of God, many of which are irrational and unsubstantiable. The Quranic description of God, not only is free from all erroneous notions, but also is in agreement with discovered facts. It is something which is more likely to appeal to the scientific mind than to a scholastic theologian. Allah, is described as the Singular Originator of this universe, the Creator of matter and energy, the *First Cause*, the *Uncaused cause*, the *Immovable Mover* — the Creator who is not subject to gender, plurality, culture and personification.

The New Humanism

> *Say: Allah is One, Allah is the Eternal and the Uncaused Cause of all being. He[199] begets not, and neither is He begotten; and there is nothing that could be compared to Him.[200]*

Furthermore, the Quranic concept is universal and culture free:

> *All praise belongs to Allah alone, the Cherisher and Sustainer of all worlds.[201]*

2) The Quranic message presents itself as the Absolute Truth.

> *This is the book which is free of doubt and involution — a guidance for all those who are actually cognisant of the Creator ...[202]*

> *This is the book whose verses are indeclinable and distinct, which comes from the One who is most wise and all-knowing, so that you may worship none but Allah.[203]*

3) This world view must be transcultural, transnational and universal.

> *Say: "We believe in God, and in that which has been revealed to us, and in that which has been revealed to Abraham, Ishmael,*

---

[199]. The quality of gender does not apply to this Intelligence (Allah). However, due to the limitations of the English language, for the purpose of communication, the masculine pronoun is used.

[200]. (Quran Ch: 112)

[201]. (Quran 1:2)

[202]. (Quran 2:2)

[203]. (Quran 11:1,2)

> Isaac, Jacob and their descendants, and that which has been given to Moses and Jesus and that which has been vouchsafed to all the [other] prophets by their Sustainer: we make no distinction between any of them. And it is unto Him that we submit ourselves."[204]
>
> O Humankind! Indeed, We have created you out of a male and a female, and have made you into nations and tribes, so that you might come to know one another. Assuredly, the noblest of you in the sight of God is the one who is the most conscious of Him. Surely, God is all-knowing, all-aware.[205]
>
> Verily, this community of yours is a single community, and I am the Sustainer of you all; therefore, worship Me alone[206]

4) The views in the Quran are contrary to personal or unquestioned faith. Islam has no doctrines that are contrary to reason. For example, it does not require one to believe in illogical doctrines such as the Trinitarian concept of 1+1+1=1. It represents an unadulterated rational way of examining things, a world view which completely rests on the foundation of reason alone, and is in consonance with the results of free inquiry, without any conflict or contradiction. It specifically requires that one examine things carefully, using one's mind constantly and incessantly. One is not required to retreat to an isolated cave in the mountains to chant some mantras, or meditate for fifteen years on the sound of one

---

[204]. (Quran 2:136)

[205]. (Quran 49:13)

[206]. (Quran 21:92)

The New Humanism

hand clapping. Instead, the Quran emphatically demands the usage of the mind:

> Do you bid other people to be pious, while you forget your own selves — and yet you recite the divine writ? Will you not, then, use your reason?[207]
>
> In the origination and design of the universe, and in the alternating succession of night and day, evidence indeed exists for those who use their minds, who remember their Creator, while standing, sitting and reclining on their sides, and contemplate on the creation of the universe, exclaiming: "Our Sustainer! You have not created all this without a meaningful purpose. Glory be to You!"[208]
>
> Behold! It is God who enjoins justice, doing good, forbidding all that is shameful and runs counter to reason, as well as envy. He exhorts you repeatedly, so that you might bear all this in mind.[209]
>
> Verily, the vilest of all creatures in the sight of God are those who choose to be deaf, dumb and those who do not use their reason.[210]
>
> Have they not pondered on the Quran? If it were from other than the Singular God, surely they would find many inconsistencies and contradictions in it.[211]

---

[207]. (Quran 2:44)

[208]. (Quran 3: 190,191)

[209]. (Quran 16:90)

[210]. (Quran 8:22)

[211]. (Quran 4:82)

From Facts to Values

> *Do not follow that of which you have no knowledge. Assuredly, you will be held accountable for all your hearing, seeing, and thinking.*[212]
>
> *Say: Produce, then another revelation from God which would offer better guidance than either of these two*[213] *- and I shall follow it, if you speak the truth.*[214]
>
> *Anyone who worships a deity beside the One God, without proof, will be held accountable for such worship.*[215]
>
> *They will say: If only we had listened or used reason, we would not have ended up as inmates in this awful place of suffering.*[216]

These few verses amplify the strong usage of reasoning, questioning, researching, testing by consistency, building on evidences and acquiring knowledge as a means towards attaining Certainty. Prophet Muhammed himself is recorded to have said that: "God has not created anything better than Reason, or anything more perfect, or more beautiful than Reason, the benefits which God gives are on its accounts, and understanding is by it, and God's wrath is caused by disregard of it."

5) On the issue of consistency, for example, in the Quran, 1,400 years ago, we are informed that the universe originated

---

[212]. (Quran 17:36)

[213]. Referring to the original revelation to Prophet Moses and the Quran.

[214]. (Quran 28:49)

[215]. (Quran 23:17), Also see: (31:15) & (18:5)

[216]. (Quran 67:10)

with the 'Big Bang', it is expanding, that the nebular early universe coalesced from gaseous and dust particles and that even the sun follows an orbital path around our galaxy.

> *Have those who deny the truth not seen that the earth and the rest of the universe were joined together in one piece; then We ripped them apart? And that We made every living thing from water? Will they then not believe?*[217]
>
> *We have built this universe with a force; We are most certainly expanding it.*[218]
>
> *Moreover, He turned to the universe when it was smoke and said to it and to the earth: Come (together) voluntarily or involuntarily.*[219]
>
> *... It is He who has created the night, the day, the sun and the moon; each travelling in an orbit.*[220]

In fact, the Quran is full of well established scientific facts on a variety of subjects, many of which describe the natural world with an incredible degree of accuracy only recently discovered.[221] The Quran also claims to be free from any

---

[217]. (Quran 21:30)

[218]. (Quran 51:47)

[219]. (Quran 41:11)

[220]. (Quran 21:33)

[221]. Wadud, Sayed Abdul. (1971), *Phenomena of Nature and the Quran*.
Bucaille, Maurice. (1979), *The Quran, the Bible and Science*.
Rahman, Afzalur. (1981), *Quranic Sciences*.
Moore, Keith L. (1982), *The Developing Human*.

internal and external inconsistencies, a claim which is open to challenge. Indeed, the Quran invites and encourages its readers to take up this challenge.

> *Have they not pondered on the Quran? If it were from other than the Singular God, surely they would find many inconsistencies and contradictions in it.* [222]

6) All laws in the Quran, whether they deal with ecology or sociology exist to maintain the socio-ecological balance.[223]

> *It is God who has raised up the universe and established the balance, in order that you might not transgress it. Institute the just balance, and do not fall short of it.* [224]
>
> *Behold! Everything that We have created is in due measure and proportion.* [225]
>
> *... the earth! We have spread it out and set on it stabilizing mountains, sprouting from it, all kinds of things in due balance.* [226]

7) When an integrated methodology based on global consistency is realized and employed, then 'Physics' and what

---

Bucaille, Maurice. (1983), *What is the Origin of Man? The Answers of Science and the Holy Scriptures.*

Nurbaki, Haluk. (1989), *Verses From the Glorious Koran and the Facts of Science.*

[222]. (Quran 4:82)

[223]. Masri, B.A. and Haque, Nadeem. (1995), *Nature in Islam: The Concern for Ecological Balance.*

[224]. (Quran 55:7-9)

[225]. (Quran 54:49)

[226]. (Quran 15:19)

The New Humanism

is usually called 'Metaphysics' can never be separated and polarized. Yet, it must be mentioned that only a system of thought which employs the very methodology mentioned in this book, brings about the unicity between 'Physics' and 'Metaphysics'. In such a system there is no dichotomy between 'science' and 'religion' in the sense of an unintegrated world view. Both must tell us the same thing and point us to the same direction. Unlike most other 'belief systems', in Islam, there is no artificial dichotomy between interrelated things such as between Church and State, between 'scientific knowledge' and 'religious knowledge'. There is not even any distinction made between the 'sacred' and the 'profane'. For a Muslim, every act in life, no matter how trivial it may seem, is considered 'sacred'. Islam is, in fact, a comprehensive system which incorporates within its fold all facets of life from A to Z in everyday individual behaviour, collective management and future planning. For example, it incorporates dress, greetings, rules of hospitality, table manners, diet, personal hygiene, sexual relations in marriage, business ethics, settlements of dispute, taxation, justice and punishment, the educational system, the economic system, the financial and banking system, the political system, the legal system, the treatment of nature, care of domestic animals and livestock, family relationships, rules of marriage and divorce, inheritance, funeral procedures, etc.

From Facts to Values

Islam: The Misrepresented 'New Humanism'

The most pertinent question at this stage is: If the Truth of Islam as the 'new humanism' is so clear, why do so many people fail to identify and accept it? There are two reasons for this reluctance. Islam has no substantiative problems; on the contrary, its substance firmly revolves around the orbit of commonsense. The perceived problems with Islam have never been with its doctrine, but with its associated image. Its negative image is generated by both internal and external factors.

First, let us discuss the internal factors. The major stumbling block towards the realization of this 'New Humanism' is the psychological blocking mechanisms which have been impeding humanity to see the interconnections that reveal the nexus between the ordered design of nature and its Originator on the one hand, and that value system which arises from and is based upon this order. This value system, or in actuality Islam, is not favoured by many, because Islam is directly against an attachment to the pleasure principle at the expense of the avoidance of reality. These blocking mechanisms basically operate through undisciplined desires. However, human desires could fall under the category of being either useful motivational factors or destructive forces, created by disregarding the limits and the required contexts. Human desires are inextricably influenced by our cognitive processes and vice versa. Human cognition is also very much influenced by desires. Therefore, unwanted facts, despite their clarity are often suppressed or ignored by desires. For example, for a corporate polluter, it may be very difficult to accept the Equigenic Principle let alone the Quran — which espouses it. This is because the polluter's vested interests, such as the income earned from such activities, are 'threatened'. What is basically happening in such a situation is that the person refuses to submit to the Creator and flow with the process of the balance in nature. On the contrary, the individual chooses to submit to desires for transient things which tends to narrow the scope or the universe in which that individual exists. In order to operate in this manner, the thought and concomitant behavioural structure of that individual must be contorted to be inconcordant with reality and concordant with an illusory construct. In other words, such an individual will develop a 'belief system' that is far from consistent with the nature of this universe of cause and effect. Indeed, any information which seeks to shatter this 'belief structure' will be blocked in various ways, or, if even allowed to enter into the cognitive structure, will be filtered in such a way that it is dissimulated into insignificance. It is, therefore, not surprising to see that in most societies on earth, at the present time, which are, in one form or another, operating on relativism and the pleasure principle, should be in dogmatic opposition to a belief system such as Islam which fosters the Equigenic Principle.

The *second factor* is an external one, and is due to a hidden conspiracy. It is a deliberate distortion of this 'New Humanism' by the elite through the 'straw man fallacy' — one of the major strategies applied to discredit a formidably strong opponent. Through these strategies, distorted images become the reality for uninformed individuals and thus abound. For example, one is certainly not hardpressed these days to find misconceptions and inaccuracies about Islam. Such misconceptions usually appear in the form of some news article about how a certain 'Islamic' state oppressing its citizens by denying them certain fundamental rights. If one were to form an image of Islam merely by the information that these articles present, it would surely be distasteful and misleading. For example, Muslims are continuously portrayed as being irrational, retrogressive, suppressive to women, barbaric, intolerant, terrorists, and above all brutally violent. However, could Islam, which literally means peace be responsible for the rise of violence and terrorism? Or could it be that Islam has come to be largely misrepresented, not only by various prejudiced commentators in the media, but also by many of its claimed adherents?

From Facts to Values

That the second factor is an obvious conspiracy can be seen from the conspicuous way in which the Western media refers to Islam, but not to other religions and groups. For example, they never refer to the IRA terrorists as Christian terrorists, despite the fact they consider themselves Catholic. Nor do they ever refer to armed Jewish settlers, or members of Jewish militia groups like Kach, Hashmona'im and the Gideon's Sword, who attack and shoot at women and children in the occupied territories as Jewish terrorists.[227] Of course, needles to say, the concept of Jewish or Christian terrorists is an imaginary concept with no biblical basis. However, when it comes to Islam, this simple logic is often abandoned. Islam is continuously presented as a modern day monstrous bogeyman. In the headlines, we constantly see the oxymoronic concepts such as 'Muslim terrorists', 'militant Muslims', 'Muslim fundamentalists' and so on, who are always ready to assault Westerners.[228] All to the contrary, since Islam is very confident of its logical precepts, it is, therefore, most tolerant of non-Islamic ideologies and their adherents. Islam sees itself as an ethical ideal, rather than as a repressive and coercive system. The Quran emphatically states that:

> *There is no coercion in matters of belief. The right way is, henceforth, distinct from error. He who rejects the powers of evil and believes in the Originator has indeed grasped a firm handhold which will never break. God is All-hearing, All-knowing.*[229]

---

[227]. See the U.S. Department of State report on 'Patterns of Global Terrorism: 1992', p. 24.

[228]. Said, Edward W. (1981), *Covering Islam: How the media and the experts determine how we see the rest of the world,* Ch. 1.

[229]. (Quran 2:256)

The New Humanism

However, while individual freedom is very much respected under the Islamic law,[230] it does not condone systems or modes of conduct that may cause and spread harm to the global family. The Islamic position of zero tolerance is not based on dogmatic authoritarianism, but on the consideration of the harm a particular action may cause. Opposition is exercised by exposing the abusive system and peacefully taking away its opportunity to gain momentum.

Why then do the upper echelons in the media falsely portray Islam in a harsh manner? The simple reason is that it is due to the blatant fact that Islam poses a deadly threat to the existing oligarchical structure of most societies. For assuredly:

If Islam arises, it would neither allow nor tolerate any system which would continuously pile-up a massive amount of arms and arsenal for its own profit and protection, while leaving its own grandmothers and grandfathers, begging homelessly on decrepit streets.

If Islam arises, it would neither allow nor tolerate any banking system that would callously and unjustly force a dispossession of one's property, because of missed mortgage payments.

If Islam arises, it would neither allow nor tolerate any economic system which makes a huge profit by the degradation and destruction of the environment in various ways.

If Islam arises, it would neither allow nor tolerate the present unjust socio-economic set-up that sustains the current unfair system of distribution of wealth and resources.

---

[230]. For more details see the *Universal Islamic Declaration of Human Rights* (1981). The 23 Articles in this charter of rights are based on the Quran and example of the Prophet.

From Facts to Values

If Islam arises, it would neither allow nor tolerate any move towards a control of the world economies and political systems by a cabal of power-hungry elites.

If Islam arises, it would neither allow nor tolerate a colossal alcohol industry that, like a vampire, drains the life-blood by providing a habituative obnoxious fluid to society at the expense of the predominant health, family and social complications.

If Islam arises, it would neither allow nor tolerate an industry which strips women off their clothes and dignity, and perpetuates promiscuity and immorality in society in order to inflate the wallets of executive pimps.

If Islam arises, it would neither allow nor tolerate a multi-billion dollar cosmetic and fashion industry, which replaces the intrinsic values of women with instrumental values, since its lifeline depends upon spreading illusory images to brainwash women to market themselves for men.

If Islam arises, it would neither allow nor tolerate an educational system which produces regurgitative automatonic relativists, who conform to machine-like systems and are blind to all of the above problems from cradle to grave.

Therefore, it would indeed be an exceedingly naive presumption that anything good will ever be said about Islam by the media which is indeed only an octopus-like arm of the elites and their psychophantic cohorts. We will always hear about pseudo-intellectual puppets like the Salman Rushdies and the Nasreens, who have the audacity to dubiously distort Islam by spurious misrepresentations in order to prevent the public from identifying this 'New Humanism'.

Allan Bloom points out that the most coercive form of tyranny is not that of the Eastern Block style, "but the one that removes the awareness of other possibilities, [the one] that makes it seem inconceivable that other ways are viable, [the one] that removes the sense that there is an outside."[231] It is indeed the dynamics of the cumulative actions of the arrogant and corrupt elitists with a common avaricious world view which avoids reconciliation with their Creator that has prevented the public identifying Islam as the 'New Humanism' — a wholesome way of life based on the wholly rational precepts of the Equigenic Principle. There is, in fact, a retrogressive dialectic between the elite and the non-elite and the latter cannot be exonerated, by any means, for being swayed by the elite into not aligning themselves with the realization of these wholesome precepts. This is exactly what has led to the quagmire described in the first chapter, which ultimately leads to the decay of society. Indeed, the rate of the downfall of a disintegrating society is directly proportional to its arrogant resistance against the realization of such a globally rational scheme.

On the other hand, the idiotic behaviour of a great many of the so-called Muslims has also contributed to the creation of this distorted image. Thus, Islam has been suffering from the malfeasance of the actions of those who purport to be following it, but who contradict its very teachings in principle. This is poignantly captured in George Bernard Shaw's astute remark to the effect that, although Islam was the most beautiful thing he had come across, the so-called Muslim as a persona was the ugliest. In another occasion, he referred to Islam as a beautiful garden and the so-called Muslims like a wall blocking the attractive view inside. Yet, the media always selectively publicizes the irrational behaviour of nominal Muslims as being Islamic in essence, thereby misleading the non-Muslims in the process.

Due to the media misrepresentation, a common mistaken assumption is often made in the minds of Westerners and others, that whatever is fomenting in some of the Middle

---

[231]. Bloom, Allan. (1987), *The Closing of the American Mind,* p. 249.

From Facts to Values

Eastern countries is based on Islamic law. However, it needs to be clearly divulged that there is absolutely no relationship, whatsoever, between Islam and the Middle East. On the contrary, in some of these so-called Islamic states, it is almost illegal to be a Muslim. The best Muslims in this region are in prison if they have not already been tortured to death. Such countries that do not follow the basic principles of Islam, either pretend to be doing so, or apply some minor aspect of Islam only for political expediency. In some of these states there is an appearance of Islam only at the superficial level. However, because these states contradict the Quran at the foundational level, they cannot be Islamic states as envisioned by the Quran.

The thoughts and actions of one who claims to be a Muslim, must be totally consistent with the Quran and Muhammed's pattern of behaviour, which was in complete conformity with the Quran and the Equigenic Principle. If an individual's behaviour violates the Islamic principles, he cannot be called a Muslim, even though he comes from the Middle East, may have an Arabic name, sports a long beard and has been consuming Falafel all his life.

Any state which claims to be an Islamic State, has to follow Islam in its entirety, not selectively. If this does not happen, grave internal inconsistencies in that state's policies will arise, and that system, which appears to be ideal in writing, will fall abysmally short in practice. Subsequently, all their social, political, educational, environmental and economic plans will naturally be inadequate to solve the problems at the root levels, leading to structural and functional injustices. In fact, a closer examination of the external and internal policies based on their constitutions, reveals that these policies are not only oppressive, but also are contrary to the very basic Islamic principles. Take the example Saudi Arabia, a quasi-Islamic state in which an elite ruling class holds sway — a place where even the country is named after its asinine rulers, something which is the exact opposite of the Quranic model of what a society should be. Or

The New Humanism

take the example of Iran, a country which is being run by a motley bunch of ruthless moronic clergymen who adorn flowing garbs, while according to the Quran, priesthood is forbidden.[232] The situation in these countries is no different than that of Medieval Europe during the dark ages, where authoritarianism and oppression were disguised in the name of God and religion. Such examples would remind us that we should always examine whether actions and beliefs are in parallel with each other, or whether they are distinctively separate? In the event that they are truly unparallel, we must not blame the belief system for the shortcomings, when it comes to wrong practices.

To liberate the convoluted understanding of Islam, the belief system founded on the Equigenic Principle, from the political violence of the Middle East and other similar environments, it is most imperative to investigate the genesis of political turmoil. One of the root causes of such turbulence, is the absence of the freedom of thought. The very absence of such conducive environments in the Middle East and other such regions, is the underlying causative factor for the emergence of political violence. However, the unbridled violence in those regions does not have any bearing at all with the tenets of Islam. In fact, Islam is often perceived to be antithetical to democracy, and therefore, at the root of the violence. However, Islam has no reason to fear democracy, nor has the rational aspect of democracy any reason to fear Islam, for Islam actually fosters it, among its adherents.

> *The believers are those whose affairs are guided by mutual consultation.*[233]

The Islamic notion of democracy as the reader would know by now, however, entails freedom of choice based on rationality, as opposed to the mere whims of the majority. It foundationally incorporates the consideration of that which is

---

[232]. (Quran 57:27, 9:31, 9:34)

[233]. (Quran 42:38)

optimal for the totality of life — both human and nonhuman. However, when the best is not sought, optimality is unobtainable, and injustice permeates into every single facet of life, the end result being violence. Therefore, while on the surface, it appears that the cause of conflict in regions such as the Middle East, Northern Ireland and the Punjab is rooted in religious fundamentalism, in South Africa based on tribalism and racism, and in the Balkans arising from ethnic nationalism, the reality is that, deeper causes lurk behind the causes of the immediate conflicts. These turmoils are due to a network of branchlike causes. For example, whenever people are systematically subjugated, their rights violated and their cries ignored, then the conditions that are created by the oppressors are ripe for an escalation in violence, resulting in the rise of nationalism or racism. Yet, even under this scenario, when socio-political obligations are obliterated and oppression and injustice become rampant, Muslims are not without guidance. It is only in such an atmosphere that the Quranic injunction concerning fighting and war should be understood.

> *Killing even a single person unrightfully is as though one has killed the whole of humanity, unless it be punishment for murder or for spreading corruption on earth; while to save even a single person is as though one has saved the whole of humanity.*[234]
>
> *Never let hatred towards anyone lead you to the error of deviating from the path of justice. Be just: this is closest to being God-conscious.*[235]

---

[234]. (Quran 5:32)

[235]. (Quran 5:8)

The New Humanism

> *Do not allow your hatred of people incite you to aggression.*[236]

This Islamic concept of war, is far more humane and democratic than that of Mr. Bush and his Allies, who annihilated an entire modern state, turning it into a premodern one, by indiscriminately obliterating innocent civilians and intentionally destroying life sustaining infrastructures and the environment. This whole disastrous episode was facilitated under the supportive auspices of a public deemed to be civilized. In Islam, however, war can only be fought for defensive purposes, or for the alleviation of oppression, where the only combatants involved are the military — not the civilians, nonhuman inhabitants and their habitats.

The drive for justice in Islam is based on a peaceful approach, meant to educate both the governors and the governed. There is a famous saying of Prophet Muhammed: "The ink of a scholar is more precious than the blood of a martyr". We have a prime example of this in Sayyed Qutb of Egypt. Qutb was a Muslim intellectual, a prolific writer of numerous books on Islam dealing with social justice, democracy and peace — all in dialogue with the modern age.[237] Yet in 1966, after a long imprisonment, Sayyed Qutb was hanged like a common criminal, by the then Soviet and Western backed Egyptian dictator — Jamal Abdul Nasser. With Qutb, the cream of the Muslim intellectuals that had grown and prospered was effaced. The Muslim Brotherhood movement in Egypt, of which he was a part, had flourished until the Egyptian army seized power in 1953. The army helped transform Egypt into a dictatorial state which it has remained up to the present time. However, the methodology

---

[236]. (Quran 5:3)

[237]. Qutb, Sayed. (1977), *Islam and Universal Peace.*
Qutb, Sayed. (1979), *In the Shade of the Quran.*
Qutb, Sayed. (1993), *Milestones.*

of peace (Islam), which involves intellection, is still alive and well today as the outcome of recent democratic elections under the current oppressive regime in Algeria and Turkey vividly attest.

By looking into the genesis of violence it must not be ignored that those undemocratic countries which hold sway over the Muslim masses, had once been and are still often set-up, backed and supported by the democracy and human rights loving Western governments and the social justice loving former Soviet Union. The populace strongly needs to be reminded, that the tragical victims of these undemocratic governments have always included Quranic intellectuals who have been the main driving force towards a holistically productive growth for society.

Many people are unaware of the indisputable historical fact that Islam, through the Quranic methodology, based on rationality, fostered the emergence of modern science and technology from the Dark Ages, by appraising and preserving thought heritages, mainly of the Greeks and others, and creatively adding its own unique contributions. This gave rise to periods in Europe such as the Renaissance and the Enlightenment. In fact, science progressed because of Islam, rather than in spite of it. Historian Thomas Goldstein, states: "Every single specialized science in the West owes it origins to the Islamic impulse — or at least its direction from that time onwards."[238]

It is even fitting to identify Islam with the 'New Humanism', especially when one ponders the early use of the word humanist. In the thirteenth century (A.C.) those who were reacting against severely authoritarian and dictatorial policies of the Church in Europe — which did not allow the expression of free thought that went against mystical doctrines — rebelled against the unjust practices of the

---

[238]. Goldstein, Thomas. (1980), *Dawn of Modern Science: From the Arabs to Leonardo da Vinci,* p. 99.

The New Humanism

Church and followed the Muslim Philosopher, namely, Ibn Rushd (Averroes) who had lived in Spain about a century earlier. They called themselves the Averroeists. Ibn Rushd believed that things occurred by cause and effect, by laws which the Creator had set in motion. Now if this was true, then certain practices of the Church, such as transubstantiation in the Eucharist, where the consecrated wine is supposed to transmute into the blood of Christ, was charged by these Averroists to be an utter impossibility. In arguing this, they were in effect, challenging the foundation upon which the Church rested. These Averroists used the term 'Humanist' for their philosophical movement. However, Humanism later on came to be identified with atheism, since a great many of those who considered themselves rationalists, reacted against the mystical conception of God as expounded by Christianity, but then failed to see the genuine Islam due to the straw-man falsities perpetrated by the Orientalists.

It would be utterly ludicrous, in light of all this historical and direct Quranic evidence, to refer to a belief system which reformed pre-Islamic society steeped in the gutter of superstition and debauchery, into a society elevated by the highest standards of moral and intellectual conduct, as being dogmatic, irrational and retrograde. Assuredly, a system that risks losing its followers by fundamentally basing its claims on mind and rationality cannot be called dogmatic.[239]

Islam considers itself as a timeless, transcultural, transnational and universal message, not the religion of the Arabs. This is because the primary source of Islam is the universe itself. The design in the universe which points to an intelligence is an open vista for investigation by anyone. It is possible, in fact, for a person to be a Muslim, by having the

---

[239]. See (Quran: 28:49) and (17:36).

essential belief in a Singular Creator, and yet never have actually heard of the Quran or the word Islam[240].

Epilogue

In this age of conflict and chaos, a vision of tolerance and accurate representation of Islam and all other belief systems is required, so that they can be judged on their actual merits. Indeed, an emergence and reinforcement of a critical media consciousness, where there is a realization of the possible misconceptions, is vital, if we are to foster anything which is capable of guiding rational human achievement. In this connection, an evidential analysis of Islam, would be useful for unfolding its latent potentialities. What is needed is the emergence or reinforcement of a media consciousness where there is a realization of possible misrepresentations. If those who write for the media attack a pseudo-version of 'Islam' — which has nothing to do with Islam itself, but more to do with local culture or the agenda of some political groups merely using Islam as a facade — then an immeasurably harmful disfavour is being committed to the whole of humanity because of the gross violation and identification of the Equigenic Principle upon which Islam is founded. On the contrary, an evidential analysis of Quran would be crucial not only for geopolitical awareness, but also for examining the potentiality of Islam as a rationally based moral force capable of solving our mounting multifarious socio-environmental problems. This wider concern for the global community is something that no thinking individual should ignore any longer. It is only with this understanding and clear vision that can the whole of humanity be led towards a healthy global society — healthy in the true sense of the word. The mental health, for instance, that would be generated is so extensive and comprehensive, so sublime and beautiful, so happy and contented that it permeates every facet of human existence,

---

[240]. See (Quran: 2:62) and (28: 52,53).

The New Humanism

affecting the individual both internally and externally, and then collectively transforming the whole of human society.

Just prior to his assassination, Malcolm X, the social justice activist, in the midst of American racial crisis pristinely recognized one of the many benefits of this 'new humanism'. He said:

> America needs to understand Islam, because this the one religion that erases from its society the race problem... I have never before seen *sincere* and *true* brotherhood practised by all colors together, irrespective of their color.[241]

American mathematician and Muslim educator, Jeffrey Lang remarks on universality of the Islamic egalitarian principle, needed to fight the ills of the entire society:

> For Muslims, the community of believers is the place where Islam's equalitarian principles are to be implemented in practice, where those committed to its worldview are to participate — through faith, government, and law — in translating them into a socio-political order. But Islam's concern is not exclusively with its adherents, for it is meant for all mankind. It is important to observe that when the Quran enjoins charity for the poor, just dealings, caring for orphans, defending the oppressed, freeing slaves, and helping the wayfarer, no mention is made of the sufferers' religion.[242]

---

[241]. Haley, Alex. (1989), *The Autobiography of Malcolm X*, p. 340.

[242]. Lang, Jeffrey. (1994), *Struggling to Surrender*, p. 132.

From Facts to Values

James Baldwin, another American social justice activist has this to say about the impact of Islam on the transformation of Afro-American community in the United States and the rest of the western world:

> And now suddenly people who have never before been able to hear this message hear it, and believe it, and are changed... [Islam] has been able to do what generations of welfare workers and committees and resolutions and reports and housing projects and playgrounds have failed to do: to heal and redeem drunkards and junkies, to convert people who have come out of prisons and keep them out, to make men chaste and women virtuous, and to invest both male and female with the pride and serenity that hang about them like unfailing light.[243]

George Bernard Shaw assessed Muhammed and the message of Islam, concluding that:

> I have always held the religion of Muhammad in high estimation because of its wonderful vitality. It is the only religion which appears to me to possess that assimilating capacity to the changing phases of the existence, which can make itself appeal to every age. I have studied him — the wonderful man and in my opinion, far from being an anti-Christ, he must be called the Saviour of Humanity. I believe that if a man like him were to assume the dictatorship of the modern world, he would succeed in solving its problems in a way that would bring it the much needed peace and happiness: I have prophesied about the faith of Muhammad that it would

---

[243]. Baldwin, James. (1962), *The Fire Next Time*, p. 68.

be acceptable to the Europe of tomorrow as it is beginning to be acceptable to the Europe of today.[244]

As these pristine experiences explicitly attest, Islam as the discovered new humanism, is, in fact, nothing but our disregarded guiding rescuer. Its dynamic principles of life are characterized by the balancing precepts of the Equigenic Principle, which, as Shaw astutely recognised, alone possess that indispensable assimilating capacity which has the natural propensity to incorporate the changing phases of the ages, making Islam appeal to every time and place. As such, its equigenic worldview is the optimal remedy readily available to emancipate our wills, by disengaging us from a blurred vision of reality. Its ennobling vision allows us to move unfettered, from facts to values, based on certainty, order and balance. Nevertheless, the universal implications of such a transition from facts to values can only be actualized if we cease to infest our hearts and minds with ephemeral paltry desires, which only lead to the omnidirectional disintegration of humanity and the rest of the earth. As such, Islam is the only worldview which can and ought to re-emerge as the solution for directively uplifting our rapidly collapsing human society.

---

[244]. Shaw, George Bernard. (1936), *The Genuine Islam*, Singapure, Vol. 1, No. 8.

Bibliography

Abubaker, Ahmad. (1989), *Africa and the Challenge of Development: Acquiescence and Dependency Versus Freedom and Development*, Praeger, New York.

Ackerman, Bruce. (1980), *Social Justice in the Liberal State*, New Haven, CT: Yale University Press, New York.

Adelman, Howard. (1992), "Justice, Immigration and Refugees", Centre for Refugee Studies, York University, Toronto.

Anderson, John Ward and Moore, Molly. (1993), "Murdered at Birth–for Being Female", *The Sunday Star*, Toronto, April 4.

Attenborough, David. (1990), *The Trials of Life*, Little, Brown and Company, London.

Augros, Robert and Stanciu, George. (1988), *The New Biology: Discovering the Wisdom in Nature*, New Science Library, Boston.

Ayer A. J. (1982), *The Central Questions of Philosophy*, Penguin Books, New York.

Bailey, J. M. and Pillard, R.C. (1991), "A Genetic Study of Male Sexual Orientation", *Archives of General Psychiatry*, December, Vol. 48, pp. 1089-1096.

Baldwin, James. (1962), *The Fire Next Time*, Penguin Books, London.

Barrow, John D. and Tipler, Frank J. (1988), *The Anthropic Cosmological Principle*, Oxford University Press, New York.

Belsey, Andrew. (1992), "World Poverty, Justice and Equality", in the *International Justice and the Third World*, Edited by Robin Attfield and Barry Wilkins, Routledge, London.

Bennett, Jon. (1987), *The Hunger Machine: The Politics of Food*, Polity Press, Cambridge.

Bentham, Jeremy. (1843), *Anarchical Fallacies*, in the *Nonsense upon Stilts*, edited by Jeremy Waldron (1987), Methuen, London.

Bentham, Jeremy. (1823), *Introduction to the Principles of Morals and Legislation*, Oxford at the Clarendon Press, London.

Bentham, Jeremy. (1984), "An Essay on Paederasty", in the *Philosophy of Sex,* edited by Robert Baker and Frederick Elliston, Prometheus Books, Buffalo.

Bergman, Charles. (1990), *Wild Echo*, Alaska Northwest Books, Seattle.

Berry, Thomas. (1988), *The Dream of the Earth*, Sierra Club Books, San Francisco.

Bloom, Allan. (1987), *The Closing of the American Mind*, Simon & Schuster Inc., New York.

Bohm, David and Peat, David F. (1987), *Science, Order and Creativity: A Dramatic New Look at the Roots of Science and Life*, Bantam Books, London.

Bonnet, Monique and Bonnet, Gerard. (1984), *Feeding Your Baby*, Prentice-Hall, Inc., Englewood Cliffs, New Jersey.

Bowring, John. (1962), (ed.) *Pennomial Fragments, in the Works of Jeremy Bentham*, Vol. 3, Russell & Russell Inc., New York.

Boyd, Richard & Gasper, Philip & Trout, J. D. (1991), *The Philosophy of Science,* Bradford Books, Cambridge, Massachusetts.

Brewster, David K. H. (1855), *A Short Scheme of the True Religion,* in *Memories of the Life, Writings, and Discourse of Sir Isaac Newton*, Vol. 2, Edinburgh: Thomas Constable and Co., Little Brown and Co., Boston.

Bright, Michael. (1984), *Animal Language,* Published by the British Broadcasting Corporation, London.

Bucaille, Maurice. (1979), *The Quran, the Bible and Science*, American Trust Publications, Indianapolis, IN.

Bucaille, Maurice. (1983), *What is the Origin of Man? The Answers of Science and the Holy Scriptures,* (9th ed., revised and expanded), Seghers, Paris.

Buchanan, Allan and Mathieu, Deborah. (1986), "Philosophy and Justice", in the *Justice: Views from the Social Sciences*, edited by Ronald L. Cohen, Plenum Press, New York.

Chalmers, Alan. (1990), *Science and Its Fabrication*, University of Minnesota Press, Minneapolis.

Chomsky, Noam. (1990), *Pirates & Emperors: International Terrorism in the Real World*, Amana Books, Brattleboro, Vermont.

Cohen, Joel E. (1989), "Big Fish, Little Fish: The Search for Patterns in Predator-Prey Relationships", *The Sciences*, March/April, Vol. 29, pp. 36-42.

Cohen, Morris and Nagel, Ernest. (1934), *An Introduction to Logic of Scientific Method*, Harcourt, Brace & World Inc., New York.

Cohen, Ronald L. (1986), *Justice: Views from the Social Sciences*, Plenum Press, New York.

Cohen, Jack and Stewart, Ian. (1994), *The Collapse of Chaos: Discovering Simplicity in a Complex World*, Viking, New York.

Coleman, Gerald D. (1992), *Human Sexuality: An all-embracing gift*, Alba House, New York.

Copi, Irving M. (1978), *Introduction to Logic*, MacMillan Publishing Co., New York.

Cori, Baill and Money, John. (1980), "Physiological Aspects of Female Sexual Development", in *Women's Sexual Development*, edited by Martha Kirkpatrick, M.D., Plenum Press, New York.

Cranston, Maurice. (1979), "What Are Human Rights?", in *The Human Rights Reader*, edited by Walter Laqueur and Barry Rubin, New American Library, New York.

Davies, Paul. (1982), *The Accidental Universe*, Cambridge University Press, Cambridge.

Davies, P.C. and Brown, R.R. (1989), *The Ghost in the Atom*, Cambridge University Press, Cambridge.

From Fact to Values

Dennett, Daniel C. (1995), "Darwins's Dangerous Ideas", *The Science,* May/June, Vol. 35, No. 3, pp. 36-37.

Denton, Michael. (1986), *Evolution: A Theory in Crisis*, Adler & Adler, Bethesda, MD.

Durkheim, Emile. (1951), *Suicide: A Study in Sociology*, Translated by J.A. Spauldig and G. Simpson. The Free Press, Glencore, Illinois.

Dynes, Wayne R. (1987), *Homosexuality: A Research Guide*, Garland Publishing, New York.

Eccles, John and Robinson, Daniel N. (1985), *The Wonder of Being Human: Our Brain & Our Mind*, The New Science Library, Shambhala, London.

Edwards, Tryon and Catervas, C.N. and Edwards, J. and Browns, R.E. (1959), *The New Dictionary of Thoughts: A Cyclopedia of Quotations,* Standard Book Company, U.S.A.

Eldredge, Niles. (1985), *Time Frames,* A Touchstone Book, Published by Simon & Schuster Inc., New York.

Eldredge, Niles. (1989), *Macro-Evolutionary Dynamics,* McGraw-Hill Publishing Company, New York.

Elton, Charles. (1968), *Animal Ecology*, Methuen Books, London, England.

Fanon, Frantz. (1961), *The Wretched of the Earth,* translated by Constance Farrington, reprint (1968), Grove Press, New York.

Forsyth, Adrian. (1989), "Togetherness: The Logic of the Herd", *Equinox,* January/February, Vol. 8, No. 43, pp. 48-57.

Fowler, W.S. (1962), *The Development of Scientific Method*, Pergamom Press, New York.

Gamlin, Linda. (1983), (ed.), *Nightwatch: The Natural World from Dusk to Dawn*, Michael Joseph Ltd., London.

George, Susan. (1977), *How the other Half Dies: The Real Reasons for World Hunger,* Allanheld, Osmun & Co. Publishers, Montclair, New Jersey.

From Facts to Values

George, Susan. (1978), *Feeding the Few: Corporate Control of Food*, Institute for Policy Studies, Washington, D.C.

George, Susan. (1984), *Ill Fares the Land: Essays on food, hunger and power*, Writers and Readers Publishing, London.

Gerety, Tom. (1988), "Sanctuary: A Comment on the Ironic Relation Between Law and Morality", in *The New Asylum Seekers: Refugee Law in the 1980's*, edited by David A. Martin, Martinus Nijhoff Publishers, Boston/Dordrecht, Netherlands.

Gewirth, Alan. (1981), "The Basis and Content of Human Rights", in *Human Rights*, Edited by J. Roland Pennock and John W. Chapman, New York University Press, New York.

Gewirth, Alan. (1982), *Human Rights Essay on Justification and Application*, Chicago University Press, Chicago.

Gewirth, Alan. (1984), "Are There Any Absolute Rights?", In Jeremy Waldron, *Theories of Justice*, Oxford University Press, Oxford.

Gibson, Eleanor J. (1969), *Principles of Perceptual Learning and Development*, Appleton-Century Crofts, New York.

Gibson, James J. (1966), *The Senses Considered as Perceptual Systems*, Houghton Mifflin, Boston.

Gibson, James J. (1979), *The Ecological Approach to Visual Perception*, Houghton Mifflin, Boston.

Giller, Paul S. (1984), *Community Structure and Niche*, Chapman and Hall, New York.

Giere, Ronald N. (1984), *Understanding Scientific Reasoning*, Holt Rinehart and Winston, New York.

Goldstein, Thomas. (1980), *Dawn of Modern Science: From the Arabs to Leonardo da Vinci*, Houghton Mifflin Co., Boston.

Goodwin, Brain. (1994), *How the Leopard Changed its Spots: The Evolution of Complexity*, Charles Scribner's Sons, New York.

Gorman, Christine. (1992), "Invincible Aids", *Time*, August 3, Vol. 140, No. 5., pp. 16-25.

Gould, Stephen Jay. (1990), "Darwin and Paley Meet the Invisible Hand", *Natural History*, November, pp. 8-16.

Haldane, E.S. and Ross, G.R.T. (1968), *The Philosophical Works of Descartes*, Two Vols., Cambridge University Press, London.

Haley, Alex. (1989), *The Autobiography of Malcolm X*, Ballantine Books, New York.

Hansell, Michael H. (1984), *Animal Architecture and Building Behaviour*, Longman Inc., New York.

Harrel-Bond, B. E. (1986), *Imposing Aid: Emergency Assistance to Refugees*, Oxford University Press, New York.

Harris, James F. (1992), *Against Relativism*, Open Court, La Salle, Illinois.

Hart, H.L.A. (1984), "Are There Any Natural Rights?", in *Theories of Rights*, edited by Jeremy Waldron, Oxford University Press, Oxford.

Havel, Vaclav. (1989), "Politics and Conscience", in: *Living in Truth*, J. Vladislav (ed.), London/Boston.

Hawking, Stephen W. (1988), *A Brief History of Time*, Bantam Books, London.

Herman, Edward S. and Chomsky, Noam. (1988), *Manufacturing Consent: The Political Economy of the Mass Media*, Pantheon, New York.

Herman, Edward S. (1992), *Beyond Hypocrisy*, Black Rose Books Ltd., Cheeyktowaga, New York.

Higgins, Rosalyn. (1983), "The European Convention on Human Rights", in the *Council of Europe, a concise guide: Text of the Convention and Protocols*, pp. 495-511.

Hitching, Francis. (1982), *The Neck of the Giraffe:Darwin, Evolution, and the New Biology*, The New American Library Inc.

Hogg, Peter. (1991), "On Being a Positivist: a Reply to Professor Vaughan", *Osgoode Hall Law Journal*, Vol. 29, No. 2, Toronto.

Horgan, John. (1993), "Eugenic Revisited", *Scientific American*, June, Vol. 268, No. 6, pp. 122-131.

Huff, Darrell. (1954), *How to lie with statistics*, W.W. Norton & Company, Inc., New York.

Hume, David. (1888), *A Treatise of Human Nature*, Edited by L.A. Selby-Bigge, Clarendon Press, Oxford.

Huntley, H. E. (1970), *The Divine Proportion*, Dover Publications, New York.

Jatkola, Barbara. (1981), *Violence Against Women in Five Erotic Magazines*, University of Wisconsin, Madison.

Johnson, R. H. and Blair J. A. (1983), *Logical Self-Defense*, McGraw-Hill Ryerson Ltd., Toronto.

Johanson, Sue. "Anal Sex", pamphlet released by Rogers Cable and Sunday Nights Sex Show, Rock Radio Network, Toronto, Ontario.

Johanson, Sue. (1995), *Sex, Sex and More Sex: 101 Questions and Answers*, Viking, Toronto.

Joly, Daniele & Nettleton, Clive & Poulton, Hugh. (1991), *Refugees: Asylum in Europe?*, Minority Rights Publications, London.

Jordan, Michael. (1992), *The Encyclopedia of Gods*, Kyle Cathie Ltd., London.

Kant, Immanuel. (1951), *Critique of Judgement*, Translated By J.H. Bernard, Hafner Press, New York.

Kaplan, Helen S. (1974), *The New Sex Therapy: Active Treatment of Sexual Dysfunctions*, Times Books, New York.

Kauffman, S.A. (1993), *Origins of Order: Self-Organization and Selection in Evolution*, Oxford University Press, Oxford.

Keun-Young Yoo et al. (1992), "Independent Protective Effect of Lactation against Breast Cancer: a Case-Control Study in Japan", *American Journal of Epidemiology*, 135:7:726-733.

King, Alexander and Schneider, Bertrand. (1991), *The First Global Revolution: A Report by the Council of the Club of Rome*, Pantheon Books, New York.

Koestler, Arthur and Smythies, J.R. (1972), *Beyond Reductionism: New Perspectives in the Life Sciences: Proceedings of the Alpbach Symposium*, (New ed.), Hutchinson of London, London.

Kruuk, Hans. (1972), *The Spotted Hyena: A Study of Predation and Social Behaviour*, The University of Chicago Press, Chicago.

Kuhn, Thomas S. (1962), *The Structure of Scientific Revolutions*, University of Chicago Press, Chicago.

Kuppers, Bernd Olaf. (1990), *Information and the Origin of Life*, The MIT Press, Cambridge, Massachusetts.

Lang, Jeffrey. (1994), *Struggling to Surrender*, Amana Publications, Beltsville, Maryland.

Lappe, France Moore and Collins, Joseph. (1986), *World Hunger: The Twelve Myths*, Grove Press, New York.

Layde, Peter M. et al. (1989), "The Independent Associations of Parity, Age at First Full Term Pregnancy, and Duration of Breastfeeding with the Risk of Breast Cancer", *Journal of Clinical Epidemiology*, Vol. 42, 963-973.

Lerner, Eric J. (1991), *The Big Bang Never Happened: A Startling Refutation of the Dominant Theory of the Origin of the Universe*, Vintage Books, New York.

LeVay, Simon. (1991) "A Difference in Hypothalamic Structure Between Heterosexual and Homosexual Men", *Science*, August 30, Vol. 258, pp. 1034-1037.

Livingston, John. (1984), "Rightness or Right?", *Osgoode Hall Law Journal*, Volume 22, No. 2.

Livingston, John. (1986), "Ethics as Prosthetics", in the *Environmental Ethics: Philosophical and Policy*

Perspective, edited by Philip P. Hanson, Institute for the Humanities/SFU Publications, Burnaby, British Columbia.

Locke, John. (1963), *The Works of Locke: A New Edition, Corrected,* Volume V, Scientia Verlag Aalen, London.

Locke, John. (1963), *Two Treatises of Civil Government,* With an Introduction by W. S. Carpenter, (E.L.), London.

Lucas, L.R. (1980), *On Justice,* Clarendon Press, Oxford, 1980.

MacMahon, B. et al. (1970), "Age at First Birth and Breast Cancer Risk", *Bull. W. H. O.,* Vol. 43, 209.

Makrides, M.; Neumann, M.A.; Byard, R.W.; Gibson, Bob; Simmer, Karen. (1994), "Fatty acid composition of brain, retina, and erythrocytes in breast- and formula-fed infants", *American Journal of Clinical Nutrition,* August, 60 (2): 189-194.

Mander, Jerry. (1978), *Four Arguments for the Elimination of Television,* William Morrow & Company, New York.

Margenau, Henry and Varghese, Roy Abraham. (1992), *Cosmos, Bios, Theos: Scientists Reflection on Science, God and the Origins of the Universe, Life and Homo sapiens,* Open Court, La Salle, Illinois.

Margolis, Joseph. (1991), *The Truth about Relativism,* Blackwell, Oxford, U.K.

Maslow, Abraham H. (1984), *Religions, Values and Peak-Experiences,* Penguin Books, New York.

Masri, B. A. and Haque, Nadeem. (1995), *Nature in Islam: The Concern for Ecological Balance,* Optagon Publications Ltd., Toronto.

Masters, Roger D. (1993), *Beyond Relativism: Science and Values,* University Press of New England.

Masters, William & Johnson, Virginia & Kolodny, Robert C. (1982), *Human Sexuality,* Little, Brown and Company, Boston.

Mayr, Ernst. (1988), *Toward a New Philosophy of Biology: Observations of an Evolutionist,* The Belknap Press of Harvard University Press, Cambridge, Massachusetts.

From Fact to Values

McTiernan, Anne and David B. Thomas (1986), "Evidence for a Protective Effect of Lactation on Risk of Breast Cancer in Young Women", *American Journal of Epidemiology*, Vol. 124, 353-358.

Messenger, Maire. (1984), *The Breastfeeding Book*, Deneau Publishers, Ottawa.

Miller, Scott A. (1987), *Developmental Research Method*, Prentice-Hall, Inc., Englwood Cliffs, New Jersey.

Milton, Richard. (1992), *The Facts of Life: Shattering the Myth of Darwinism*, Fourth Estate Ltd., London.

Mohr, Richard D. (1988), *Gay Justice: A Story of Ethics, Society and Law*, Columbia University Press, New York.

Moore, Keith L. (1982), *The Developing Human*, 3rd ed., Saunders Co., Philadelphia.

Morris, Desmond. (1990), *The Animal Contract: Sharing the Planet*, based on BBC television series, Virgin Books, London.

Morrison, Cressy A. (1944), *Man Does Not Stand Alone,* F. H. Revell, Westwood, N.J.

Morrison, Cressy A. (1988), "Does God Exist?" in the *Philosophy and Contemporary Issues*, by John R. Burr and Milton Goldinger, Fifth Edition, Macmillan Publishing, New York.

Neilsen, Kai. (1992), "Global Justice, Capitalism and the Third World", in the *International Justice and the Third World*, edited by Robin Attfield and Barry Wilkins, Routledge, London.

Newcomb, Polly A. et al. (1994), "Lactation and a Reduced Risk of Premenopausal Breast Cancer". *New England Journal of Medicine;* 330:2:81-87.

Newton, Isaac. (1966), *Mathematical Principles of Natural Philosophy,* translated by Andrew Motte, revised by Florian Cajori, Vol. 2, University of California Press, Berkeley.

Nobel, Peter. (1987), *Refugees and Development in Africa*, Scandinavian Institute of African Studies, Seminar Proceedings No. 19, Uppsala.

Nurbaki, Haluk. (1989), *Verses From the Glorious Koran and the Facts of Science,* Turkish Foundation for Religious Publications, Ankara.

Oakley, Ray and Charles Ksir. (1993), *Drugs, Society and Human Behaviour,* Sixth edition, Mosby, St. Louis.

Orians, Gordon H. (1972), "The Strategy of the Niche", in *The Marvel of Animal Behaviour*, edited by Thomas B. Allen, National Geographic Society.

Page, George. (1991), *Horse Tigers*, The Nature Series, PBS television production.

Pagels, Heinz R. (1984), *The Cosmic Code: Quantum Physics as the Language of Nature,* Bantam Books, New York.

Pagels, Heinz R. (1986), *Perfect Symmetry*, Bantam Books, New York.

Penrose, Roger. (1989), *The Emperor's New Mind,* Oxford University Press, New York.

Percy, Walker. (1983), *Lost in the Cosmos: The Last Self-Help Book*, Farraar, Straus and Giroux, New York.

Pimm, Stuart L. (1991), *Balance of Nature*, Chicago University Press, Chicago.

Popper, Karl R. (1975), *The Logic of Scientific Discovery,* Hutchinson, London.

Potter, Gary W. (1989), "The Retail Pornography Industry and the Operation of Vice", *Journal of Deviant Behaviour,* Vol. 10, No. 3, pp. 233-251.

Powell, Corey S. (1992), "More Proof for the Big Bang: The Golden Age of Cosmology", *Scientific American*, July, Vol. 267, No. 1, pp. 17-22.

Putnam, Hilary. (1978), *The 'Corroboration' of Theories,* in *The Philosophy of Science*, edited by Richard Boyd, Philip Gasper and J. D. Trout, (1991), Bradford Books, Cambridge, Massachusetts.

From Fact to Values

Putnam, Hilary. (1981), *Reason, Truth and History,* Cambridge University Press, New York.

Quine, W. V. (1953), *From a Logical Point of View,* Cambridge Harvard University Press, Cambridge.

Qutb, Sayed. (1977), *Islam and Universal Peace,* American Trust Publications, Indianapolis, In.

Qutb, Sayed. (1979), *In the Shade of the Quran,* (30 Volumes), The MWH Publishers, London.

Qutb, Sayed. (1993), *Milestones,* Revised ed., American Trust Publications, Indianapolis, In.

Raeburn, Paul. (1993), "Breast-Cancer Risk Higher for Lesbians", *The Globe and Mail*, February 5.

Rahman, Afzalur. (1981), *Quranic Science,* The MWH Publishers, London.

Raup, David M. (1991), *Extinction: Bad Genes or Bad Luck?,* Norton & Company, New York.

Rawls, John. (1971), *Theory of Justice,* Harvard University Press, Cambridge, Massachusetts.

Ray, Colette and Michael Baum. (1985), *Psychological Aspects of Early Breast Cancer,* Springe-Verlag, New York.

Rollins, L. A. (1983), *The Myth of Natural Rights*, Loompanics Unlimited, Port Townsend, Wash.

Rowan-Robinson, Michael. (1993), *Ripples in the Cosmos,* W.H. Freeman and Company Ltd., New York.

Russell, Diana E. H. (1993), *Making Violence Sexy: Feminist Views on Pornography,* Teachers College Press, New York.

Said, Edward W. (1981), *Covering Islam: How the media and the experts determine how we see the rest of the world,* Pantheon Books, New York.

Said, Edward W. (1993), *Culture and Imperialism*, Alfred A. Knopf, New York.

Schneck, Marcus. (1991), *Patterns in Nature: A World of Colour, Shape and Light,* Crescent Books, New York.

From Facts to Values

Schwartz, Mark F. & Masters, William H. (1984), "The Masters and Johnson Treatment Program for Dissatisfied Homosexual Men", *American Journal of Psychiatry*, February, Vol. 141, No. 2, pp. 173-181.

Shaw, George Bernard. (1936), *The Genuine Islam*, Singapure, Vol. 1, No. 8.

Siegal, Harvey. (1987), *Relativism Refuted: A Critique of Contemporary Epistemological Relativism*, D. Reidel Publishing Company, Boston.

Singer, Peter. (1990), *Animal Liberation*, Avon Books, New York.

Slattery, Brian. (1991), "Aboriginal Sovereignty and Imperial Claims", *Osgoode Hall Law Journal*, Winter, Vol. 29, No. 4.

Sober, Moshe. (1990), *Beyond the Jewish State: Confessions of a Former Zionist*, Summerhill Press Ltd., Toronto.

Spinoza, Baruch. (1951), *A Theological-Political Treatise*, Translated with an introduction by R.H.M. Elwes, Dover Publications, New York.

Suzuki, David. (1991), *Running for their Lives*, CBC Production from "The Nature of Things" television series, Toronto.

Thagard, Paul. (1992), *Conceptual Revolutions*, Princeton University Press, Princeton, New Jersey.

Thaxton, Charles B. & Bradley, Walter L. & Olsen, Roger L. (1984), *The Mystery of Life's Origin: Reassessing Current Theories*, Philosophical Library, London.

Thayer, H. S. (1953), *Newton's Philosophy of Nature: Selection from his Writings*, Hafner Publishing Co., New York.

Thompson, D'arcy. (1990), *On Growth and Form*, Cambridge University Press, New York.

Thor Dahlburg, John. (1994), "Where killing baby girls 'is no big sin'", *Toronto Star*, February 28, reprint from the *Los Angles Times*.

Toulmin, Stephen E. (1969), *The Uses of Arguments*, Cambridge University Press, Cambridge.

Valverde, Mariana. (1985), *Sex, Power and Pleasure,* Women's Press, Toronto.

Vaughan, Frederick. (1991), "On Being a Positivist: Does it Really Matter?", *Osgoode Hall Law Journal,* Toronto, Vol. 29, No. 2.

Wadud, Sayed Abdul. (1971), *Phenomena of Nature and the Quran,* Khalid Publishing, Lahore, Pakistan.

Wainwright, S. A., Biggs, W. D., Currey, J. D., Gosline, J. M. (1982), *Mechanical Design in Organisms,* Princeton University Press, Princeton, N.J.

Walzer, Michael. (1983), *Spheres of Justice: A Defence of Pluralism and Equality,* Basic Books, New York.

Whitam, F.L. et al. (1993), "Homosexual orientation in twins: a report on 61 pairs and three triplet sets", *The Archives of Sexual Behaviour,* Vol. 22, No. 3. pp. 187-206.

Winchester, A. M. (1973), *The Nature of Human Sexuality,* Bell & Howell Company, Columbus, Ohio.

No Primary Authors

Toronto Board of Education. (1992), *"Sexual Orientation: Focus on Homosexuality, Lesbianism and Homophobia",* A Resources Guide for Teachers of Health Education in Secondary Schools, Toronto.

"The Breast Care Test", with Jane Pauly, a PBS television documentary on breast cancer among American women, 1993.

"The European Convention on Human Rights and Its Five Protocols", (1955), Council of Europe Treaty Series No. 5, Strasbourg.

Pornography and Sexual Violence: Evidence of the Links, (1988), The complete transcript of Public Hearing on Ordinances to add pornography as discrimination against women, Minneapolis City, December 12-13, 1983.

The United Nations Universal Declaration of Human Rights, (1948), (U.N. Doc. A/811), New York.

The United Kingdom National Case-Control Study Group, (1993), "Breastfeeding and Risk of breast cancer in young women", *British Medical Journal,* 307:17-20.

The United States Immigration Reform and Control Act of 1986, (1986), Pub. L. No. 99-603, § 112, 100 Stat. 3359, 8 U.S.C. § 1324(a)(1982).

The United States Department of Health and Human Services, (1981), *Special Report to the Congress on Alcohol and Health,* Washington, D.C.: Government Printing Office (DHHS Pub. No. [ADM]81-1080(b).

The United States Department of State, (1992), "Patterns of Global Terrorism: 1992", Office of The Secretary of State, Office of the Coordinator for Counterterrorism, Washington, D.C.

The *Universal Islamic Declaration of Human Rights,* (1981), published by the Islamic Council of London, England.

UNHCR, (1988), *Handbook on Procedures and Criteria for Determining Refugee Status: Under the 1951 Convention and the 1967 Protocol relating to the Status of Refugees,* Geneva.

"*Let Her Die*", (1994), A joint BBC & CBC television documentary, London & Toronto.

"The Gay Science of Genes and Brains", (1992), *The Economist,* December 5, Vol. 325, No. 7788, pp. 87-88.

From Facts to Values

Index

Animal Rights, 141, 192-200
Anthropic Principle, 102, 154, 162
Ayer, 88, 101

Bentham, 135, 139-143, 213
Big Bang, 14-65, 74-77, 81-83, 101, 113, 153, 155, 240-249
Bloom (Allan), 15, 17, 52, 256
Bohm (David), 109
Breast Cancer, 189-190
Breast feeding, 185-190

Certainty, 18, 25, 31-34, 38, 40, 46-47, 51, 53, 58, 63, 70, 71, 88, 108-109, 113, 115-117, 120-121, 231, 235, 248, 267
Chomsky, 178, 226-228
Christianity, 53, 75, 263
Competition, 12, 116, 137, 181, 183, 197
Consistency, 3, 4, 45, 213
Cooperation, 136-137, 166, 197

Darwin, 61, 66-68, 86-87, 106, 136, 153, 233
Davies (Paul), 50, 72
Deduction, 39-40, 46-47, 52-53
Democracy, 135, 156, 225-228, 259, 261-262
Descartes, 40, 43, 46-47

Distribution of Resources, 158, 173-182
Dogma, 35-39
Dogmatism, 18, 37-38, 58, 61-63

Einstein, 69, 79, 108
Equigenic Principle, 157-163, 165, 171-172, 183, 192-193, 195, 199-200, 207, 213, 216-218, 224, 239, 243-244, 252-253, 257-259, 264, 267
Ethics, 110, 115-117, 120, 251
European Convention on Human Rights, 126-127, 147, 173
Evolution, 61, 64, 66-69, 74, 77, 84, 86, 89-104, 137, 153-155

Facts, 64-65, 71, 112, 120-123, 146
Falsification, 48-49, 52, 54-56, 70, 80
Freud, 52-53, 99, 111, 233

God, 52, 75, 78, 89, 91, 110-113, 231-232, 241
Gould, 67, 96, 100

Homosexuality, 201-218
Human Rights, 126-132, 147, 149, 161, 168-169, 173-174, 234, 262

Humanism, 12-14, 156, 239, 252-253, 257, 262-263, 267

Induction, 39-46
Islam, 239-246, 251-267

Justice, 123-130, 133, 138, 141, 144-157, 159-162, 167-169, 173-177, 179, 181, 183-184, 193, 216, 244, 247, 251, 260-262

Knowledge, 34-35, 113-114, 223
Kuhn, 19-21, 58-59

Malcolm X, 265
Morrison, 71, 72,
Mysticism, 24-27, 109, 142, 156

Nationhood (Nationalism), 164-172, 181
Natural Rights, 133, 135-142, 150, 162, 195, 204, 229-230
Newton, 22, 49, 54-55, 69, 79, 231, 232, 243
Nietzsche, 51-53, 111

Popper, 48-50, 53-59, 70
Pornography, 130, 219-220
Positivism, 108, 126, 131, 143-150, 156, 169
Putnam, 54, 120

Quantum Mechanics, 49, 108-109
Quine, 19-21
Quran, 240-249, 254, 258-265
Qutb, 261

Racism, 136, 157, 164, 169-170, 183, 220, 260
Relativism, 5, 13, 15-24, 27, 33, 53, 83, 109, 126, 131, 156, 215, 253
Religion, 8, 11-12, 121-122, 231, 234, 239, 241, 244, 251, 254, 259, 263
Revelation, 122, 231, 239, 243, 248

Science, 13, 32, 36, 39-40, 46-58, 64, 75, 83, 99, 109, 115-117, 120, 127, 231, 234, 241, 244, 251, 262
Shaw, 257, 266
Spinoza, 135-136, 229

Teleological Argument, 84-104
The United Nations Universal Declaration of Human Rights, 127, 173
Theory, 32, 39, 41, 51, 64, 65